Politics in an Era of Divided Government

T0346565

POLITICS AND POLICY IN AMERICAN INSTITUTIONS

Steven A. Shull, *Series Editor*

POLITICS IN AN ERA OF DIVIDED GOVERNMENT
ELECTIONS AND GOVERNANCE IN THE SECOND CLINTON ADMINISTRATION

Edited by
Harvey L. Schantz

Routledge
New York • London

Published in 2001 by
Routledge
270 Madison Ave,
New York NY 10016

Published in Great Britain by
Routledge
2 Park Square, Milton Park,
Abingdon, Oxon, OX14 4RN

Routledge is an imprint of the Taylor & Francis Group.

Transferred to Digital Printing 2009

Library of Congress Cataloging-in-Publication Data

Politics in an era of divided government : elections and governance in the second Clinton administration / edited by Harvey L. Schantz
p. cm. — (Politics and policy in American institutions)
Includes bibliographical references and index.
ISBN: 0-8153-3583-0 (hardcover)
1. Presidents—United States—Election—1996. 2. United States. Congress—Elections, 1996. 3. Elections—United States. 4. United States—Politics and government—1993–2001. I. Schantz, Harvey L., 1951– II. Garland reference library of social science. Politics and policy in American institutions
JK526 1996L
324.973'0929—dc21   2001023028

Publisher's Note
The publisher has gone to great lengths to ensure the quality of this reprint but points out that some imperfections in the original may be apparent.

To Our Families

Contents

List of Tables

Acknowledgments

I must thank all of the authors for contributing to the intellectual breadth of this project. This book would not be possible without their work and specialized knowledge. In addition to his own chapter, Milton Cummings provided wise counsel and a critique of each chapter.

At Routledge, I am in debt to social science editors Amy B. Shipper and Maria C. Zamora for their support and suggestions. I also benefited greatly from the insights of Professor Steven A. Shull, editor of the Routledge series on "Politics and Policy in American Institutions." I would also like to thank production editor Jeanne Shu and her team for helping to turn the manuscript into a book.

Abbreviations Used In Notes

AJPS	*American Journal of Political Science*
AP	Associated Press
APQ	*American Politics Quarterly*
APSR	*American Political Science Review*
CD	*Columbus (Ohio) Dispatch*
CQWR	*Congressional Quarterly Weekly Report*
CSM	*Christian Science Monitor*
DMR	*Des Moines Register*
JOP	*Journal of Politics*
NJ	*National Journal*
NYT	*New York Times*
RC	*Roll Call*
USA	*USA Today*
WP	*Washington Post*
WSJ	*Wall Street Journal*

Series Editor Foreword

The Routledge series, "Politics and Policy in American Institutions" strives to show the interaction of American political institutions within the context of public policy-making. A public policy approach often by definition is all-encompassing. Admittedly, my own interests focus on national policy-making, but the series will also include works on all levels of government. Indeed, I do not want my own specialties to define the series. Therefore, we seek solid scholarship incorporating a wide range of actors, including those outside the usual definition of government actors. The policy concerns, too, are potentially quite broad, with special interests in the policy process and such substantive issue areas as foreign and defense policy, economic and budget policy, health care, social welfare, racial politics, and the environment. The series will publish a considerable range of works, ranging from upper division texts to scholarly monographs, including both hard and soft cover editions.

Some might argue that we do not need another edited book on the topic of divided government. However, *Politics in an Era of Divided Government* concentrates on elections and governance during the second Clinton administration. In this valuable collection of original essays, editor Harvey L. Schantz focuses heavily on the results and the aftermath of the 1996 elections of Congress and the president. The volume covers party nominations, the general election, and subsequent government organization, arguing that these three processes are highly interrelated. The individual authors describe events but also make provocative arguments about the implications of elections for government structure and policy-making.

Perhaps not surprisingly, *Politics in an Era of Divided Government* finds a blurred boundary between elections and governance. At the end of the volume, Schantz sets the stage for the 2000 congressional and presidential elections. He contends that "impeachment and electoral politics have overshadowed policy during the second Clinton administration." As the first edited volume in this series, *Politics in an Era of Divided Government* provides an assessment of the important connection between elections and governance. Those linkages are crucial in understanding the relationship between American political institutions and public policy, the primary focus of this Routledge series.

Steven A. Shull

Introduction

HARVEY L. SCHANTZ

The Constitution of the United States directs that the American electorate choose a president every four years; a House of Representatives every two years; and one-third of the Senate every two years. In 1996, U.S. political leaders and voters complied with this mandate, as the electorate chose a president for the fifty-third time and also elected the members of the 105th Congress. The Clinton presidency, along with the 106th Congress elected in the 1998 midterm election, will complete 212 years of governance under the Constitution of the United States.

The national election of 1996 and its aftermath occurred in an era of divided government. In the eight presidential administrations since 1969, there has been divided partisan control of the Congress and president for 26 of 32 years. In 1995, though, Bill Clinton became the first Democratic president since Harry Truman in 1947-1948 to share control of the government with a Republican Congress. The 1996 and 1998 elections maintained this political lineup.

This book describes, explains, and reflects upon the 1996 presidential and congressional elections, devoting equal coverage to three phases of the political process: the major party nominations, the general election, and the subsequent government organization. In so doing, this study links elections and governance.

THE PARTY NOMINATIONS FOR THE PRESIDENT AND CONGRESS

The first two chapters of this book address the party nominations for the presidency and Congress. Although not called for in the Constitution, the major party nomination process is the crucial first step for any candidate seeking the presidency or a seat in the U.S. House or Senate. All presidents, aside from George Washington, have won the presidential general election as the nominee of a major political party. Throughout U.S. history, and especially in the twentieth century, the number of third party and independent candidates winning seats in Congress has been minimal.

To formally gain their presidential nomination, the Democratic and Republican parties require a candidate to win a majority of the delegate support at their national party conventions, both of which are held in the summer of election years. The delegates to the national convention are mostly selected between February and June of the election year in a local caucus–state convention process or by presidential primaries in each of the fifty states, the District of Columbia, and those territories allocated delegates by the national party committees.

Emmett H. Buell Jr., in his chapter, "Some Things Are Predictable: Nominating Dole, Clinton, and Perot," provides a detailed description of how the 1996 presidential nominating process unfolded, with special attention to the Republican nomination contest won by former U.S. Senator Robert Dole. Buell's account of the Republican nomination contest covers all the major phases of the process but emphasizes the importance of the invisible primary—the extended period before formal delegate selection begins. During the invisible primary, the field of candidates is finalized. Candidates lay the groundwork for their campaigns: raising funds, organizing their staff, and clarifying their message. The role of the media is most important at this stage, since the public does not yet know all of the individual candidates. Through polls and candidate coverage, the press judges the viability of the various candidates.

The invisible primary period can last as long as five years. By contrast, the visible part of the nomination process, in part because of the frontloading of delegate selection caucuses and primaries, often proceeds quickly and dramatically. In 1996, for example, delegate selection began with the Louisiana caucuses on February 6. By March 19, 1996—only about six weeks after the state caucuses and primaries began—Dole commanded a majority of the delegates to the Republican National Convention and thus could lay claim to the presidential nomination.

Among the Democrats, the pace was even quicker: President Bill Clinton's only challenger withdrew in April 1995. Clinton's renomination campaign was thus much easier than that of the last Democratic president, Jimmy Carter, in 1980, or that of Republican president George Bush in 1992. And the Reform Party nomination, as Buell indicates, was a foregone conclusion: "the party of Ross Perot" unsurprisingly nominated Ross Perot as its presidential candidate. In all three cases, it was the work that took place before the first primaries and caucuses that allowed the 1996 presidential nomination process to proceed as predictably as it did.

Virtually all congressional nominations in each of the fifty states are made by direct primary elections, a method of nomination that developed and spread throughout most of the United States in the first two decades of the twentieth century. However, there are differences in the primary election systems used by the states. These differences, as described by Harvey L. Schantz, include state variations in voter eligibility, in the role of party organizations in endorsing candidates, and in the margin needed for victory.

In his chapter on congressional nominations, Schantz also looks at primary candidates in 1996. He finds that incumbent representatives and senators did very well in primaries, and were rarely challenged by other current office-holders. Current office-holders gravitated to open districts, since they are viable candidates in the absence of a congressional incumbent. The weakest candidates in primaries were non-office-holders, who generally only won nominations when their party was not expected to win in November. A few non-office-holders did, however, win a congressional seat in 1996; included in this group were celebrity candidates, who had earned high name recognition outside of politics.

A third focus of the chapter on congressional nominations is electoral patterns in the primaries. Schantz finds that in 1996, margins of victory were almost always substantial when incumbents sought renomination. In the absence of an incumbent, however, there was frequently a close contest. Voter turnout in congressional primaries was very low, almost always less than half of the turnout in the ensuing general election.

THE GENERAL ELECTIONS FOR THE PRESIDENT AND CONGRESS

The middle three chapters of this book focus on the general elections for the national executive and legislature. Presidential elections are indirect: voters at the polls do not vote directly for their preferred candidate but, rather, pull the lever for a party's slate of electors. These electors are pledged—but not legally bound—to support the candidate preferred by the voters in their state. Every state is allocated electoral votes equal to its representation in Congress (the House and Senate). To be elected president, a candidate must receive a majority of electoral votes.

Milton C. Cummings Jr., in his chapter, "The Presidential Campaign and Vote in 1996: Job Ratings of Presidents—and Success or Failure at the Polls," provides a succinct description of the political setting and campaign leading up to the presidential election. Cummings devotes much attention to the pattern of the popular vote and the electoral vote verdict. An important social factor in the voting pattern in 1996 was once again the gender gap, whereby women were more likely than men to support Clinton. Both major parties once again shared all the electoral votes, as Clinton won 379, over 100 votes more than the necessary 270. Perhaps the most important aspect of the 1996 electoral verdict was that it continued divided government in Washington, with a Democratic president and a Republican Congress.

Cummings views the 1996 election as a referendum on the incumbent, and thus to explain the outcome of the election, Cummings consults popular approval of presidential job performance. According to Cummings, presidential approval ratings are a reliable predictor of presidential election outcomes. Therefore, Clinton's reelection is predicted by his 54 percent job approval rating. Finally, using an important typology of presidential elections, Cummings classifies the 1996 election as a "reaffirmation of support by a vote of confidence" in the Clinton administration.

The Constitution of the United States initially provided for indirect election of U.S. senators. But since 1914, due to the seventeenth amendment, senators have been directly elected. For electoral purposes, senate seats are divided into three classes, and every two years one of these classes is up for reelection. Thus, the senate seats up for election in 1996 were last filled in 1990.

Douglas B. Harris, in his chapter, "Strategic Partisan Decisions and Blunted National Outcomes: The 1996 Senate Election Campaign and Vote," describes the backdrop for the senate elections and the outcome on election day. In the 1996 senate elections, the Republicans, who were defending 19 seats—four more than the Democrats were trying to retain—were most successful in senate elections, extending their majority from 53 to 55.

Yet according to Harris, these numbers do not tell the whole story, for two reasons. First, turnover usually occurs when an incumbent retires. In this regard, the Republicans had the upper hand in 1996, since they had to defend only five open seats, while eight Democratic senators were retiring. Moreover, despite Clinton's 31-state victory, the senate races were evenly divided between states won by Dole and states won by Clinton. Thus, in Harris's view, rather than accomplishing a surprising feat by extending their majority in 1996, the Republicans did less well than might have been expected before the government shutdowns of November 1995–January 1996 turned public opinion against them.

Altogether, four senate seats changed parties in 1996. In the Plains states, Republicans lost in South Dakota but gained in Nebraska. In the South, Republicans gained two seats, Alabama and Arkansas. This turnover continued a trend of Republican gains in the South, and, as Harris points out, these gains are an integral part of the Republican senate majority.

The Republican senate majority, along with the reelection of President Clinton, continued one of the major trends in U.S. government in the second half of the twentieth century: the increased frequency of divided party control of the president and one or both chambers of Congress. In his chapter, "Sideshows and Strategic Separations: The Impact of Presidential Year Politics on Congressional Elections," Garrison Nelson examines congressional elections, especially those for the U.S. House, from the vantage point of divided government. As he notes, most explanations for the rise of divided government point to changes in electoral behavior. But Nelson persuasively contends that the increased frequency of divided government is, rather, the result of strategic decisions made by recent presidents, especially Richard M. Nixon and Bill Clinton, and recent Speakers of the House of Representatives, especially Thomas P. "Tip" O'Neill and Newt Gingrich.

Most of the recent academic discussion about the results of divided party government has centered upon its impact on the amount, quality, and responsibility for legislation. But Nelson suggests that divided government has other effects: most particularly, under divided government, presidents usually enjoy greater public approval, benefiting from the public's negative perception of Congress.

In addition, divided party government allows political leaders in both branches to better realize their electoral goals. Leaders are able to run against each other and not have to shoulder the responsibility for the performance of the government. As divided control in Washington, D.C. has become the typical political lineup, according to Nelson, politicians have more frequently followed the lead of President Harry Truman in 1948, and have used divided government as a reelection tool. In 1996, the chief beneficiaries of this strategy were Speaker Newt Gingrich and President Clinton; both seem to have benefited from a learning curve in this regard.

ORGANIZING THE NEW ADMINISTRATION AND CONGRESS

As soon as the elections are over, political leaders and the media turn their attention to the tasks of organizing the new Congress and presidency. The headline in the *New York Times* on Thursday, November 7, 1996, just two days after election day was "Clinton Preparing for 2D Term With Shuffle of Top Officials." In Congress, also, attention quickly shifts from the election to organization.

The organizing for a new presidential administration takes place during the transition, which may begin even before election day and stretches past the inauguration. In this crucial period, the new or reelected president nominates and appoints cabinet-level officials and the White House staff, and also should develop a policy agenda for the new term of office. The importance of presidential transitions was formally recognized by the Congress in the Presidential Transition Act of 1963, which provides funding for transitions involving a new president, to both the incoming and outgoing administrations.

The presidential transition of 1996–1997 did not bring major change because it was an inter-term transition, involving the same president. Nevertheless, as Margaret Jane Wyszomirski shows in her chapter, "Clinton's Second Transition: Historic Aspirations Amidst Divided Government," crucial decisions of personnel and policy were made during the presidential transition period. These personnel decisions involved replacing seven of the fourteen Department Secretaries, as well as filling key positions in the White House staff, including selection of a new Chief of Staff. Special care was taken by the president to assemble effective staff teams in the areas of national security and economic policy.

Of special interest to Wyszomirski is the process by which Clinton set his second term policy agenda. Wyszomirski shows that Clinton's agenda emerged from events that transpired during the election campaign, particularly the Democratic party platform, as well as his 1997 inaugural and State of the Union addresses. During the first 100 days of his new term, Clinton's policy agenda, aided by growing government revenues stimulated by economic growth, set the stage for bipartisan cooperation in congressional policy-making.

Discussions of presidential administrations often suggest that the first 100 days or six months are the most propitious time for presidential legislative success with Congress. But Wyszomirski argues that the dynamics of policy-making may be different in divided government. In these circumstances, she suggests, the first six months of a new administration may have to be dedicated to working out a bipartisan agenda with the Congress. Thus, rather than an initial outburst of policy followed by a decline, lawmaking in divided government may take longer and most likely will be achieved in a more piecemeal fashion.

The 105th Congress, elected in the November 1996 election, convened on January 3, 1997. But much of the organizing for the new Congress took place in the months between election day and the new year. In this period, the four congressional parties held their conferences—meetings of all the legislative members of the party—in which they decided basic organizational matters such as the selection of party leaders and committee chairs and assignments. These conference decisions were then ratified by the full chambers, along a party line vote, when the Congress convened.

At the outset of the 105th Congress, in both the House and Senate, there was stability in the standing committee system and the party leadership. The standing committees of Congress are permanent legislative committees that prepare legislation for the full chamber. In the 105th Congress, the House retained the same 19 and the Senate the same 16 standing committees employed in the previous Congress. Similarly, all four congressional parties retained the same leaders: in the House, Republican Speaker Newt Gingrich—despite ethics charges which threatened his position—as well as Republican Majority Leader Richard Armey and Democratic Minority Leader Richard A. Gephardt; in the Senate, Republican Majority Leader Trent Lott and Democratic Minority Leader Tom Daschle.

However, every Congress brings some change to Washington, D.C. In their chapter, "The Irony of the 105th Congress and Its Legacy," Roger H. Davidson and Colton C. Campbell examine the new Congress and also contrast it with its predecessor. The 104th Congress, elected in 1994, brought revolutionary change to Congress, as the Republicans won control of the House for the first time since Dwight Eisenhower was swept into office in 1952. The Republicans also captured the Senate, after losing control of this chamber in the second Reagan midterm, 1986. Compared to its predecessor, the 105th Congress brought a minimal amount of change to Washington, as the Republicans retained control of both chambers.

According to Davidson and Campbell, the 1996 elections set the stage for the Congress which was to follow. A number of trends in House elections and campaigns made it more difficult for the Republican party to legislate on its own. Chief among these was the net loss of Republican seats, leaving the GOP with the narrowest House majority since Republican control of the first Eisenhower-era Congress. Between the elections of 1994 and 1996, the Republican majority declined from 230 to 227, but the loss of seats in 1996 was actually nine, for in 1995 Republicans had gained five Democratic defectors and won an additional seat in a 1995 special election.

The policy environment of the 105th Congress differed greatly from the previous Congress. After the 1994 election congressional Republicans, especially in the House, aggressively sought to pass the items contained in the "Contract with America." But as Davidson and Campbell point out, the Republican congressional majority in 1997 had not been elected on the basis of an agreed-upon policy agenda, and thus Republicans did not move quickly to pass mandated legislation. Rather, the first months of the new Congress were spent developing party priorities and formulating a balanced budget agreement with Democratic President Clinton.

In Congress, there is frequently a tension between the power of the party leadership and the committees. In the 104th Congress, the House leadership was ascendant, dominating the policy process. But in the 105th Congress, according to Davidson and Campbell, committee leaders began to exert themselves. Moderate House Republicans also gained in power, as the Republican leadership needed all available votes in order to produce winning coalitions.

By comparison, the Senate was "an island of relative tranquillity." Although Republicans increased their party advantage to 55-45, the rules of the Senate, which carefully protect the rights of the minority and individual members, leave it less open to party government.

By early 1998, Congress devoted most of its attention to the Clinton impeachment. These proceedings, according to Davidson and Campbell, were aided by two basic principles of congressional politics—party and committee. That is to say, the autonomy of the extremely partisan House Committee on the Judiciary provided a congenial setting for the beginning of the effort to impeach President Clinton. Although the impeachment effort ultimately failed, these proceedings continued the partisan era on Capitol Hill. Ironically, the 105th Congress turned out to be even more partisan that the revolutionary 104th Congress.

Although this book is organized around three distinct steps of the political process—nominations, general elections, and transitions—the chapters demonstrate that these steps are highly interconnected. Most directly, the nominations set the stage for the general elections, and the elections are the prelude to organizing the new Congress and administration. The decisions of political leaders will in turn influence the next nomination and electoral cycle. And of course, there are reciprocal influences between all three stages. More generally, though, this book once again reminds us that there is not a clear boundary between elections and governance.

Politics in an Era of Divided Government

CHAPTER 1

Some Things Are Predictable

Nominating Dole, Clinton, and Perot

EMMETT H. BUELL JR.

This is an account of how the Republican, Democratic, and Reform parties chose their respective presidential nominees in 1996. As memories of the last nominating cycle fade, we tend to forget how slim the odds of a second Clinton term once seemed or how much H. Ross Perot frightened both major parties. Ever adaptable, President Clinton reinvented himself after disaster struck his party in the 1994 midterm elections and he eventually swept to renomination unopposed. No event astonished election analysts less than Perot claiming the nomination of a party of his own making.

Most of what follows is about the Republicans who experienced the only seriously contested nomination of the three. I argue that the Republican choice was highly likely if not wholly predictable owing to what the nominating process has become. Presumably a front-runner can still self-destruct in such a system, but, if 1996 is any guide, process-related advantages will cancel out short-term factors like candidate style or weak message. Much depends on who else is running, of course, but that, too, is increasingly determined by the process. In 1996, unprecedented "front-loading" of the primary calendar, combined with the associated lack of viable rivals, extraordinary media exposure, and related leads in the polls and fund-raising set Dole up as the inevitable nominee.

NOMINATING STAGES AND FRONT-LOADING

Put simply, the increased resort of state parties to front-loading has changed the dynamics of presidential nominating politics in both of the major parties. The proliferation of February and March primaries now impels aspirants to start campaigning years in advance of the first votes to select convention delegates. Long familiar to pundits as the "invisible primary," this lengthy run-up to the first caucuses and primaries truly has become the most critical phase of the whole process.[1] This is the time when presidential hopefuls must raise huge sums, recruit activist supporters, build campaign organizations in key primary states, articulate a message, and impress the news media. More often than not, aspirants drop out after discovering that they lack the will, the resources, the stamina, or some other essential reason to continue campaigning.

Owing to the degree of front-loading now practiced by state parties, a seemingly interminable run-up to the first act of delegate-selection is followed by an incredible rush to judgment in a clutch of primaries. Rather than sort these primaries into multiple phases on the assumption that each importantly bears on the choice of the nominee,[2] it makes more sense nowadays to distinguish between "de facto" and "ex post facto" primaries. De facto contests occur only weeks into the presidential election year and decide the nomination in six weeks' time or less. Voters go to the polls in ex post facto primary states after one candidate has captured enough delegates to claim the nomination.

Front-loading also has wreaked havoc with the traditional distinction between the nominating and electing stages of presidential selection. Unencumbered by a primary challenge to Clinton in 1996, the Democrats began their general election campaign more than a year before the San Diego convention nominated Dole. The sooner a candidate captures the de facto nomination, the earlier the general election campaign begins. Thanks in great measure to reforms of delegate-selection rules after the 1968 Democratic convention (which indirectly but importantly affected the GOP as well), 1972 marks the beginning of a dramatic rise in the total number of Republican primaries.[3] Republican front-loading also picked up, so that, by 1988, the GOP held more presidential primaries before April 1 than afterwards.[4]

Today most of the convention delegates needed for formal nomination are selected by the end of March. The early yield of delegates increased dramatically when big states changed their primary dates from May and April to March. In 1980, for example, only 40 percent of the Republican delegates were chosen before April 1. That figure soared to 61 percent in 1988 before subsiding to 51 percent in 1992.[5] Front-loading reached a new high in 1996, when New York, Ohio, and California switched to March. In the end, 29 primary states (including eight of the twelve most populous) selected roughly 64 percent of all 1,990 Republican delegates before April 1. By March 26, Dole had accumulated 1,126 delegates, or 127 more than the simple majority needed for nomination.[6]

A LONG INVISIBLE PRIMARY FOR THE GOP

It is impossible to date the exact start of an invisible primary, but as good a marker as any is when the national press starts paying attention to likely candidates in the next round of presidential nominating contests. Major newspapers began speculating on the GOP's 1996 lineup more than a year before the 1992 New Hampshire primary.[7] By December 1991, the media list of presidential aspirants included General Colin Powell, Secretary of Defense Dick Cheney, Vice President Dan Quayle, Secretary of State James Baker, Secretary of Housing and Urban Development Jack Kemp, pundit Pat Buchanan (who only twelve days earlier had entered the 1992 nominating race), Governor Pete Wilson of California, Senator Phil Gramm of Texas, and former Tennessee governor Lamar Alexander.[8] Ostensibly called to renominate Bush, the Houston convention also showcased Quayle, Buchanan, Baker, Cheney, Gramm, Kemp, Wilson, and still other 1996 possibilities.[9]

Although generally omitted from the earliest lists, Dole's stock rose when he became the party's principal spokesman after the 1992 presidential election.[10] In February 1993, Dole signaled his interest in a third try for his party's nomination (he had run unsuccessfully in 1980 and 1988) by accelerating the fund-raising of Campaign America, his own political action committee. He also set up The Better America Foundation, yet another vehicle for raising pre-presidential money beyond the reach of campaign finance limits.[11] Dole boosted his standing among Republicans by leading the fight against the Clinton stimulus package in the 103d Congress. August 1993 found him "vacationing" in New Hampshire.[12] By year's end he had campaigned for Republican candidates in 39 states.[13] Campaign America also dispatched Dole organizers to Iowa and New Hampshire by early 1994. Dole began mapping out a general strategy shortly after the 1994 elections.[14] On January 12, 1995, he registered as a candidate with the Federal Election Commission (FEC).[15]

QUAYLE, POWELL, AND OTHERS OPT OR DROP OUT

Consistent with Arthur Hadley's disclosure that as many or more aspirants opt or drop out of the invisible primary as stay on to compete for delegates,[16] House speaker Newt Gingrich and five former members of the Bush administration—Baker, Cheney, Quayle, Kemp, and labor secretary Lynn Martin—assessed their 1996 chances before opting out. Quayle looked almost certain to run after undertaking a national book-promotion tour in June 1994. Slow to organize in key states, beset by health problems, and evidently discouraged by initial efforts at fund-raising, the former vice president departed the race on February 9, 1995.[17] Several governors—Carroll Campbell of South Carolina, Tommy Thompson of Wisconsin, and William Weld of Massachusetts—also seriously considered running before deciding against it. Two others, Governor Pete Wilson of California and Senator Arlen Specter, actually declared candidacy but withdrew in the last quarter of 1995 after failing to rise in the polls or raise the sums necessary to wage serious campaigns.

All of these early departures aided Dole enormously, but none helped more than Colin Powell's. A few conservatives in the GOP, most notably Kemp and William Bennett, former education secretary and drug czar, openly welcomed a Powell candidacy. Ralph Reed of the Christian Coalition, Speaker Gingrich, Republican National Committee (RNC) Chairman Haley Barbour, and talk-show host Rush Limbaugh carefully avoided criticizing him. Dole extolled Powell's accomplishments but warned that the party would not remake itself to suit Powell; Gramm and Buchanan charged that he was a Democrat in all but name.[18]

Powell's most outspoken opposition issued from conservative pundits and leaders of groups constituting the Republican right. To support someone so bereft of basic beliefs, George Will wrote, was to embrace a "watery Caesarism—trust the leader, well, because he is the leader." Paul Weyrich of the Free Congress Foundation declared that, if Powell got the nomination, "it would be as if Ronald Reagan never lived and Nelson Rockefeller never died." Gary Bauer of the Family Research Council blasted Powell as "Bill Clinton with ribbons," an opponent of smaller government, and an advocate of failed social programs. David Keene of the American Conservative Union castigated Kemp and other Powell supporters in the GOP willing to "sacrifice the work of decades on the altar of celebrity." Oliver North declaimed that "this guy is not a Republican." Carol Long of the National Right to Life Committee vowed to oppose a Powell candidacy.[19]

How much this reaction influenced Powell's decision not to run may never be known. How much he would have hurt Dole in the primaries is also a matter of considerable speculation. Powell looked strong in some polls but weak in others. Gallup put him even with Dole in September 1995, and one percentage point behind in early November.[20] One October poll showed him besting Dole among likely Republican primary voters. The same poll found Powell winning and Dole losing in respective trial heats against Clinton.[21] Still another sampling commissioned by Clinton consultant Dick Morris showed Powell losing to Dole in a two-man race.[22] Powell cut Dole's support in half in New Hampshire, but consistently trailed in polls of likely Iowa caucus participants.[23] Powell in any event opted out of the race on November 8, admitting that the political life required a calling that he did not yet hear.[24]

On balance it appears that Powell mania helped as much as it hurt Dole. On the one hand it confirmed that Dole's support was soft. On the other hand it deprived the other candidates of press attention and activist support. Contributors held back from giving to Alexander, Indiana Senator Richard G. Lugar, and Specter as long as a Powell candidacy looked likely.[25]

The Final Field: Insiders And Outsiders

By September 1995, all eight of the challengers who would formally contest Dole's nomination at least through the Iowa caucuses had thrown their hats into the ring. In addition to Gramm, Alexander, Buchanan, and Lugar, they included Congressman Robert Dornan of California, former ambassador to the Economic and Social Council of the United Nations Alan Keyes, and two multimillionaires with little or no experience whatever in public office—Steve Forbes and Morry Taylor. Dole and Lugar won respect in most party circles as accomplished legislators.

Recent "outsiders" typically have not held public office at the point of starting their presidential bids, although some had previously served in government or enjoyed considerable access to high public officials.[26] Posing as outsiders naturally obliged the 1996 outsiders to paint Dole and Gramm as charter members of the party establishment. Lugar escaped most of these attacks because of his low standing in the polls.

Some outsiders looked more convincing than others. Heir to a vast fortune, Forbes arguably belonged to the GOP "establishment" despite lack of experience as an office-holder. Alexander had worked for Senator Howard Baker and Richard Nixon before serving as governor of Tennessee, president of the University of Tennessee, and Bush's education secretary. His approach was to attack incumbents in offices he had not yet held. Buchanan had spent nearly all of his life inside the Beltway, achieving notoriety as a conservative activist, Nixon aide, syndicated columnist, and television personality. Buchanan came across as a more authentic outsider than Alexander or Forbes, however, because of his 1992 bid to deny President Bush renomination and his passionate criticism of orthodox Republican views on trade. Although a House member since 1977(except for 1983-84), Dornan nonetheless was widely regarded as no less a fringe candidate than Keyes and Taylor.[27]

The Republican finalists often differed strongly on policy matters, even though each billed himself as a conservative.[28] Though much mentioned during the campaign, the outsider-insider distinction had remarkably little connection with candidate stands on the issues. True, most outsiders favored term limits while all of the insiders opposed them. Still, no outsider except Forbes offered any tax plan as radical as Lugar's proposal to supplant income taxes with a national sales tax. Alexander's call for massive transfers of federal power to state and local governments elicited no more support from outsiders than insiders. Alexander, Buchanan, and Taylor joined Dole and Gramm in attacking the Forbes flat tax. Alexander and Forbes supported free trade along with Dole, Gramm, and Lugar. Every candidate wanted to dismantle the Department of Education. With the possible exceptions of Dornan and Keyes, every candidate favored Senate passage of a balanced budget resolution. All favored voluntary prayer in public schools and rejected race quotas. True, Lugar did not go much beyond quotas when speaking out on affirmative action, but neither did Forbes. Meanwhile, insider Gramm joined outsider Buchanan in calling for an end to affirmative action. (Dole sometimes made this argument too.) The outsider-insider distinction also had little if anything to do with which candidates pledged to make life tougher on imprisoned felons, oppose gun control, or resist gay rights. Outsiders Forbes and Taylor wrote off the Christian right while outsiders Buchanan and Keyes identified with it.

The Money Chase And Early Spending

No activity of the invisible primary affects the rest of the nominating process more importantly than fund-raising, and this is especially true when front-loading reaches 1996 proportions. Conventional wisdom maintained that the 1996 aspirants had to raise at least $20 million by the end of 1995 to become viable.[29] Any candidate in the contemporary system who counts on taxpayer money must abide by Federal Election Campaign Act (FECA) contribution limits, including a cap of $1,000 per individual, up to $250 of which is matched when the contribution is made by check. These caps have not changed since the FECA took effect in 1976, forcing candidates to raise huge sums from many individuals in small amounts capped by limits oblivious to inflation.

Every Republican candidate except Forbes and Taylor filed for matching funds and agreed to abide by FECA caps on contributions, total spending, and state spending. By not filing, Forbes and Taylor freed themselves to spend whatever amounts they wished. For all other Republican candidates, state spending limits varied by population rather than by importance in the process. Theoretically, for example, no federally financed candidate could spend more than $618,200 on the first primary in New Hampshire, exactly the same limit set for Alaska and a dozen other small states.[30]

From 1976 (the first race regulated by the FECA) through 1992, the general rule for contested Democratic nominations was that the candidate who raised the most money during the invisible primary went on to claim the nomination. Republican history suggests a slightly different conclusion: The race cannot be won without amassing a great deal of money, but raising more than any rival is neither necessary nor sufficient to win the nomination.[31]

Dole largely owed his nomination to highly successful fund-raising during the invisible primary. Without $25 million in seed money, his campaign could not have gone all out to compete in several straw votes, build state organizations, commission polls, conduct focus groups, and counter Forbe's massive advertising assault in Iowa and other early-bird states. Table 1.1 shows that Dole topped the list in individual contributions reported through the end of January 1996, surpassing Gramm by nearly $10 million, Alexander by almost $15 million, and all others by $17 million or more.[32] He also led in matching funds, outpacing Gramm, his closest competitor, by more than $1.5 million.

Table 1.1: 1996 Invisible-Primary Finances of Declared Republican Candidates

Candidate	Individual Contributions	Matching Funds	Adjusted Receipts	Adjusted Spending	Spending Subject to Limit	Cash on Hand	Campaign Debt
Alexander	$10,294,257	$1,933,475	$12,535,861	$12,050,711	$9,245,489	$425,806	$94,070
Buchanan	$7,540,444	$2,383,252	$10,731,288	$10,630,098	$10,630,098	$101,192	$1,398,234
Dole	$25,113,989	$5,552,297	$31,988,345	$27,152,687	$21,660,153	$4,835,659	$5,447,981
Dornan	$245,444	$0	$288,444	$285,951	$0	$2,491	$173,640
Forbes	$2,074,564	$0	$25,440,564	$25,136,300	$0	$304,264	$23,650,979
Gramm	$15,648,123	$3,987,412	$25,715,538	$24,119,921	$16,342,012	$1,515,050	$1,781,363
Keyes	$2,073,531	$0	$2,083,545	$1,841,638	$0	$204,428	$511,747
Lugar	$4,503,489	$1,363,342	$7,367,800	$6,805,507	$5,672,510	$539,666	$1,381,905
Specter	$2,283,651	$592,651	$3,203,441	$3,188,768	$3,188,769	$29,121	$311,366
Taylor	$36,236	$0	$5,354,351	$5,340,807	$0	$3,244	$5,442,408
Wilson	$5,123,841	$953,654	$6,362,258	$6,051,190	$2,448,884	$290,369	$1,503,680
Totals	$74,937,569	$16,766,083	$131,071,435	$122,603,578	$69,187,915	$8,251,290	$41,697,373

Source: Data kindly supplied by Robert Biersack of the Federal Election Commission.

Note: Data from inception of each campaign through January 31, 1996.

For all of its undeniable importance, if early money determined everything, a close correlation should always show up between how much
money the candidate raised or spent and how well that candidate did. Political reality belies such simplicity.[33] Gramm was the first casualty of the
Louisiana and Iowa caucuses, despite having raised more from individual
contributors, received more in matching funds, and reported more cash-on-
hand than any other candidate abiding by the FECA except Dole. The com-
paratively impecunious Buchanan actively contested Dole's nomination
longer than anyone else, including the biggest spender of them all.

Forbes withdrew before Buchanan, but not before setting new spending
records for the invisible primary. A candidate only since September 22,
Forbes nonetheless laid out $14 million in the final quarter of 1995, most
of which went into radio and television advertising in Iowa, New Hampshire, and Arizona. By mid-December, he had spent more on ads in the Des
Moines media market than had all of the Republican *and* Democratic candidates at the same point in the 1988 nominating cycle.[34]

NATIONAL POLL STANDINGS

Another barometer of likely candidate success is standing in the national
polls. Writing about the 1976 invisible primary, Arthur Hadley maintained
that the last Gallup poll released before the first voting in New Hampshire
always predicted the Democratic and Republican nominees.[35] Although
wrong about the Democrats in 1976, Hadley's law has stood up remarkably well for every contested nomination since. Substituting Iowa for New
Hampshire, every Democratic and Republican front-runner in the final
Gallup poll before Iowa has gone on to win his party's nomination. Still, as
I have argued elsewhere, it is unwise to regard the last poll of the invisible
primary as representative of all polls preceding it. Democratic front-runners typically emerge quite late in the invisible primary, while eventual
Republican nominees typically lead in the polls for most if not all of the
invisible primary.[36] Dole's standing in the *national* polls adhered closely to
the Republican pattern. The unannounced Powell, as previously noted,
posed the only threat to Dole's otherwise impressive lead in every Gallup
poll taken between March 1994 and January 1996. In the polls with only
announced candidates, Dole always received between 45 and 55 percent of
all the support.[37]

TELEVISION NEWS EXPOSURE

Coverage in the news media constitutes yet another measure of candidate
success during the invisible primary. Publicity closely follows the polls,
with most of it going to front-runners, runners-up, and potential upstarts,
while candidates written off as hopeless receive remarkably little notice.[38]

Seldom, if ever, has an early front-runner not already in the White House enjoyed more of a media advantage than Dole, who exploited his position as Senate Republican leader to the hilt. In 1993 alone, he appeared on 31 weekend television news and talk shows, including seven interviews on CNN's *Newsmaker/Late Edition* and six on *Larry King Live;* in 1994 Dole marked his 50th appearance on NBC's *Meet the Press.*[39]

At a point when poll standings signified little more than name recognition, no other candidate came close to matching Dole in television exposure. The number of stories naming him on all three networks more than doubled the total for all other aspirants during the early phase of the campaign.[40] He also predominated during the latter part, albeit less impressively. Altogether, he showed up in a total of 765 stories over a period of 109 weeks, averaging seven stories per week. Gramm, his closest rival in the polls, appeared in only 227 stories, or only two per week.[41]

Dole's coverage looked all the more impressive for its variety. During the latter phase of the invisible primary, for example, the networks turned to him more often than all of his rivals combined for pronouncements on the 103d Congress and the 1994 midterm elections. He dominated in coverage of the budget battle and associated government shutdowns (100 stories or ten times the coverage of all other Republican candidates on this issue), the balanced budget amendment (15 stories to Gramm's 2), welfare reform (27 Dole stories compared to 14 mentioning Gramm, Buchanan, or Wilson), and health care (59 stories compared to 23 for Gramm and Specter). All three networks aired a total of 61 nightly news stories mentioning his Bosnia views, compared to 25 paying similar attention to his rivals. Even in the case of the U.S. takeover of Haiti, which Powell helped broker, Dole got the most coverage.[42]

STRAW POLLS: "IS ANYBODY HERE FROM IOWA?"

Though yielding no delegates, the invisible primary indicators mentioned thus far do forecast who eventually wins the nomination. The same cannot be said of straw polls. Of the 18 Republican and Democratic straw votes that took place during the invisible primaries of 1976–92, in which 1,000 voters or more participated, eventual nominees won only nine.[43] The Republicans staged a record 11 of these contests during the 1996 invisible primary. Dole won only three, including the crucial Presidency III showdown in Florida. Gramm won five and tied Dole in the much publicized Ames, Iowa poll. Buchanan prevailed in two others. Table 1.2 summarizes the outcome of each straw vote.

Table 1.2: 1994–1996 Republican Presidential Straw Polls

Date	Event	Winners and Losers	Particulars
June 24, 1994	Iowa GOP convention in Des Moines	Dole 27%, Alexander 15%, Gramm 15% of 1,349 votes cast	Voting limited to holders of $25 tickets.
January 7, 1995	Louisiana GOP convention	Gramm 72%, Buchanan 12%, and Alexander 5% of 1,247 votes cast	Gramm launched a major effort to contact every delgate; Dole did not compete.
March 3, 1995	South Carolina GOP "Silver Elephant" fundraiser	Gramm 35%, Alexander 25%, Dole 21% of 1,200 votes cast	Voting limited to ticket-holders; blocs of tickets purchased by campaigns and distributed to supporters.
April 8, 1995	Oklahoma GOP state convention	Gramm 50%, Keyes 22%, Dole 15% of 1,439 votes cast	Each participant paid $10 "delegate fee" to vote.
June 17, 1995	Virginia Republicans	Buchanan 59%, Keyes 11%, Gramm 8%, Lugar 8%, Dole 7% in vote of 1,083 participants	Participants paid $25 each to vote at a fundraiser in Tyson's Corner.
August 19, 1995	Iowa GOP convention in Ames	Dole and Gramm tied with 24% each of 10,598 votes cast; Buchanan got 18%, Alexander 11%, and Wilson only 1%	Each participant paid $25 to vote; news reports of extensive voting by activists from other states; widely interpreted as Dole setback.
September 17, 1995	National Federation of Republican Women convention meeting in Albuquerque	Gramm 35%, Alexander 17%, Dole 17% (1 vote less than Alexander), Wilson 15%, Keyes 8%, Lugar 5%, Buchanan 2% of about 1,200 votes cast	New York Times described delegates as a "fairly good cross section of the Republican party;" interpreted outcome as a plus for Gramm and a setback for Dole.

Table 1.2 continued

Date	Event	Winners and Losers	Particulars
November 4, 1995	Maine GOP	Gramm 42%, Lugar 21%, Dole 10%, Specter 8% with 1,500 votes cast	Participants paid $15 to vote.
November 18, 1995	Florida's Presidency III	Dole 33%, Gramm 26%, Alexander 23% of 3,325 votes cast	Voting limited to registered Florida Republicans, mostly chosen by lot or party office as delegates to state convention.
January 30, 1996	Alaska GOP	Buchanan 33%, Forbes 31%, Dole 17%, Keyes 10%, Gramm 9% of about 10,000 votes cast	Buchanan waged an extensive television campaign in contest open to all registered voters.
February 11, 1996	California GOP mail poll	Dole 36%, Buchanan 25%, Forbes 18%, Gramm 9% of 21,329 votes cast	Participants paid $25 per ballot; of 390,000 invitations mailed out to Republicans, 20,000 were returned along with fee; more than 100 delegates to the GOP state convention also voted.

Sources: "Dole Wins Early Nod in Race for President," *Des Moines Register*, June 25,1994, IA; "Texas Senator Has a Victory in Louisiana," *New York Times*, January, 1995, 12A; "As South Carolina GOP Uses 'Straw Poll' Dinner to Raise Cash, Hungry '96 Hopefuls Crowd Table," *Wall Street Journal*, March 3, 1995, 12A; "Gramm is Winner in South Carolina GOP Straw Ballot," *Washington Post*, March 5, 1995, 7A; "Buchanan Big Winner in Va. Poll," *Washington Post*, June 18, 1995, 1B; "Freewheeling Iowa Straw Poll Even Has Out-of State Voters," *Washington Post*, August 19, 1995, 1A; "Dole or Gramm? Iowa GOP Says Yes," *Washington Post*, August 20, 1995, 9A; "Maine GOP Backs Gramm in Straw Poll," *Washington Post*, November 5, 1995, 18A; "Dole Narrowly Wins Florida GOP Straw Poll," *Washington Post*, November 19, 1995, 1A; "Buchanan, Forbes Top Dole in Alaska GOP Straw Poll," *Washington Post,* January 31, 1996, 4A; "Dole Wins Calif. Straw Poll," Associated Press release, February 11, 1996; author's telephone interview with Oklahoma GOP staff.

At least seven of these limited voting to purchasers of tickets costing between $10 and $25. Voting early and often was a common practice. In Ames, for example, anyone from anywhere could cast as many votes as he had tickets.[44] The Alexander, Gramm, and Taylor campaigns brought in voters from out of state by the bus- and plane-load.[45] Small wonder that master of ceremonies Dan Quayle opened the gathering by asking, "Is anybody here from Iowa?"[46]

No candidate took these pseudo-events more seriously than Gramm. Like the early losers of past nominating races, Gramm hoped to parlay a string of straw poll wins into a firm grip on second place. Accordingly, the Gramm campaign invested heavily in the Louisiana straw vote of January 1995.[47] Gramm competed with Alexander to buy up tickets for the "silver elephant" poll in South Carolina; Gramm bought more than Alexander and won.[48] His organization in Iowa admitted to having spent at least $200,000 on the Ames vote alone, although half a million is a more likely figure.[49] Gramm likewise bought the vote in the Maine straw poll.[50]

Any benefit accruing to Gramm from these synthetic victories proved evanescent. The vast sums spent on contesting straw polls probably exceeded whatever new money they attracted. Moreover, his inability to rise in the real polls gave pundits additional reason not to take his ersatz wins seriously.[51]

The book on straw polls should not be closed before making note of Presidency III, a conspicuous exception to the other contests just described.[52] Participation in this straw poll was restricted to Republican delegates registered to vote in Florida who had been chosen in county caucuses and lotteries. GOP office-holders and state party officials also got to vote, as did contributors of $5,000 or more.[53] Dole went all out to win this November showdown by flying in 21 out-of-state politicians, wooing delegates, and lavishing money on social events. Like Gramm, Alexander, and Buchanan, he took time off from Iowa and New Hampshire to meet with the delegates. After extravagant spending by all four campaigns,[54] Dole won with 33 percent. Gramm finished second, Alexander third.

EARLY CAUCUSES AND DE FACTO PRIMARIES

For all his early advantages in fund-raising and the polls, Dole suffered greatly during the invisible primary. Much of the problem was of his own making. At no point during the campaign did Dole make a substantive argument for nominating him. His utterances raised doubts that he possessed any vision whatever. When asked what he would do first if elected, for example, Dole answered, "If I get elected, at my age, you know, I'm not going anywhere. It's not an agenda. I'm just going to serve my country."[55]

Changing stands on key issues increased this concern. Having built a reputation in the Senate as a consummate deal-maker and dedicated pragmatist, Dole now tried to pass himself off as no less ardent a conservative than Gramm, the rival he feared most during the invisible primary. Dole endorsed Oliver North for the U.S. Senate, signed the same no-new-taxes pledge in New Hampshire that he had spurned in 1988, began opposing affirmative action, decried welfare for unwed mothers in their teens, blasted multiculturalism, and assailed the gratuitous violence and explicit sex in films and recordings.[56]

Incredibly, for all of his experience with the news media, Dole repeatedly gave the press openings to point out contradictions and inconsistencies in his rhetoric. It soon came to light that he had not seen the films he had criticized and that he had avoided attacking Hollywood moguls who had contributed to his campaign.[57] Another flap erupted when his campaign aides first solicited and then returned a contribution from the Log Cabin Republicans, a gay caucus in the GOP. Dole contradicted his own aides before lapsing into an uneasy silence on the matter. By that time, however, his "flip flopping" had drawn criticism from all parts of the GOP.[58] Dole also angered the religious right by campaigning for the right-to-life vote while refusing to take an absolute stand against abortion.[59]

As front-runner, Dole naturally drew fire from his rivals. Alexander, Buchanan, and Gramm repeatedly disputed his credibility as a conservative and frequently called attention to his advanced age (72 in 1995). Dole gave Republicans fresh basis for concern on both counts when he delivered the GOP's response to Clinton's 1996 State of the Union address. Almost everyone agreed that he looked old and sounded tired compared with Clinton. Many Republicans saw the speech as yet another demonstration of his infirmities as a candidate, a sentiment his rivals pounced upon. "Senator Dole," Alexander assured an Omaha audience, "is too decent to fake a vision he does not have."[60]

Dole endured much worse from the ceaseless barrage of Forbes attacks in Iowa, New Hampshire, and Arizona. In the final week of January 1996, for example, Forbes aired 526 spots in Iowa and another 630 in New Hampshire, most of which flayed Dole as a Washington insider, a toady of the special interests, and a tax-hiker.[61] Before Forbes got into the race, Dole had enjoyed a comfortable lead of 40 percent in Iowa. Scarcely six months later, Dole had dropped to 28 percent and Forbes had moved up to second place with 16 percent. Forbes passed Dole in some New Hampshire polls and in Arizona.[62]

On January 12, Dole effectively declared total war against Forbes. In Alabama to address the Southern Republican Leadership Conference, Dole pointed out that Forbes had held only one minor post in government. A Dole ad attacking Forbes's inexperience and "risky ideas" aired the same day in Iowa. Another grossly distorted Forbes's stand on the imprisonment of violent criminals. Yet another branded him as "just too liberal on welfare," "untested," and "more liberal than you think." One week before the

Iowa caucus vote, the Dole campaign bought 138 half-minute spots on Des Moines television.[63]

Dole settled on the flat tax as the riskiest Forbes idea, charging that it would burden ordinary Americans while making moguls like Forbes even richer.[64] He released his tax returns of the last 29 years and repeatedly challenged Forbes to do the same. Dole even floated a flat tax of his own with deductions for home mortgages and charitable contributions. He ridiculed Forbes for prescribing the flat tax as a remedy for almost every ailment: "If you've a got a headache, the cure is the flat tax. If your feet hurt, the cure is the flat tax. If you don't want to pay any taxes, the cure is the flat tax." Beginning February 1, the Dole campaign ran an effective if inaccurate ad featuring Governor Stephen Merrill of New Hampshire warning that the Forbes tax would cost the typical New Hampshire household $2,000 more in taxes. A similar Dole spot featuring Senator Charles Grassley aired in Iowa.[65]

Dole attacked on other fronts as well. He repeatedly accused Forbes of trying to buy the nomination and branded him a liberal for taking on the Christian Coalition. The Dole campaign sent flyers to 40 percent of all registered Republicans in Iowa and New Hampshire denouncing Forbes's support of welfare for illegal immigrants and distorting his position on imprisoning violent criminals.[66] Extensive "push polling" supplemented these attacks.[67] The consequences of all this could be seen in the Iowa polls. In two months' time, Forbes's negative ratings among likely caucus participants soared from 26 percent to 46 percent while Dole's rose from 9 percent to 29 percent.[68]

Gramm despaired of the polls even more than Dole. Forbes had displaced him as Iowa runner-up in November, and by January Gramm had fallen to fifth place in the final poll of likely caucus participants. He remained frozen at 5 or 6 percent in the New Hampshire polls. Arizona and California also looked grim for Gramm.[69]

Gramm hoped to turn things around by winning the Louisiana caucuses on February 6. Though boycotted by most candidates out of deference to Iowa, Louisiana nonetheless marked the actual start of 1996 delegate-selection. Buchanan saw these rogue caucuses as a golden opportunity to knock Gramm out of the race and thereby become the conservative alternative to Dole. Gramm, however, had built a strong organization there and fully expected Louisiana conservatives to back a Texas conservative. Inexplicably, however, he spent most of the final week elsewhere while Buchanan worked Louisiana hard and won a key endorsement from Governor Mike Foster.[70]

Returns from Louisiana revealed that Gramm had badly underestimated Buchanan, who trounced him in the preference vote and ended up with 13 of the 21 delegates. The Voter News Service (VNS) poll of caucus participants disclosed that about 90 percent identified themselves as "conservative," and that most of these claimed to be "very conservative." Buchanan won big among conservatives of every description; he also appealed to elderly, less educated, low-income, and anti-abortion activists.[71] In a single stroke Buchanan changed the dynamics of the Republican race.

When the Iowa precinct caucuses took place six days later, only 96,451 of a projected 130,000 turned out, a dropoff some attributed to all the negative campaigning.[72] Dole "won" with 26 percent in a straw poll taken just before the actual selection of delegates to county conventions. Buchanan finished a strong second at 23 percent, and Alexander rounded out the top three with 18 percent.[73] Forbes came in a dismal fourth, after spending $407 per vote.[74] Gramm quit two days later.

The Iowa results must have alarmed Dole, for he had barely bested Alexander among self-identified moderates and fared poorly with the conservatives.[75] Moreover, he had been judged less electable than Alexander in the VNS poll. The poll also showed that half of his early supporters had backed somebody else on caucus day. Less than one-third of the majority of caucus attenders who did not identify with the religious right had supported him. R.W. Apple compared Dole's 1996 vote to the 36 percent he won in the 1988 caucuses and pronounced it "dangerously narrow."[76]

"Narrow" likewise described the support for Buchanan and Forbes. Buchanan owed his strong showing to an intense but overlapping following consisting of the very conservative, those who identified with the religious right, those who wanted a nominee with conservative convictions, those who wanted the GOP to oppose abortion, and those who had not supported Dole at any point in the race. Forbes fared well only with those most opposed to nominating a career politician and those most concerned about tax plans. Perceived electability surfaced as Alexander's most noteworthy asset in the VNS poll, probably the result of his endlessly reiterated claim that only he could beat Clinton.

All attention was now riveted on the final eight days of the New Hampshire campaign. The daily tracking polls showed Dole peaking at 32 percent six days before the primary vote.[77] He fell steadily thereafter to 23 percent on the eve of the primary. Buchanan rose from 19 percent to 25 percent where he remained until he gained a point in the final sampling. Forbes's support dropped from 25 percent to 13 percent between February 11 and 16. Meanwhile, Alexander rocketed from 11 percent to 23 percent on February 16. With this kind of momentum, he looked almost certain to finish second if not first.

Facing the prospect of finishing third in New Hampshire, which almost certainly would have driven him from the race, Dole shifted his fire from Buchanan to Alexander in a desperate bid to finish no worse than second. He filled the airwaves with ads branding Alexander a liberal on taxes, crime, and spending. Massive push-polling embellished these charges. The

Alexander campaign had expected something of this sort, for everyone now appreciated that whoever beat Buchanan in New Hampshire would in all probability become the nominee.[78]

Dole's change of primary targets paid off. Alexander dropped by three crucial points in the last three days of the New Hampshire campaign. Dole ended up in second place, with 26 percent to Buchanan's 27 percent, a difference of only 2,090 votes out of 208,993 cast. Alexander got 23 percent while Forbes finished a dismal fourth. Buchanan picked up six delegates to four for Dole and two for Alexander.[79]

The VNS exit poll showed Buchanan scoring impressive majorities among the very conservative, the religious right, those who had voted for him in the 1992 primary, pro-life plank advocates, those who based their vote mainly on abortion, and those who wanted a strong and principled conservative as nominee.[80] Buchanan also captured a majority of the small number most concerned about foreign trade.

Dole garnered a majority from the 10 percent who viewed Washington experience as a plus and from those mentioning the deficit as the most important issue in their vote. Nearly half of all voters most concerned about nominating an electable candidate backed him, a big improvement over the Iowa poll numbers. On the debit side, only 10 percent who felt strongly that the nominee should have a vision of the future voted for him, as did 15 percent of those wanting a champion of conservative values.

Alexander fared well among liberals and moderates, those wanting a candidate with a vision for the future, and those most offended by negative advertising. He even carried a majority of those voters wanting someone "not too extreme" to win the nomination, an interesting comment on Dole's attempt to brand Buchanan as "too extreme" to carry the Republican standard. Almost half of those citing education as the biggest factor in their choice of candidates voted for Alexander. As in Iowa, he lost out to Forbes among voters most desirous of an outsider nominee. And, in a near perfect reversal of the Iowa entrance poll, Alexander lagged well behind Dole among those looking for a winner against Clinton. Forbes found little to celebrate except his majority among the voters wanting an outsider as nominee and his plurality among those who regarded taxes as the most important issue.

Many in the GOP took fright at Buchanan's apparent strengths and Dole's demonstrated weaknesses.[81] Celebrating in New Hampshire, Buchanan rightly anticipated that party leaders would "come after this campaign with everything they've got."[82] Indeed, within 48 hours of his victory, Buchanan had been attacked by Newt Gingrich, New York Mayor Rudolph Giuliani, House GOP conference chairman John Boehner, Colin Powell, George Will, Senator Olympia Snowe, Rush Limbaugh, Senator John McCain, and Senator Alfonse D'Amato.[83]

Playing to Republican fears of another debacle on the scale of Barry Goldwater's nomination in 1964, the winless Alexander asked Dole to withdraw so that he could unify the party against Buchanan and Clinton, a proposal that Dole promptly spurned.[84] Lugar rebuffed Dole's entreaties to get out.[85] At this point, of course, the process precluded the entry of new candidates. Even in defeat, Dole looked like the only viable alternative to Buchanan. Alexander's only hope of altering this perception was to win something soon. For his part, Dole announced that "the real Bob Dole" would now make his appearance to save the GOP from the "extremist" Buchanan.[86]

Four primaries now loomed in the immediate future: Delaware on February 24; Arizona, North Dakota, and South Dakota on February 27. Dole should not have been surprised by the Delaware outcome, for he and almost every other candidate had agreed not to campaign there out of respect for New Hampshire. (Delaware Republicans scheduled their contest to occur four days after the New Hampshire vote, thereby violating the tradition of allowing New Hampshire an entire week unto itself before the next primary. The New Hampshire party retaliated by pressuring the candidates to ignore Delaware. Forbes and Keyes refused.[87]) Forbes made a major effort in Delaware, capturing all 12 delegates under winner-take all rules. Dole came in second.

Although declared an easy winner in North and South Dakota on February 27, Dole suffered through a long night of network predictions that he would lose to both Forbes and Buchanan in Arizona.[88] In the final tabulation, however, Dole edged out Buchanan to finish second. He now vowed to win the South Carolina primary on March 2.[89] A new Gallup poll of registered Republicans nationwide showed that he was still the front-runner.[90]

Arizona hurt Buchanan much more than it did Dole. Buchanan had spent nearly all of his time there since winning New Hampshire. A win in Arizona, Buchanan told the press, "would give us such a propulsion it would be very, very difficult to stop us from winning the nomination." After receiving false reports of victory, Buchanan told ecstatic followers that he was going "all the way to the White House."[91] The actual outcome, however, suggested that he was going nowhere.

Up to this point, Alexander had raised substantial sums by selling the scenario that Dole would collapse just as he had in 1980 and 1988.[92] This time, however, front-loading dictated the outcome almost as much as the pace. In the week following New Hampshire, Alexander finished fourth in Delaware, fourth in Arizona, fourth in South Dakota, and fifth (behind even the departed Gramm) in North Dakota. Indeed, having failed to win 10 percent of the preference vote in any of these primaries, Alexander now risked losing his federal matching funds.[93] Polls in South Carolina and the Super Tuesday South held out little hope of his recovery.[94]

Reestablished as a contender, Forbes concentrated on the South Carolina primary, on the New England states voting in the "Junior Tuesday" primaries of March 5, and on New York, where he won a protracted battle to get his name on the March 7 ballot. Though still pushing the flat tax and advertising on a lavish scale, Forbes let up on the attacks and supplemented his message with foreign policy themes.[95]

Thanks largely to the overwhelming support of Republican officials and party regulars, Dole won big in the South Carolina primary. He picked up 45 percent of the preference vote, compared to 29 percent for Buchanan, 13 percent for Forbes, and 10 percent for Alexander. According to the VNS exit poll, he won outright majorities among senior citizens (a 15-percent improvement over his New Hampshire showing), deficit hawks (a 30-percent improvement), those most concerned about nominating a winner in the general election (a 34-percent gain), those who prized Washington experience (97 percent for Dole, a gain of 7 percent), and free traders (no comparable question asked in New Hampshire). Dole also made inroads into Buchanan's base. Among South Carolina voters identifying with the religious right, he captured 40 percent of the vote against Buchanan's 43 percent.[96]

South Carolina sent a clear signal to Buchanan that he could not win a two- or even three-man race against Dole. Compared to the New Hampshire vote, his support among voters wanting an avowedly conservative nominee dropped by 18 percent. The Palmetto primary also cast a pall over Alexander and Forbes. Alexander got enough votes to become eligible again for federal money, but in every other respect he suffered a devastating loss.

Finally on the fast track, Dole captured outright majorities of the preference vote in Connecticut, Maryland, and Rhode Island and won a plurality in all of the other Junior Tuesday primaries on March 5.[97] Two days later Dole picked up all 93 of the delegates at stake in the New York primary, even though 45 percent of those sampled in an exit poll expressed dissatisfaction with the choice of candidates, and 57 percent complained that he lacked new ideas.[98] By this time, Alexander and Lugar had dropped out and endorsed him. Dole romped through the Super Tuesday primaries on March 12, forced Forbes out of the race on March 14, and trounced Buchanan in a Midwestern regional primary on March 19. Dole may well have gone over the top in delegates at this point, but he did not claim the prize until sweeping the California Tuesday primaries on March 26. This meant that primary voters in Pennsylvania, Indiana, North Carolina, the District of Columbia, Nebraska, West Virginia, Arkansas, Idaho, Kentucky, Alabama, Montana, New Mexico, and New Jersey would play no meaningful part in deciding the 1996 Republican nomination. Dole racked up huge majorities in all of these ex post facto primaries, garnering more than 70 percent of the vote in nine of the thirteen.

By that time, however, even Buchanan had given up, suspending his candidacy six days before the Pennsylvania primary.[99] He had lost all of the primaries since New Hampshire, prevailing only in the little-noted caucuses in Missouri on March 9.

THE UNCONTESTED DEMOCRATIC NOMINATION

Analysts on the Republican "Tsunami" of 1994 typically counted Clinton's presidency as part of the debris. Rightly or wrongly, much of the blame for this electoral debacle fell on Clinton. In 1992 he had posed as a centrist "new Democrat" who would end chronic welfare dependency, make communities safe, and promote the interests of the great middle class. Once in office, however, he made common cause with liberal Democrats in the Congress to push a tax-and-spend program of economic recovery. At the same time he backtracked on promises to open the armed forces to gays and to appoint Lani Guinier Assistant Attorney General for Civil Rights. Early accounts of his administration reported a White House awash in consultants and consumed by interminable and inconclusive meetings.[100]

More problems followed when he set welfare aside to concentrate on a massive overhaul of the nation's health-care system. The end product of a task force headed by wife Hillary Rodham Clinton was so lengthy and complicated that it bewildered even members of his own administration.[101] Congressional Democrats haggled over approaches while congressional Republicans and allied interest groups pounced on the plan's ambiguities. Clinton suffered a stinging defeat and Clinton health care became a nightmarish caricature of what liberal Democrats like Hillary had in mind for the nation.[102]

Accusations of marital infidelity, fraudulent dealings, misuse of FBI files, and concealing evidence in the suicide of a key aide all added to the President's woes, as did the killing of American soldiers in Somalia. Clear signs of economic recovery helped his job approval rating remarkably little. Less than 40 percent of the public approved of his performance at one point during the summer of 1993. Some improvement could be seen at year's end, but, for most of 1994, Clinton remained below 50 percent.[103]

Massive Democratic defeat in 1994 generated a conventional wisdom that Clinton would not be reelected. Prominent Democrats talked openly of dumping him. Liberal columnist Jack Newfield scourged him as an unprincipled liar and called on him to bow out. Pundit Jack Germond described him as "politically naked" for want of a following in the Democratic party. One poll found that 66 percent of the Democrats interviewed did not want Clinton to escape a primary challenge. Matched against a generic Republican and an unidentified independent in this poll, Clinton lost to the Republican, 33 to 40 percent.[104]

Although not immediately apparent, the electoral setback of 1994 did have a positive side for Clinton. It undermined any primary challenge from the left. With liberal Democrats in disrepute, potential rivals like Jesse Jackson saw little point to fighting him for a worthless nomination. Indeed, even as Democrats bewailed Clinton's failings, pundit Fred Barnes noted the curious absence of primary challengers. "Is there anybody organizing?" Barnes asked. "Is there anybody talking about organizing?"[105] Meanwhile Clinton embarked on a strategy of "triangulation" that moved him back to the center and distanced him from liberal Democrats as well as conservative Republicans in Congress.[106]

The closest thing to a challenge issued from an old enemy, Robert Casey, the former governor of Pennsylvania. Casey had gained national attention for his opposition to abortion and attacks on "left-wing ideologues" in his party. He had also undergone massive heart and liver transplant surgery and lacked both the stamina and resources to make an all-out effort. Less than a month after forming an exploratory committee, Casey admitted that he could not keep up the pace of fund-raising and speechmaking.[107] His withdrawal in April 1995 marked the end of organized Democratic opposition to Clinton's renomination.

Clinton by this point already had achieved an astounding comeback, surpassing Dole in most polls. His resurrection began with an effective show of presidential leadership immediately after the Oklahoma City bombing in April 1995. Two months later, Clinton stunned liberal Democrats and stole some of the Republicans' thunder by proposing to balance the budget within ten years.[108] The State of the Union address in January 1996, with its reference to ending "the era of big government," further strengthened his credibility as a centrist. (By this time Clinton had raised more prenomination money than Dole.[109]) Shortly before the Republican convention in San Diego Clinton let it be known that he would sign a compromise version of the Republican welfare-reform bill. Dole had hoped to make welfare reform an issue in the fall campaign.[110]

Little need be said about 33 uncontested primaries in which Clinton won 87 percent of nearly 11 million votes cast. His support ranged from 76 percent in his home state of Arkansas to nearly 100 percent in Georgia and Indiana.[111]

THE PRE-CONVENTION PHASE OF THE GENERAL ELECTION CAMPAIGN

Usually the winner of an early nomination has cause to celebrate. More time exists to reunite the party, refine the message, scrutinize potential running-mates, and script the convention—all essentials of success in the fall campaign. Unfortunately for Dole, the long interval between the actual and the official nomination became an ordeal of straitened finances and Republican infighting, exacerbated by unanswered Democratic attacks, frustration in the Senate, and his own blunders.

The most immediate consequence of Dole's costly wars against Forbes, Buchanan, and Alexander came to light in April disclosures that his campaign had spent all but $2 million allowed under the FECA limit. Moreover, at least a quarter of what still could be legally spent was reserved for the San Diego convention nearly four months distant, at which point Dole would receive his federal grant for the general election.[112] Although party coffers could be tapped for so-called "generic" campaigning in the interim, Dole recognized the depths of his predicament. Clinton, he lamented on CNN, "has $25 million in the bank and we're broke."[113]

Democratic money was already taking a toll on Dole support in California, Ohio, Michigan, Illinois, Florida, and other key electoral states. There Democratic ads continually tarred Dole as opposed to the welfare of senior citizens, students, and the environment. From October 1995 up to the Chicago convention, the Democratic National Committee (DNC) spent $42.4 million on these so-called "issue advocacy" ads. Dole depended heavily on Republican National Committee (RNC) money to answer these attacks. The RNC did respond in eight of a dozen states targeted by the Democrats, but only in California did it come close to matching the Democrats dollar for dollar.[114]

With the race basically decided by Super Tuesday, Dole returned to the Senate in hopes of showcasing his leadership ability. After achieving initial success on giving the next president an item veto and on raising the debt ceiling, Dole learned that his interests as presidential nominee did not always coincide with congressional Republicans. This became apparent when House Republicans embarrassed him by passing a repeal of the assault weapons ban. Dole angered them and the gun lobby by refusing to schedule a Senate vote. Five Senate Republicans helped the Democrats kill a medical savings account bill important to Dole's presidential campaign. Incredibly, given his own time in Congress, Dole got bogged down in a battle over term limits that few senators wanted to fight. Democrats took full advantage of Senate rules to thwart his initiatives, and they forced him repeatedly to block a popular bill to revise the minimum wage.[115]

Although accounts differ on Dole's reluctance to resign from the Senate,[116] they agree that his strategy of campaigning for president on the Senate floor had not worked. Rather, it had inspired more Republicans in and out of Congress to express misgivings about their nominee. Falling in the polls, Dole announced on May 15 that he would give up his seat and "seek the presidency with nothing to fall back on but the judgment of the people and nowhere to go but the White House or home."[117]

Back on the campaign trail Dole got into fights that distracted him and dismayed the GOP. One such flap erupted after Dole revealed his doubts that cigarettes were addictive and that the tobacco industry should be more regulated. The Democrats carried on as if their candidates had never taken tobacco money or fought for tobacco in Congress.[118]

Dole stumbled again when declining an invitation to speak to the National Association for the Advancement of Colored People (NAACP). President Bush had passed up a similar opportunity in 1992, and nobody denied that an NAACP convention was less than an ideal venue for conservative views on affirmative action. Dole, however, made headlines by bluntly accusing chairman Kweisi Mfume of trying to set him up.[119]

Although his share of the anti-abortion vote had increased since New Hampshire, the issue itself had not gone away. Ralph Reed warned Republicans just before the March 19 primaries that "you cannot, you should not, and you must not retreat from the pro-life and pro-family stand[s] that have won you that majority in the first place."[120] When Reed hinted in May that the Christian Coalition might support a change in the GOP platform to permit an exemption for mothers in danger of dying in childbirth, Bay Buchanan, sister and campaign manager of Pat Buchanan, avowed that "no words can be changed, no words can be added. There is no compromise, there is no negotiating, there is no appeasement."[121]

Moderate Republicans seized this opportunity to call for an open debate on abortion in the platform committee. Senator Olympia Snowe maintained that "the more we suppress debate on this issue, the more it hurts the Republican party. It's not the abortion issue in and of itself, but what the Republican party says about women—less government is better, except in the case of women." Congressman James Greenwood of Pennsylvania argued that the platform should not even mention abortion.[122] Dole spoke out on June 6. "I expect to run for president with the existing pro-life language from our 1992 platform," he said, "and with the declaration of tolerance for different points of view on such issues as abortion."[123]

On June 11, Dole argued that tolerance language belonged in the pro-life plank itself because abortion was a moral issue, not to be equated with the likes of taxes and trade.[124] This statement dismayed Congressman Henry Hyde, the platform committee chairman, who had been led to believe that general language in the preamble would be acceptable to all. "There are enough contentious issues," Hyde warned Dole, "when you put a major one to rest, you like to see that it stays there."[125]

By early August a floor fight looked likely when moderates repeatedly failed to win any concession from the platform committee. Rebuffed on the plank itself, Dole supporters tried to insert tolerance language elsewhere in the platform. Fearing more adverse publicity if the issue went to the whole convention, Dole settled for a general statement of tolerance and an appendix listing all of the proposals defeated in the platform committee. The right-to-life language remained unchanged from 1992. "The unborn child has a fundamental individual right to life which cannot be infringed. We support a human life amendment to the Constitution and we endorse legislation to make clear that the Fourteenth Amendment's protections apply to unborn children."[126]

Although hints of a flat tax in Dole's economic package turned up in the press as early as March,[127] the Dole team appeared to make little progress over the next several months. Dole headquarters finally released the long-awaited plan on August 4. It contained major concessions to Forbes and accordingly contradicted Dole's career as a deficit hawk. Rather than adopt a single tax rate as advocated by Forbes, the plan called for $548 billion in tax cuts—achieved principally by a 15-percent slash for every tax bracket and a reduction in the capital gains from 28 percent to 14 percent. The plan also called for a $500-per-child tax credit and repeal of the 1993 increase in Social Security taxes on higher-income Americans. Little was said about balancing the budget.[128] The plan came under Democratic attack even before Dole first revealed its particulars, in a speech to the Chicago Chamber of Commerce.[129]

THE NATIONAL NOMINATION CONVENTIONS

The most vestigial of presidential nominating institutions is the national convention. Presidential nominations in a front-loaded system are decided long before the delegates are called to order. Typically the nominee picks a running-mate shortly before the convention begins. Contemporary conventions have been likened to operas, scripted and scored mainly for benefit of the audience.[130] Certainly Byron Shafer's description of the convention as "bifurcated" remains apt in the era of massive front-loading.[131] Indeed, the televised version now amounts to little more than prime-time coverage of selected speeches (when not interrupted by pundits interviewing themselves). Only those in attendance or watching C-SPAN experience the real convention.

Convention platforms, however, still retain value as guides to party principles and priorities. The Democratic platform adopted August 27 in Chicago echoed Clinton themes of limited government offset by rejection of "the misguided call to leave our citizens to fend for themselves." Americans, according to Democrats, wanted a "course that is reasonable, help that is realistic, and solutions that can be delivered—a moderate, achievable, common sense agenda that will improve people's daily lives and not increase the size of government."[132] Most of the Democratic plank on economic growth lauded Clinton's version of a balanced budget. The fact that the Democrats had embraced the principles of smaller government, a balanced budget, tax relief, and even welfare reform spoke volumes about liberal disarray and how much Clinton's stock had improved since 1994.

This is not to say that voters lacked a choice in 1996. The Republican and Democratic platforms clashed on what to do about Medicare, funding of the arts, and support for National Public Radio and Legal Services. The Republicans' manifesto called for constitutional amendments requiring a balanced budget, recognizing the unborn child's right to life, denying automatic benefits to children of illegal immigrants, and enhancing the rights of crime victims. It also proposed to terminate the Departments of Commerce, Education, Energy, and Housing and Urban Development. In contrast, the Democrats talked about "reinventing government" and saving programs from the Republican ax. The parties also differed on gun control and other "hot button" issues. Taking aim at the Republican right-to-life plank, the Democrats lauded "the right of every woman to choose, consistent with *Roe v. Wade,* and regardless of ability to pay." No reference was made to partial-birth abortions, prominently mentioned in the Republican platform. Responding to the Republican plank on illegal immigration, the Democrats decried "those who used the need to stop illegal immigration as a pretext for discrimination." After professing support for the ideal of equal treatment under law, the two parties offered opposing views of how the law should regard race, gender, and sexual orientation in the workplace and universities. In these and other respects the platforms pointed up important differences between a predominantly liberal and a preponderantly conservative party.

Previous research has shown that convention delegates are more ideologically intense and unified than are registered voters of the same party or the electorate as a whole.[133] As documented in earlier studies, in 1996, Republican and Democratic delegates positioned themselves at opposite ends of the ideological continuum while registered voters in the aggregate occupied the center.[134] On issues of policy and ideology, Republican delegates more often identified themselves as conservative than registered Republican voters, and Democratic delegates were always more liberal than registered voters of their party.

Interviewed before they learned that Kemp was the vice-presidential pick, barely half of the San Diego delegates offered positive assessments of Dole's campaign. By putting Kemp on the ticket Dole finally electrified a convention desperate for something to celebrate. Spirits lifted as convention orators extolled the economic plan, remembered Ronald Reagan, plugged family values, and ridiculed Clinton. In Chicago the euphoric Democrats shrugged off news of Dick Morris's sex scandal, danced in the aisles, and renominated their ticket by acclamation.

THE PEROT PARTY NOMINATES PEROT

Nothing aids prediction better than repetition, and, in key respects, the Perot candidacy of 1996 resembled the Perot candidacy of 1992. Both times Perot sought to endow his candidacy with the appearance of popular demand. Perot launched his first campaign during a guest appearance on CNN's *Larry King Live.* He turned again to the King show to make his 1996 announcement. In 1992 Perot ran as an independent and transformed his United We Stand organization into an electoral machine. Four years later he chose to run as a third-party candidate and thereby needed a party to nominate him. Perot looked almost certain to run in 1996 after having won nearly 19 percent of the popular vote in 1992 and having helped the Republicans recapture the House in 1994.

The tip-off to what Perot had in mind for 1996 came when he summoned the Republican aspirants and Clinton surrogates to address the 1995 convention of United We Stand. Ostensibly the point of these invitations was to promote discussion of key issues with Perot followers. Nearly every Republican spoke, as did Thomas McLarty III of the White House and DNC chairman Christopher Dodd. True to form, Perot laid down an impossible ultimatum at the end of the proceedings: unless the Republicans and Democrats balanced the budget, solved the problems of Medicare and Social Security, curbed the special interests, and imposed term limits on themselves—all of this to be accomplished by Christmas—he might well take up the torch.[135]

Perot waited only until September before launching the Reform party, the principal purpose of which was to nominate a presidential standard-bearer. Its platform would champion campaign finance reform and propose solutions to other problems discussed in Dallas. Perot promised to find "world-class" bidders for the presidential nomination, and, when asked, pointedly refused to rule out his own candadicy.[136]

By this time a major effort was already underway to get his party on the 1996 ballot in California. State law gave Perot little more than three weeks to acquire the necessary names of "party members" for a line on the presidential ballot. Paid and volunteer workers collected more than the 89,007 needed. Eventually, under one name or another, Perot or the Reform party got on the ballot in 44 states. Perot ran as an independent, rather than as a third-party candidate in Alaska, Mississippi, South Dakota, Tennessee, Texas, and Wyoming.[137]

Gordon Black, Perot's pollster, summed up the conventional wisdom about who would get the nomination: "It has to be Perot." Perot said as much himself. "Let's assume the dust clears, and that's what the members of this party want," he said in March 1996. "Then certainly, I would give it everything I have because probably there's not a luckier person alive in this country today." Days later, after decrying the evils of deficit spending and high national debt, Perot declared: "You and I are going to have to climb back in the ring again and make sure that it gets done, otherwise we're leaving a mess to our children."[138]

Nearly every potential candidate mentioned in the news wanted no part of a Perot party. Former Connecticut governor Lowell Weicker, former Oklahoma senator David Boren, and former Minnesota congressman Tim Penny all declined the honor. Reportedly, Jack Kemp considered running but decided against it after receiving little encouragement from Perot. Richard Lamm, a Democrat and former Colorado governor, expressed interest if Perot would only disavow an interest in running. Perot gave him no such assurance, but Lamm announced anyway on July 9, 1996. After inveighing against "big money, big influence, and narrow elite interests" in his announcement speech, Lamm acknowledged that he would have no credibility if Perot funded his campaign.[139]

Perot waited only a day before declaring his own candidacy in yet another appearance on *Larry King Live*. "If anybody should do this," he avowed, "I should do it." He reiterated this line on ABC's *Good Morning America* before adding: "And I will do it, and I'm in a unique position to do it."[140]

As worked out by Perot, the nomination would be decided in several stages. First, everyone who signed a petition to get the Reform party on a state ballot, or who applied to become a party member, would be sent a preference form. Respondents could propose anyone, but only persons named in at least 10 percent of these responses would get on the ballot. The finalists would speak at the first of two conventions in Long Beach, California, on August 11. A second vote limited to these finalists would occur by mail, telephone, or other means. Elaborate precautions would be taken to count the ballots and prevent fraud. The winner would be announced August 18 at a second convention in Valley Forge, Pennsylvania, where the nominee would deliver his acceptance speech.[141]

The problematic nature of this process first became apparent when 10 percent of the 979,882 preference forms proved undeliverable, and only 43,135 completed forms were filled out and returned. Nearly two-thirds of these respondents backed Perot, but Lamm also qualified as Perot's only rival on the ballot.[142] By this time an exasperated Lamm was complaining to reporters about the low response rate in the first round of voting, Perot's unwillingness to share his mailing list, the sending of more than one ballot to some individuals, apparent favoritism for some states over others, putting Perot's picture on the ballot, Perot's initial reluctance to divulge the names of the firms hired to distribute the ballots and tabulate the vote, and Perot's unwillingness to debate him in Long Beach.[143]

The Long Beach convention turned out to be little more than a rally for Perot, and he claimed the nomination one week later after winning 65 percent of 49,266 votes cast in all 50 states and the District of Columbia. The total amounted to a meager return of 4 percent on more than a million ballots mailed out, or about half of the Republican turnout for the 1996 Iowa precinct caucuses. The electorate exceeded 1,000 in only 12 states and fell below 100 in five states and the District of Columbia. California alone cast 35 percent of the total vote, more than the combined returns from New York, Texas, Ohio, Michigan, and Pennsylvania. Perot won by more than 60 percent in 41 states while losing to Lamm in Alaska, Colorado, Minnesota, and the District of Columbia.[144]

If this process was meant to legitimate Perot's candidacy, it had quite the opposite effect. Lamm's well-publicized carping coincided with a big jump in Perot's polling negatives. Perot also suffered in the trial-heat comparisons with Dole and Clinton, falling from an average of 16 percent in the earliest polls to only 6 percent in mid-August. Subsequent polls showed him stuck at 7 percent. His efforts to find a running-mate met with refusal until author Pat Choate accepted.[145]

CONCLUSIONS AND CODA

How much did Dole owe his nomination to the front-loaded process described above? True, the primary calendar is only one part of the overall situation, but it does figure importantly in who runs and who does not. Clearly the massive front-loading of the 1996 primaries largely accounts for the paucity of strong Republican candidates at a time when it looked like almost any Republican could defeat Clinton. Significant back-loading would have reduced the criticality of the invisible primary by allowing candidates time to raise money and to make strategic adjustments *after the actual primary season had started*. Dole would not have become the prohibitive favorite by default, nor would he have remained the only realistic choice after losing the New Hampshire, Delaware, and Arizona primaries.

Significant back-loading in any event is not in the immediate future of presidential nominating politics. Although the GOP has approved a plan to encourage late contests,[146] the dates of 2000 primaries and caucuses are about as front-loaded as 1996. More than the simple majority needed for nomination will have been chosen by March 14, and more than two-thirds of all 2,061 delegates will be corralled by March 21. Unless the front-runner stumbles badly, the Republican race should effectively end with the March 7 primaries. Republican winner-take-all rules of delegate selection should help in expediting an early decision.

As in 1996, the invisible primary is proving to be the most critical stage of the process in both parties. The run-up to 2000 has already winnowed Republicans Senator Fred Thompson, Governor Pete Wilson, Senator John Ashcroft, Senator Robert Smith, Congressman John Kasich, and Lamar Alexander. Aschroft, Smith, Kasich, and Alexander waged extensive campaigns before departing. Smith departed the GOP as well. Still other Republican withdrawals appear likely before 2000. On the Democratic side, a once-crowded field has narrowed to Vice President Al Gore and former senator Bill Bradley. Congressman Richard Gephardt, Senator Bob Kerrey, Senator John Kerry, and Senator Paul Wellstone ventured out on the campaign trail before withdrawing.

Even more so than in 1996, a prohibitive favorite dominates the Republican version of the invisible primary. Gallup polls taken in the first six months of 1999 showed that Texas governor George W. Bush increased his support from 42 percent in January to 59 percent in June. Elizabeth Dole's standings over this same period dropped from 22 percent to 8 percent. None of the other aspirants—including Pat Buchanan, Steve Forbes, Senator John McCain, and Dan Quayle—got more than 9 percent in any of these polls.[147] Moreover, in marked contrast to Dole at the same point in the 1996 race, Bush hit upon an attractive theme ("Compassionate Conservatism") and exploited a near consensus among Republicans to pick a winner.

Bush also set a new record for fund-raising. On July 15, 1999, his campaign reported receipts of $37.3 million from 74,000 contributors in only six months, $5 million more than the total amount that Bob Dole took in during his entire campaign. Forbes ranked second with $9.4 million ($6.6 million of which was his own money) while McCain placed third with $6.3 million. Receipts for the remaining active candidates ranged from $3.5 million for Elizabeth Dole to $1.9 million for Alan Keyes.[148]

Clearly mindful of what happened to Bob Dole, Bush announced that his campaign would not accept federal matching funds. This freed him from the FECA spending limits that hobbled Dole in 1996. "You've got limits that constrain a candidate," he said with Forbes clearly in mind. "I want to be in a position to respond."[149] Taking a page from the Clinton playbook, Bush has also raised so-called soft money for an early start to the general election, as well as for his nominating campaign. Worried by the early polls, Clinton, Gore, and the DNC have launched a soft-money drive of their own.[150]

Several other parallels from the Republican process of 1996 deserve passing mention. It is a safe bet that Bush has gotten far more coverage in the news media than any and perhaps all of his rivals. Alexander, Buchanan, Forbes, and Keyes again cast themselves as outsiders, as did Quayle and family-values advocate Gary Bauer. Not surprisingly, front-runner Bush has come under attack as the establishment candidate, albeit for raising so much money and getting so many endorsements rather than for government service. Much of the debate centers on competing notions of conservatism since all of the candidates claim to be conservative. Abortion is central to this discussion, trade evidently less so. As of June 1999, Forbes had spent nearly $3 million on advertising in four early-voting states.[151] At least one straw poll took on great importance in the 2000 Republican race when Alexander decided to quit after a poor showing in Ames.

Thanks to Perot's decision to accept a federal grant and abide by spending limits in the 1996 general election, the Reform party is entitled to $12 million of public money for its 2000 convention and fall campaign. Nearly 70 and discredited by his comparatively weak showing in 1996, Perot's future in the Reform party appears to have dimmed with his political star. Attempts to loosen his hold on the party began only two weeks after the 1996 election and have continued since.[152] Perot acquired a formidable rival for control of the party in 1998, when Reform candidate Jesse Ventura won election as governor of Minnesota. A former Navy Seal, professional wrestler, and actor, the flamboyant Ventura has since eclipsed Perot in media exposure. He disavows any interest in claiming the presidential nomination for himself and disapproves of another Perot candidacy. Perot, of course, has not taken himself out of contention and still commands a loyal if diminished following. "As long as I am helpful to the organization," Perot proclaimed at the 1999 Reform party convention, "I am certainly happy to help and participate in any constructive way."[153] The next day Perot lost out to Ventura in the Reform party's choice of a new national chairman.

NOTES

ACKNOWLEDGMENTS: I researched and wrote initial drafts of this chapter while on sabbatical at the Institute of Governmental Studies (IGS), University of California, Berkeley. I am indebted to Nelson W. Polsby for admitting me to so productive a workplace and am deeply grateful to Nelson, the talented library staff, and many other friends at IGS for making my time there so productive and enjoyable. Robert Biersack of the Federal Election Commission, Linda Fowler of Dartmouth College, and Mark Acton and Catherine Tyrell of the Republican National Committee kindly provided essential data. None of the above is in any way responsible for any errors or omissions on my part.

1. Arthur Hadley, *The Invisible Primary* (Englewood Cliffs, NJ: Prentice-Hall,1976).

2. See, for example, John H. Kessel, *Presidential Campaign Politics*, 4th ed. (Pacific Grove, CA: Brooks/Cole, 1992).

3. See Nicol C. Rae, *The Decline and Fall of the Liberal Republicans: From 1952 to the Present* (New York: Oxford University Press, 1989), 127-56. William G. Mayer provides useful data on how the number of primaries on both sides increased in tandem. See *The Divided Democrats: Ideological Unity, Party Reform, and Presidential Elections* (Boulder, CO: Westview Press, 1996), 12-13.

4. The same held true for the Democrats. See Emmett H. Buell Jr., "The Invisible Primary," *In Pursuit of the White House*, ed. William G. Mayer (Chatham, NJ: Chatham House, 1996), 7.

5. Elaine Ciulla Kamarck and Kenneth M. Goldstein, "The Rules Do Matter: Post-Reform Presidential Nominating Politics," in *The Parties Respond: Changes in American Politics*, 2d ed., ed. L. Sandy Maisel, (Boulder, CO: Westview Press, 1994), 183.

6. "The National Tally," *CQWR*, 1996, 577, 650, 727, 826, 907, 1183, 1329, and 1704.

7. Maureen Dowd, "Stars of War Room Are Auditioning for the Presidential Battles to Come," *NYT*, February 11, 1991, 7A; "Washington Wire: Gramm in '96," *WSJ*, September 20, 1991, 1A.

8. Andrew Rosenthal, "Weary of '92 Campaign? Now Try Pondering '96," *NYT*, December 22, 1991, 10A.

9. Jack Anderson and Michael Binstein, "Buchanan Aims Right Toward 1996," *WP*, August 3, 1992, 16C; Clara Germani, "Jockeying for '96 Is in Full Swing," *CSM*, August 21, 1992, 7; Michael McQueen and John Harwood, "With '92 Presidential Race Just Begun, GOP Hopefuls Line Up at the '96 Gate," *WSJ*, August 21, 1992, 8A. Other potentials for 1996 included South Carolina Governor Carroll Campbell, former drug czar and education secretary William Bennett, Wisconsin Governor Tommy Thompson, Massachusetts Governor William Weld, and Elizabeth Dole of the Red Cross and wife of Senator Robert Dole.

10. John Dillin, "Front-Runners Emerge in '96 GOP Free-for-All," *CSM*, November 20, 1992, 2.

11. James A. Barnes, "Whoosh! There Goes Bob Dole!" *NJ*, February 2, 1993, 351.

12. See Ann Devroy, "Not 'Fishing'—Just Testing New Hampshire Waters," *WP*, August 20, 1993, 8A.

13. AP, "Bob Dole's Everywhere as GOP Point Man," *CD*, January 2, 1994, 4A.

14. Bob Woodward, *The Choice* (New York: Simon & Schuster, 1996), 27-39.

15. Evan Thomas, et al., *Back From the Dead: How Clinton Survived the Republican Revolution* (New York: The Atlantic Monthly Press, 1997), 48.

16. Buell, "The Invisible Primary," 3 for a brief discussion of dropouts in the 1988 and 1992 invisible primaries.

17. Richard L. Berke, "Citing Financing, Quayle Drops Out of '96 Campaign," *NYT*, February 9, 1995, A1.

18. AP, "Powell Finds Fault With GOP Leaders," *CD*, September 18, 1995, 8A.

19. George Will, "Powell Couldn't Run for President on Character Alone," *CD*, April 16, 1995, 3B and "If Powell Runs, He'll Face Difficult Questions—Such as These," *CD*, October 29, 1995, 3B; R. W. Apple Jr., "Powell Stirs Waves on Republican Right," *NYT*, October 3, 1995, 11A; Berke, "Powell Sounds Out Friends About a White House Run," *NYT*, October 27, 1995, 8A; Berke, "Right Tries to Mobilize Against Powell Candidacy," *NYT*, November 2, 1995, 11A; and Berke, "Powell Record is Criticized by Conservatives in GOP," *NYT*, November 3, 1995, 9A.

20. Data from *Gallup Organization Newsletter Archive*, Vol. 60, October 7, 1995, 21; and William G. Mayer, The Presidential Nominations," in *The Election of 1996*, ed. Pomper (Chatham, NJ: Chatham House, 1997), 33.

21. Berke, "Poll Finds GOP Primary Voters Are Hardly Monolithic," *NYT*, October 30, 1995, 10A.

22. Dick Morris, *Behind the Oval Office: Winning the Presidency in the Nineties* (New York: Random House, 1997), 156.

23. Darmouth College news releases on polls of October 1–4 and October 22–25, 1995, kindly supplied by Professor Linda Fowler. Iowa data come from Mayer, "The Presidential Nominations," in *The Election of 1996* (Chatham, NJ: Chatham House, 1997) 33.

24. Francis X. Clines, "Powell Rules Out '96 Race; Cites Concerns for Family and His Lack of A Calling," *NYT*, November 9, 1995, 1A.

25. Berke, "GOP Candidates Feel The Gen. Powell Blues," *NYT*, September 24, 1995, A18.

26. See James W. Ceaser and Andrew E. Busch, *Upside Down and Inside Out: The 1992 Elections and American Politics* (Lanham, MD: Rowman & Littlefield, 1993). For an application of this scheme to the 1996 GOP candidates, see Ceaser and Busch, *Losing to Win: The 1996 Elections and American Politics* (Lanham, MD: Rowman & Littlefield, 1997), 57–87. Elsewhere Busch lists 16 outsider candidates since 1952, of which six sought the Democratic or Republican presidential nomination while serving in public office. Since 1984, however, only one of the nine outsiders listed by Busch held public office at the point he entered the presidential nominating race. Busch, *Outsiders And Openness in The Presidential Nominating System* (Pittsburgh, PA: University of Pittsburgh Press, 1997), 24–25.

27. B. Drummond Ayres Jr., "For Dornan, Keyes, and Taylor, Low Polls Can't Dash High Hopes," *NYT*, December 30, 1995, 1A.

28. For example, see the symposium, "My Guy: Why My Presidential Candidate is Mr. Right," *Policy Review* 75 (Summer 1995): 6–17.

29. See discussion in Buell, "The Invisible Primary," 12.

30. "1996 State-by-State Expenditure Limits For Presidential Candidates," FEC document kindly provided the author by Robert Biersack.

31. Buell, "The Invisible Primary," 14–16.

32. "Hard money" comparisons hardly constitute the whole picture of pre-nomination campaign finance in 1996. See, for example, Mary Jacoby, "Dole's PAC Aided Presidential Bid," *RC*, November 2, 1995, 1; AP, "Alexander Discloses Contributors' Names," *NYT*, December 31, 1995, 10A; and Ruth Marcus and Charles Babcock, "When is a Candidate Not a Candidate?" *WP National Weekly Edition*, January 8–14, 1996, 18.

33. See Buell, "The Invisible Primary," 11–16.

34. Anthony Corrado, "Financing the 1996 Elections," in *The Election of 1996*, ed. Pomper (Chatham, NJ: Chatham House, 1997), 144–5.

35. Hadley, *The Invisible Primary*, 2.

36. Buell, " The Invisible Primary," 16–18.

37. Data from *Gallup Organization Newsletter Archive*, Vol. 60, October 7, 1995; February, June 30, August 17, September 14, October 7; also February 1, 1996 at www.gallup.com; data for November 1995, January 5–7, 1996, and January 12–15, 1996 from Table 1.3 of William G. Mayer, "The Presidential Nominations," in *The Election of 1996*, ed. Pomper, 31–32.

38. Buell, "'Locals' and 'Cosmopolitans': National, Regional, and State Newspaper Coverage of the New Hampshire Primary," in *Media and Momentum: The New Hampshire Primary and Nomination Politics* ed. Gary R. Orren and Nelson W. Polsby, (Chatham, NJ: Chatham House, 1987), 60–103; Buell, "Meeting Expectations? Major Newspaper Coverage of Candidates During the 1988 Exhibition Season," in *Nominating the President*, ed. Buell and Lee Sigelman, 150–95; Buell, "The Invisible Primary," 25–28.

39. Tim Curran, "Handicapping the Three Senate Republicans Gearing Up to Run for the White House in 1996," *RC*, November 21, 1994, 10.

40. These data cover the period October 1, 1993, to February 6, 1996, and they are based on the Vanderbilt Television News Abstracts. The early stage dates through June 30, 1994, and the late stage begins on July 1, 1994.

41. See Buell, "The Invisible Primary," and "The Invisible Primary Revisited," paper presented at the Southern Political Science Association meeting in Atlanta, November 9, 1996, for more extensive comparisons of Republican candidate coverage.

42. See Buell, "The 'Invisible Primary' Revisited" for more detailed comparisons of topical coverage. Not all of this coverage helped Dole, of course, since the flood of stories about government shutdowns linked him to the unpopular Gingrich.

43. Buell, "The Invisible Primary," 22–23.

44. Paul Taylor, "Freewheeling Iowa Straw Poll Even Has Out-of-State Voters," *WP*, August 19, 1995, 1A.

45. See Thomas, et al., *Back From the Dead*, 52. For more on behind-the-scenes maneuvering at the Ames poll, see Woodward, *The Choice*, 240–7.

46. Taylor, "Dole or Gramm? Iowa GOP Says Yes," *WP*, August 20, 1995, 9A.

47. Dan Balz, "Gramm Wins, Opponents Minimize Louisiana Presidential Straw Poll," *WP*, January 8, 1995, 4A.

48. Balz and Eric Pianin, "Gramm is Winner in South Carolina GOP Straw Ballot," *WP*, March 5, 1995, 7A.

49. Berke, "Surprising Straw Poll Gives Dole a Glimpse of the Battles Ahead," *NYT*, August 21, 1995, 1A.

50. Steve Campbell, "Straw Polls Aren't Everything They're Made Out to Be," *Maine Sunday Telegram*, October 29, 1995, 3C.

51. See, for example, Berke, "Surprising Straw Poll"; Charles Cook, "What the Iowa Straw Poll Says, and What it Doesn't Say," *RC*, September 4, 1995, 8; Morton Kondracke, "Straw Polls Aside, Dole's on Track for GOP Nod," *RC*, September 4, 1996, 6; Thomas Edsall and Balz, "Straw Poll Winner Still Falls Short," *WP*, November 20, 1995, 4A.

52. Florida has the best overall record of straw-vote victors winning the state's presidential primary and eventually capturing the nomination. See Buell, "The Invisible Primary," 22–23.

53. William March, "Florida is Place to Be for GOP," *Tampa Tribune*, July 16, 1995, 1A.

54. Michael Murphy, a key Alexander operative, later conceded that his campaign had spent about half a million on Presidency III, "money we didn't have" that should been invested in New Hampshire. Remarks at a George Washington University symposium on the 1996 presidential election, April 20, 1996.

55. AP, "Dole Willing to be Another Reagan," *CD*, July 16, 1995, 9A; Charles Cook, "Rivals Chip Away at Granite State's Primary Electorate," *RC*, September 17, 1995, 6.

56. Berke, "Now Officially Dole Is Making a Run for '96," *NYT*, April 11, 1995, 1A; AP, "Dole Launches Presidential Bid, Vows No Tax Hike," *CD*, April 11, 1995, 3A; "Bob Dole: Where He Stands," from Dole campaign website.

57. Bernard Weinraub, "Violent Movies and Records Undercut Nation, Dole Says," *NYT*, May 31, 1995, 1A; Kevin Merida, "Dole Cites Murder in New Attack on Hollywood," *WP*, June 28, 1995, 4A.

58. Berke, "Gay Congressman of His Own Party Brings Fire on Dole," *NYT*, September 7, 1995, 1A; Berke, "Dole in Switch Says Aides Erred in Refunding Gay Gift, " *NYT*, October 18, 1995, 1A; Steven A. Holmes, "Reversal on Gay Donations Embroils Dole," *NYT*, October 19, 1995, 11A.

59. Berke, "Christian Right Issues Threat to the GOP," *NYT*, February 11, 1995, 1A; Berke "Politicians Woo Christian Group," *NYT*, September 9, 1995, 1A; Berke "Christian Coalition Ends Convention With A Dual Identity," *NYT*, September 10, 1995, 11A.

60. Michael J. Wines, "Dole's Response Gets a Response of Its Own, and It's Fairly Underwhelming," *NYT*, January 25, 1996, 8A.

61. Gerald F. Seib, "Dole's Twin Secrets: Old Style Organizing and a Newfound Cool," *WSJ*, March 11, 1996, 1A; Berke, "Wealthy Newcomer Gains His Rivals' Attention," *NYT*, January 13, 1996, 1A; and Berke, "Forbes, A Newcomer in Perot Clothing," *NYT*, January 15, 1996, 8A.

62. Mayer, "The Presidential Nominations," 39, 40–42; AP, "Polls Show Forbes Remains Close, But Must Count on Independents' Turnout," *CD*, January 30, 1996, 4A; Judy Keen, "A Two-Man Contest By Any Poll," *USA*, January 30, 1996, 4A; Berke, "Wealthy Newcomer Gains His Rivals' Attention."

63. Berke, "Wealthy Newcomer"; Elizabeth Kolbert, "GOP Candidates Struggle To Stand Out in Blur of Ads," *NYT*, January 20, 1996, 8A; Martha Moore and Judi Hasson, "Campaign '96: Dole Buying 'Awesome Amount' of Ads in Iowa," *USA*, February 7, 1996, 4A.

64. The flat tax plan as outlined by Forbes in his announcement speech of September 22, 1995, called for abolishing the federal income tax in favor of a 17 percent rate across the board. Certain exemptions provided that the head of a family of four would pay no taxes whatever on the first $36,000 of income. No taxes would be collected on Social Security, pensions, personal savings, or capital gains. "A New Conservative Vision," speech by Steve Forbes at the National Press Club in Washington, D.C., obtained from the Forbes campaign.

65. David E. Rosenbaum, "Panel Calls for a Flat Tax, But Fails to Specify the Rate," *NYT*, January 18, 1996, 10A; Katharine M. Seelye, "Dole, in Iowa, Unleashes Tough New Attacks," *NYT* January 26, 1996, 10A; Rosenbaum, "For Dole and Forbes, the Fight Is on the Air," *NYT*, February 7, 1996, 10A; Moore and Hasson, "Dole Buying 'Awesome Amount' of Ads."

66. Holmes, "Courtship of Iowans Intensifies," *NYT*, January 25, 1996, 8A; AP, "Dole Turns Up Heat on Forbes as Early Primaries Approach," *NYT*, January 28, 1996, 8A.

67. Ernest Tollerson, "Forbes Steps Up Defense Against Attack Ads," *NYT*, February 10, 1996, 8A; and Larry J. Sabato, ed., *Toward the Millennium: The Elections of 1996* (Boston: Allyn and Bacon, 1997), 74–76.

68. Elizabeth Kolbert, "Pointing Up Contrast, Lugar Points to His Campaign Ads," *NYT,* February 12, 1996, 9A.

69. Mayer, tables 1.4 and 1.5 in "The Presidential Nominations"; Roger K. Lowe, "Dole Opens Final Push for Iowa Hearts, Votes," CD, February 11, 1996, 1A; Berke, "Wealthy Newcomer Gains his Rivals' Attention"; AP, "New Poll Shows Forbes Gaining in California," NYT, February 3, 1996, 8A.

70. Kevin Sack, "In Louisiana, Church Pews Are Trenches in GOP War," NYT, January 24, 1996, 12A; Berke, "Who Knew? Louisiana Is Beginning to Choose," NYT, February 6, 1996, 10A.

71. AP, "Buchanan Deals Gramm Sharp Blow," CD, February 7, 1996, 1A; AP, "Buchanan Gets Overwhelming Support From Religious Right," CD, February 7, 1996, 2A; Keen, "Stunning Setback for Gramm," USA, February 7, 1996, 4A; Apple, "Louisiana Makes it Harder on Gramm," NYT, February 8, 1996, 13A; James Bennet, "Disappointed Gramm Says Top 3 Iowa Finish Is a Must," NYT, February 8, 1996, 13A.

72. See Keen, "Buchanan, Alexander Show Power for N.H.," USA, February 13, 1996, 1A for projected turnout; Table 2.1 of Harold W. Stanley, "The Nominations: Republican Doldrums, Democratic Revival," in The Elections of 1996, ed. Michael Nelson, (Washington, DC: CQ Press, 1997), 22. Also see Darrell M. West, Air Wars: Television Adverting in Election Campaigns, 1952–1996, 2nd ed. (Washington, DC: CQ Press, 1997), 63–64.

73. Although no delegates would be officially allocated until June, when the other steps in Iowa's caucus-convention process had been completed, the AP released a preliminary count, in which Dole received 8, Buchanan 6, and Alexander 5 out of 25 total. "Iowa Delegates, National Total," USA, February 13, 1996, 3A.

74. Berke, "Dole Tops the Field in Iowa Caucuses," NYT, February 13, 1996, 1A; Kolbert, "Campaign Spending Per Vote: Who Got His Money's Worth," NYT, February 14, 1996, 10A. According to this tabulation the per-vote cost for Gramm was $122, Alexander $47, Dole $35, and Buchanan $27.

75. The Iowa VNS poll is available at www.cnn.com/ALLPOLITICS/politics/1996/polls.

76. Apple, "Dole Ends the Race in Iowa As a Scalded Front-Runner," NYT, February 14, 1996, 1A.

77. Buell, "The Changing Face of The New Hampshire Primary," in In Pursuit of the White House 2000, ed. Mayer (New York: Chatham House/Seven Bridges, 1999), 89.

78. Woodward, The Choice, 385–6; Lowe, "Dole Stays Bright as Polls Dim," CD, February 16, 1996, 1A; Sabato, Toward The Millennium, 43–45; Robert D. Novak, "Dole Can't Blame Anyone But Himself," CD, February 22, 1996, 11A; Murphy presentation at George Washington University.

79. Rhodes Cook, "GOP Faces Uncharted Terrain In Wake of Buchanan Upset," CQWR, February 24, 1996, 438–442; updated with official returns as published in "1996 Republican Primary Results," CQWR, ugust 3, 1996, 63.

80. The New Hampshire VNS poll is available at www.cnn.com/ALLPOLITICS/politics/1996/polls.

81. Richard Wolf, "GOP Steps In to Help Dole," *USA*, February 22, 1996, 1A; Berke, "Buchanan Victory Stirs Opposition Within the GOP," *NYT*, February 22, 1996, 1A.

82. "Buchanan Victory Speech—New Hampshire," text obtained from Buchanan campaign.

83. AP, "Buchanan Edges Dole," *CD*, February 21, 1996, 1A; Steve Lee Myers, "Buchanan's Policies Assailed by Giuliani as Peril to U.S.," *NYT*, February 22, 1996, 12A; Wolf, "GOP Steps in To Help Dole;" Will, "Republican's Mission: Thwart Buchanan," *CD*, February 22, 1996, 11A; Berke, "Buchanan Victory Stirs Opposition Within the GOP," *NYT*, February 22, 1996, 1A; Robin Toner, "Radio Host Fears for Conservatism's Fate," *NYT*, February 23, 1996, 13A; Ayres, "A Rare Chance for State Republicans in Tuesday's Vote," *NYT*, February 25, 1996, 13A; Bennet, "D'Amato Attacks Vigorously On 'Extremism' of Buchanan," *NYT*, March 3, 1996, 11A.

84. Keen, "Dole Vows Fight for GOP 'Heart and Soul,'" *USA*, February 22, 1996, 6A.

85. Seelye, "A Vow to Unleash 'the Real Bob Dole,'" *NYT*, February 22, 1996, 10A; Seelye, "Dole Adopts a New Persona: Savior of the Grand Old Party," *NYT*, February 23, 1996, 1A.

86. Seelye, "Dole Adopts A New Persona."

87. Apple, "Delaware Vote to Test Forbes's Viability," *NYT*, February 23, 1996, 12A. For more on the New Hampshire primary, see Buell, "The Changing Face of the New Hampshire Primary," 88–143.

88. Bill Carter, "3 Networks Admit Error in Arizona Race Reports," *NYT*, February 29, 1996, 9A.

89. Hasson, "GOP Race Deeper in Disarray," *USA*, February 28, 1996, 4A; Jerry Gray, "Dole Counts On a Surge Of Support in the South," *NYT*, February 28, 1996, 11A.

90. Richard Benedetto, "Dole Capturing Poll Percentages, Unlike Primaries," *USA*, February 27, 1996, 2A.

91. AP, "Buchanan Says Arizona Race is Key," *CD*, February 27, 1996, 1A; "Campaign '96: Late Arizona Votes Dull Buchanan's Enthusiasm," *USA*, February 28, 1996, 4A.

92. Jessica Lee, "Alexander Aide Lives on Bottom Line," *USA*, February 27, 1996, 4A; Stephen Labaton, "When Big Money Fails to Win Some Delegates," *NYT*, March 1, 1996, 11A.

93. The FECA makes candidates for a major party nominations ineligible to receive matching funds for 30 days. Failure to attain 10 percent within the 30 days terminates matching funds unless a candidate requalifies by winning 20 percent in a subsequent primary, in which case they receive the matching funds retroactively. "Campaign '96: Alexander's Goals," *USA*, February 29, 1996, 3A.

94. Keen, "Scrambling Starts for Primary-Heavy 2 Weeks," *USA*, February 23, 1996, 4A; Rachel L. Swarns, "Southerner Places His Hopes Down Home," *NYT*, February 27, 1996, 13A.

95. Elaine Sciolino, "Forbes Offers View of His Foreign Policy Stands," *NYT*, March 1, 1996, 11A.

96. The analysis of South Carolina exit poll findings in this chapter relies on information obtained from the Hotline by Institute of Governmental Studies librarian Terry Dean.

97. Results of primaries are available at www.fec.gov.pubrec/presprim.htm.

98. Jonathan D. Salant, "One Man Corners the Ballot in N.Y.," *CQWR*, March 9, 1996, 646. The remaining nine New York delegates were slated in June.

99. Bennet, "With Cursory Nod to Dole, Buchanan Backs Off Race," *NYT*, April 18, 1996, 12A.

100. Elizabeth Drew, *On the Edge: The Clinton Presidency* (New York: Simon & Schuster, 1994); Woodward, *The Agenda: Inside the Clinton White House* (New York: Simon & Schuster, 1994).

101. Robert B. Reich, *Locked in the Cabinet* (New York: Vintage Books, 1998), 168.

102. Theda Skocpol maintains that Clinton's health care plan opened the Democrats to telling if inaccurate Republican attacks. See *Boomerang: Health Care Reform and the Turn Against Government* (New York: W.W. Norton, 1997). For a somewhat different view of the effectiveness of these attacks on public opinion, see West and Burdett A. Loomis, *The Sound of Money: How Political Interests Get What They Want* (New York: W.W. Norton, 1999.)

103. Paul R. Abramson, John H. Aldrich, and David W. Rohde, *Change and Continuity in the 1992 Elections*, rev. ed. (Washington, DC: CQ Press, 1995), 323–25.

104. Jack Newfield, "It's Time to Dump Bill," *New York Post*, November 21, 1994, 1A; Howard Kurtz, "Talk Grows of Dumping Clinton '96 Ticket," *CD*, November 25, 1994, 4A; Apple, "Clinton's Grip on '96 Ticket Not So Sure," *NYT*, November 20, 1994, 1A; Scripps Howard News Service, "Democrats Support Challenge to Clinton," *CD*, December 8, 1994, 4A.

105. "Democrats Support Challenge to Clinton."

106. Dick Morris immodestly claims the credit for this strategy in *Behind the Oval Office*; see also Thomas, et al., *Back From the Dead*, and Walter Dean Burnham, "Bill Clinton: Riding the Tiger," in *The Election of 1996*, ed. Pomper, 13.

107. AP, "Ex-Governor Explores a Bid Against Clinton," *NYT*, March 25, 1995, 8A; David Yepsen, "Casey Seen as No Threat to Clinton," *DMR*, April 1, 1995, 5M; Catherine Manegold, "Ex-Governor Ends '96 Challenge to Clinton," *NYT*, April 19, 1995, 10A.

108. See Woodward, *The Choice*, 206–10.

109. Corrado, "Financing the 1996 Election," 143.

110. Morris, *Behind the Oval Office*, 291–305; Ceaser and Busch, *Losing to Win*, 97–100; Drew, *Whatever It Takes* (New York: Viking, 1997), 97–100.

111. "1996 Democratic Primary Results," *CQWR*, August 17, 1996, 79–80. Clinton did not enter non-binding primaries in North Dakota and Michigan.

112. Ruth Marcus, "Dole Campaign Spent $3.5 Million in March," *WP*, April 20, 1996, 9A.

113. Moore, "Dems' Barrage of Ads Gets Little GOP Response," *USA*, April 18, 1996, 7A; Labaton, "Dole Campaign Nears Spending Limit for Primaries," *NYT*, March 22, 1996, 11A; Jane Fritsch, "In Dole's Race, Party's Money Now a Lifeline," *NYT*, May 22, 1996, 1A.

114. Brooks Jackson, "Financing the 1996 Campaign: The Law of the Jungle," in *Toward the Millennium*, 237–8; Corrado, "Financing the 1996 Election," 148.

115. Kolbert, "Gingrich and Dole Aides Try New Unified Party Message," *NYT*, March 20, 1996, 1A; David S. Cloud, "Tough Campaign Challenges For the Senate Leader," *CQWR*, March 30, 1996, 861; Helen Dewar, "Striving to Lead, Dole Stumbles Into a Week of Setbacks," *WP*, April 21, 1996, 6A; Thomas, et al., *Back From the Dead*, 74; Jackie Koszczuk, "Dole Leaves Senate Behind To Hit Campaign Trail," CQWR, May 18, 1996, 1359.

116. Drew, *Whatever It Takes*, 90; Woodward, *The Choice*, 421–8; Thomas, et al., *Back From the Dead*, 72–78.

117. Koszczuk, "Dole Leaves Senate Behind," 1360.

118. Thomas, et al., *Back From the Dead*, 106–7; Fritsch, "Democrats as Well as GOP Profit from Tobacco," *NYT*, July 6, 1996, 1A.

119. Keen and Gary Fields, "Dole Says He Was 'Set Up' by NAACP," *USA*, July 12–14, 1996, 1A.

120. Bennet, "Abortion Foes Warn Dole Not to Shift On Platform," *NYT*, March 17, 1996, 17A.

121. Bennet, "Top Conservative Would Back Shift on Abortion Issue," *NYT*, May 4, 1996, 1A: Bennet, "Leader of Christian Coalition Denies Shifting on Abortion," *NYT*, May 5, 1996, 1A.

122. Clines, "Abortion-Rights Supporters Fight for Their Say in GOP," *NYT*, May 6, 1996, 1A.

123. "Text of Dole's Statement On His Abortion Stance," (Provided by Dole campaign office) *NYT*, June 7, 1996, 10A.

124. Berke, "Dole, Ignoring His Advisers, Lashes Out at Abortion Foe," *NYT*, June 12, 1996, 1A.

125. Berke, "Battle Over the Abortion Plank Jolts the Republicans Yet Again," *NYT*, June 14, 1996, 1A; Berke, "In Many States, Abortion Feud Splits GOP," *NYT*, June 20,1996, 1A.

126. *Restoring the American Dream: The Republican Platform of 1996* (Washington, DC: Republican National Committee, 1996), 34–35. Seelye, "Moderates in GOP Vow Fight on Platform Abortion Language," *NYT*, August 7, 1996, 1A; Rosenbaum, "Accord Satisfies GOP Moderates on Abortion Issue," *NYT*, August 8, 1996, 1A. The general statement of tolerance declared: "While our party remains steadfast in its commitment to advancing its historic principles and ideals, we also recognize that members of our party have deeply held and sometimes differing views. We view this diversity of views as a source of strength, not as a sign of weakness, and we welcome to our ranks all Americans who may hold differing positions. We are committed to resolving our differences in a spirit of civility, hope, and mutual respect." *Restoring the American Dream*, 32

127. David E. Sanger, "Recycled Ideas Echo Forbes and Buchanan," *NYT*, March 25, 1996, 13A.

128. Adam Nagourney, "Dole to Advocate 15% Cut in Taxes, His Campaign Says," *NYT*, August 5, 1996, 1A.

129. Seelye, "Dole Offers Economic Plan Calling for Broad Tax Cut Aimed at Spurring Growth," *NYT*, August 6, 1996, 1A.

130. Larry David Smith and Dan Nimmo, *Cordial Concurrence: Orchestrating National Party Conventions in the Telepolitical Age* (Westport, CT: Praeger, 1991).

131. Byron E. Shafer, *Bifurcated Politics: Evolution and Reform in the National Party Convention* (Cambridge, MA: Harvard University Press, 1988).

132. *Today's Democratic Party: Meeting America's Challenges, Protecting America's Values: The 1996 Democratic National Platform* (Washington, DC: Democratic National Committee, 1997), 1.

133. For a review of the landmark literature and a detailed comparison of 1988 convention delegates, see Buell and John S. Jackson III, "The National Conventions: Diminished but Still Important in a Primary-Dominated Process," in *Nominating the President*, 228–35.

134. Random *Washington Post*-ABC News Telephone polls of 505 Republican delegates, 508 Democratic delegates, and 1,514 adults nationwide, as described in national convention supplements to the *WP National Weekly Edition*, August 12–18 and August 26–September 1, 1996.

135. Berke, "Perot Calls Meeting for '96 Contenders to Address Issues," *NYT*, June 3, 1996, 1A; Ayres, "Perot Leaves Door Open for '96 Presidential Run," *NYT*, August 14, 1995, 6A; Seib, "Perot's Followers Remain Frustrated, Directionless After Weekend of Wooing," *WSJ*, August 14, 1995, 14A.

136. AP, "Perot Changes Mind, Launches Third Party," *CD*, September 26, 1995, 2A.

137. Seelye, "In Quest for a Third Party, First Hurdle Is the Highest," *NYT*, September 28, 1995, 11A; Ayres, "Perot Claims Victory in Effort to Qualify Party in California," *NYT*, October 25, 1995, 12A; Tollerson, "Perot's Party Gains 2 States, New York and Arizona, in Its Campaign for Presidential Ballot," *NYT*, June 28, 1996, 11A; Sam Howe Verhovek, "Perot is in the Contest for President, Unless," *NYT*, March 19, 1996, 12A; author's interview with Richard Winger of *Ballot Access News*, September 9, 1997.

138. Verhovek, "Perot as a Political Presence: 1992 All Over Again?" *NYT*, January 23, 1996, 6A; Mini Hall, "Perot: I'd 'Give It Everything' If Asked to Run," *USA*, March 20, 1996, 4A; Nagourney, "When Perot Talks, It's Like a Campaign," *NYT*, March 25, 1996, 17A.

139. Sabato, *Toward the Millennium*, 85–8; Berke, "Perot's '96 Strategy in Setting Up Third Party Is Called Masterful, Even by Detractors," *NYT*, September 27, 1995, 1A; Tollerson, "A Third Party in the Wings Waits for a Leader to Arrive," *NYT*, June 3, 1996, 12A; Hall, "Lamm Edges Closer to '96 Race," *USA*, June 11, 1996, 7A; Hall, "Experts Put Perot Atop Reform Ticket," *USA*, June 24, 1996, 8A; Hilary Stout, "Lamm to Seek Presidential Bid of Perot's Party," *WSJ*, July 10, 1996,

18A; Tollerson, "Lamm, Ex-Governor of Colorado, Seeks Reform Party's Nomination," *NYT*, July 10, 1996, 1A.

140. Hall, "Perot Sets Up Fight for Reform Party Nomination," *USA*, July 11, 1996, 3A; Berke, "Perot Declares He Will Seek His Party's Presidential Nod," *NYT*, July 12, 1996, 1A.

141. Tollerson, "Reform Party Awaits the Mail to Determine Who the Candidates Will Be," *NYT*, July 9, 1996, 9A; "Candidate Picked by Mail Survey," *USA*, July 12–14, 1996, 6A.

142. *Ballot Access News*, August 12, 1996, 6.

143. James Brooke, "Perot Rival Protests Foul-Ups in Party's Nationwide Survey," *NYT*, August 2, 1996, 12A; and Ayres, "Reform Party's Split Is Widening as Members Head to Convention," *NYT*, August 10, 1996, 1A.

144. *Ballot Access News*, September 9, 1996, 5.

145. David Moore, "Perot Candidacy Hurt By Major Party Conventions," *The Gallup Poll Monthly*, 372 (September 1996), 4–5; Thomas, et al., *Back From the Dead*, 159–60.

146. The 1996 GOP convention approved a plan to reward late-voting states with bonus delegates. States holding their primaries between March 15 and April 14, 2000 get a 5-percent increase in the size of their national convention delegation. The bonus for states voting between April 15 and May 14 is 7.5 percent. States selecting their delegates on or after May 15 get a 10-percent boost. Alan Greenblatt and Rhodes Cook, "Nominating Process Rules Change," *CQWR*, August 17, 1996, 2299. According to the "Preliminary 2000 Delegate Allocation" breakdown released to the author on July 22, 1999, American Samoa and 20 late-voting states received a total of 56 bonus delegates.

147. Poll data accessed from *http://www.cloakroom.com/members/polltrack*, the Hotline.

148. Salant, "White House Hopefuls Report New Fund-Raising Numbers," July 15, 1999, *http://www.cnn.com/allpolitics;* Federal Election Commission, "Financial Activity of 1999–2000 Presidential Campaigns Through June 30, 1999," *http://www.fec.gov/finance/prsq.*

149. Don Van Natta Jr., "Bush Foregoes Federal Funds and Has No Spending Limit," *NYT*, July 16, 1999, A1.

150. Neil A. Lewis, "Flush Bush Turns to Soft Money," *NYT*, July 17, 1999, A9; Van Natta, "Democrats Are Trying to Double Unregulated Donations for 2000," *NYT*, July 25, 1999, A1.

151. "Forbes Leading Spending Race," July 20, 1999, *www.cnn.com/allpolitics.*

152. Tollerson, "Breather for Reform Party Is Giving Way to Discord," *NYT*, November 24, 1996, 20A; Bill Dedman, "Perot Dissidents Form A New Party," *NYT*, October 5, 1997, 17A.

153. AP, "With Ventura as Their Star, Reform Party Gathers to Chart Its Future," July 23, 1999, *www.cnn.com/allpolitics;* AP, "Ventura Again Says He Will Not Seek Presidency in 2000," *NYT*, July 25, 1999, A17; "Perot Doesn't Hint of 2000 Plans in Speech to Reform Leaders," July 24, 1999, *www.cnn.com/allpolitics.*

CHAPTER 2

Congressional Nominations in 1996
Procedures, Candidates, and Electoral Patterns

HARVEY L. SCHANTZ

Congressional election returns consistently underscore a central character-
istic of United States elections and the Congress: two-party hegemony. Virtually all members of Congress are elected as Democrats or Republicans.
Thus, although it is not called for in the Constitution, major party nominations are the crucial first step in congressional selection. This chapter is
an examination of the congressional nomination process of 1996, with an
emphasis on procedures, candidates, and electoral patterns in primaries.

CONGRESSIONAL NOMINATING METHODS

Popularly elected government has long called into existence the prior nomination of candidates.[1] In the United States, the predominant method of
nomination for offices other than the presidency changed from party conventions to direct primaries in the early years of the twentieth century.[2] The
direct primary opened up the selection of candidates to more people, for it
places the formal selection of party candidates in the hands of the electorate rather than in those of party officials or members.

The 1996 congressional nominations followed the pattern of most of the
twentieth century, as the overwhelming number of U.S. House and Senate
party nominations were made in direct primaries (tables 2.1 and 2.2).[3] One
major difference between House and Senate primaries, though, was that
most House primaries were not contested whereas most Senate primaries
were contested. There were also a few nominations decided by party conventions, party committees, and write-ins. The Democrats and Republicans
nominated candidates for all of the Senate seats, but both parties failed to
nominate in a few House districts.

Table 2.1: Nominating Methods for the U.S. House, 1996

Nominating System	Democrats		Republicans	
	N	%	N	%
Primary Election[a]				
Contested	151	35.5	156	36.5
Uncontested	235	55.3	232	54.3
	386	90.8	388	90.9
Nonprimary Nominations[a]				
Party Convention	19	4.5	17	4.0
Party Committee	1	0.2	3	0.7
Write-In	2	0.5	0	0.0
Self-Nominated	17	4.0	19	4.4
	39	9.2	39	9.1
Total Nominations	425	100.0	427	100.0
No Candidate[b]	10	2.3	8	1.8
House Elections	435	100.0	435	100.0

[a]These are the number and percentage of total nominations made by designated method.
[b]These are the number and percentage of House elections in which designated party did not offer a candidate.

Table 2.2: Nominating Methods for the U.S. Senate, 1996

Nominating System	Democrats		Republicans	
	N	%	N	%
Primary Election[a]				
Contested	20	60.6	24	72.7
Uncontested	11	33.3	7	21.2
	31	93.9	31	93.9
Nonprimary Nominations[a]				
Party Convention	1	3.0	1	3.0
Party Committee	0	0.0	0	0.0
Self-Nominated	1	3.0	1	3.0
Total Nominations	33	100.0	33	100.0
No Candidate[b]	0	0.0	0	0.0
Senate Elections[c]	33	100.0	33	100.0

[a]These are the number and percentage of total nominations made by designated method.
[b]These are the numbers and percentage of Senate elections in which designated party did not offer a candidate.
[c]Excludes twin primaries for short-term Kansas seat.

CONTEMPORARY PRIMARY SYSTEMS

Primary systems—which are regulated by state laws—vary along a number of dimensions. Three of the most crucial are party organizational control over the ballot, voter eligibility, and margin needed for victory.

Party and Ballot Access

In seven states the party organizations are granted a measure of legal control over primary ballot access, which is exercised through a preprimary convention.[4] In Utah and Connecticut a threshold of support at the party convention *is necessary* for inclusion on the primary ballot. In Utah party conventions nominate two candidates for the primary ballot, but there is automatic nomination of a candidate receiving 70 percent of the delegate support at the Republican or 60 percent support at the Democratic preprimary convention. In Utah's three congressional districts in 1996, there were three primaries and three convention nominations. In the second district there were two primaries for the seat of retiring Republican Enid Greene. Republican Merrill Cook, a perennial candidate, placed second at the party convention, but won the primary and general election.

In Connecticut nominations are made by party conventions with the provision that any unsuccessful candidate receiving 15 percent (recently reduced from 20 percent) or more of the delegate support on any convention ballot is eligible to file for a "challenge" primary. There was one challenge primary in 1996, and in this contest the endorsed candidate won. In both Connecticut and Utah there was not a Senate seat up for election in 1996.

The congressional nominating systems of Colorado and New Mexico, as well as the senatorial nominating system of New York, grant party organizations less control over candidate access to the primary ballot. In New Mexico candidates need 20 percent, in New York 25 percent, and in Colorado 30 percent (recently changed from 20 percent) of the preprimary convention or party committee support for automatic inclusion on the primary ballot. However, candidates not receiving this minimum level of support may appear on the primary ballot by fulfilling a petition requirement. In these systems, as well, the endorsed candidate does not always win the subsequent primary. In 1996, for example, Gene Nichol won the Colorado Democratic state assembly with 53 percent, but he lost the U.S. senatorial primary to Tom Strickland, who had received 45 percent support at the state assembly. Meanwhile, in the fourth district, Don Ament narrowly won the party endorsement, and with it the top spot on the ballot, but he lost the Republican primary to Bob Schaffer.

In North Dakota and Rhode Island the political parties legally endorse congressional candidates but are *not* empowered to exclude others from the ballot. "During the 1990s," in Rhode Island, according to Maureen Moakley, "in a series of high visibility races for governor and federal office, unendorsed candidates trounced their party-backed opponents."[5] One such race took place in the second district in 1996, where Democratic Lt. Governor Bob Weygand defeated the endorsed candidate in the primary and won the U.S. House seat in November.

In addition to these seven states, in a few other states, most notably Minnesota, the political parties provide "extra-legal" endorsements.[6] In 1996 though, Republicans declined to endorse a senatorial candidate because their convention was deadlocked after 14 ballots.

The direct primary has lessened the grip of party organizations over the nomination process. The preprimary nominating or endorsing convention is an attempt to insure some organizational control over the primary. But as we have seen, in 1996, at least, the preprimary endorsing convention is an unsure method of maintaining party organizational control over the nomination.

Voter Eligibility

In an open primary system registered voters may participate in the party primary of their choice. In states with a closed primary voters may only participate in the primary of the party to which they are registered. In 1996, 21 states were open primary states.[7] Sixteen states had closed primaries. Another nine states were modified-closed states, allowing nonaffiliated voters to choose the party primary of their choice. Additionally, in West Virginia the Democratic primary was closed, but the Republican primary was open to nonaffiliated voters. According to the Supreme Court, states cannot prevent state parties from opening their primaries to nonaffiliated voters; such a restriction was deemed by the Court an infringement upon the associational rights of the party and its members.[8] Three remaining states, discussed below, used a unified primary system in 1996.

Another crucial dimension is the period of time before primary day that a voter must be registered with a political party in order to be eligible for the party primary. In twenty-five states, including four closed or modified-closed states, voters may decide the party primary in which they wish to participate as late as primary day.[9] In seven states the deadline for switching partisan affiliation is 21 days or less before the primary. This deadline is about a month in nine states. There are more extended deadlines in five states, ranging from about three to six months. And, finally, New York State requires a voter to have changed partisan affiliation 30 days before the previous general election—a period of about eleven months before the September congressional primary.

The Supreme Court examined lead times in two 1973 cases.[10] In *Rosario v. Rockefeller*, the Supreme Court allowed the extended New York State registration deadline, reasoning that this law does not prevent voters from participating in primaries, even in years in which they switch party affiliation. However, in *Kusper v. Pontikes*, the Supreme Court voided an Illinois law which prevented a voter from participating in a party primary within

23 months of voting in another party's primary. The Court felt that the Illinois procedure limited a voter's right of political association by preventing participation in a party primary.

Party organizations tend to view the open primary with trepidation, fearing loss of control and pointing to the possibility of "cross-over voting" by nonpartisans in an effort to select a weak candidate for the general election. The U.S. Supreme Court saw these concerns of parties as legitimate in *Rosario*.

The Unified Primary States

Alaska, Washington, and (since 1998) California operate under a blanket primary system, in which voters may switch back and forth from party to party to select their favorite nominee for each office. Nominations are granted for each office to the leading candidate from each party.

In recent years the Republican party of Alaska has resisted the blanket primary, arguing that, in light of *Tashjian v. Republican Party of Connecticut*, a political party has the right to decide whether or not to allow independents into its primary. But in August 1996 Alaska held a blanket primary, as the Alaska Supreme Court and the U.S. Supreme Court upheld this system.[11]

In March 1996, the unified or consolidated primary system was adopted in California when voters approved Proposition 198 and this system was used for the 1998 congressional primaries. This change was opposed by the state's Democratic and Republican party leaders.[12] In 1996 California operated under a fairly closed primary, not allowing voters to change party registration within 29 days of the primary.

Louisiana since 1978 has operated with a unified primary. In Louisiana all candidates for an office are on one ballot. If a candidate receives a majority of the votes cast, that candidate is declared the winner and a general election is not held. If no candidate receives a majority, the two leaders—regardless of party affiliation—compete in the general election ballot. The law, strongly advocated by Governor Edwin Edwards (D., 1973–1980), was intended to prevent general election contests between Democratic candidates who had survived a difficult primary and run-off and Republicans nominated without opposition.[13]

In 1996, six of seven Louisiana congressional seats were won in the primary. The one runoff, in congressional district 7, was between two Democrats. This pattern is consistent with earlier years. Between 1978 and 1994—nine congressional election years—70 regular House elections took place in Louisiana. Of these 70, 60 were decided in the primary. There were ten runoffs on election day: five were Democrats versus Republicans, four were between two Democrats, and one involved two Republicans.

In 1996, a Louisiana U.S. Senate seat was decided in a runoff on election day, as Democrat Mary Landrieu beat Republican Louis "Woody" Jenkins, who had led in the first primary. However, only one of six U.S.

senate races between 1978 and 1992 was decided on election day: a 1986 runoff won by a Democrat over a Republican. The other five contests were won with a majority of the vote in the unified primary held in September.

On December 2, 1997, the U.S. Supreme Court struck down the Louisiana statute that set up the unified primary system. The Court's decision in *Foster v. Love* upheld a federal appeals court, finding that due to the lack of election day runoffs, the Louisiana system is contrary to an 1872 federal law which set a national election day for members of Congress.[14] In 1998, Louisiana held its congressional primary on election day, along with provision for a (not needed) later runoff.

Margin Needed for Victory

In the United States, general and primary elections usually require a simple plurality for victory. Two of the exceptions are southern primaries and primaries in Iowa and South Dakota. In Iowa and South Dakota a candidate must receive at least 35 percent of the total primary vote in order to win party nomination. In Iowa, a party nominating convention is held to select a nominee if no candidate garnered the required minimum.[15] In South Dakota a runoff primary is held between the two leading candidates. These infrequently employed procedures were not used in 1996.

Seven southern states and one border state—Alabama, Arkansas, Florida, Georgia, Mississippi, Oklahoma, South Carolina, and Texas—currently require a majority for victory in primaries.[16] A ninth state, North Carolina, since 1989 has required 40 percent of the total vote, rather than 50 percent. If no candidate receives at least one-half (or 40 percent in North Carolina) of the votes cast in the primary, a runoff primary is held, if the second candidate files, four weeks or so later. These states adopted the runoff between 1902 and 1939. V. O. Key Jr. and Cortez A. M. Ewing, in their era two of the closest students of southern politics, pointed to the ideal of majority rule rather than factional or personal advantage as the prime motivation for adoption of the runoff.[17] Democratic hegemony in the South required a runoff to insure a form of majority decision because of the frequent splintering of the vote in the southern Democratic primaries in these years.

In 1996 U.S. House contests, there were 15 runoff primaries held for Democratic nominations and 12 runoff primaries for Republican nominations. There was a reversal in ten of these runoffs. In U.S. House primaries from 1970 to 1986, the primary leader lost 28.6 percent of the subsequent runoffs.[18]

Only one incumbent in 1996 was involved in a runoff: Texas Republican Greg Laughlin, who led in the primary but lost the runoff primary. Incumbents are rarely in runoffs, but incumbents generally run greater risks in a runoff than in the first primary because opposition is no longer fragmented between more than one candidate.[19]

Runoff primaries are sometimes criticized for serving as an obstacle to women and minority candidates. In 1996, runoff primaries placed a heavy burden upon female candidates. No women were nominated in runoff primaries, and four Democratic female candidates and one Republican female candidate lost the runoff to a male candidate after leading in the initial primary. From 1970 to 1986, five of eight women who led in the House primary won the runoff.[20] It is difficult to identify the race of all congressional candidates, but at least one runoff resulted in the elimination of a minority candidate—a native American woman—by a white male in the seventh district of North Carolina Democratic runoff.

In Senate contests there were five runoff primaries held to determine party nominees: Alabama (both parties); Arkansas (Democrats); Georgia (Republicans); and Texas (Democrats). In all five of these nominations, the winner of the first primary was victorious in the runoff. All of these runoffs involved two white males, except for the Texas contest where a Hispanic male led in the primary and won the runoff.

NONPRIMARY NOMINATIONS

In every election year a number of congressional nominations by both major political parties are made by means other than the direct primary. In 1996, four Senate and 78 House major party candidates were nominated by nonprimary methods, including self-nomination in unified primaries in Texas and Louisiana (tables 2.1 and 2.2).

Convention Nominations

By the second decade of the twentieth century, nominating conventions had given way to the direct primary as the most common way of nominating party candidates. In a few states and among southern Republicans, though, the party convention persisted.[21] However, the party convention was abandoned by southern Republicans during the 1960s and it was forsaken for statewide nominations by New York, Delaware, and Indiana in 1968, 1970, and 1974, respectively.

Today, "pure" convention nominations for Congress are made only in Virginia. In Virginia, responsibility for the selection of a nominating method is shared by party committees and elected officials. District and state party officials have, for House and Senate nominations respectively, the option of choosing a direct primary or other nominating method. However, an incumbent office holder nominated by, or filing papers for, a direct primary in the previous election year may veto the selection of a nominating method other than a primary. In 1996, all but two party nominations for the U.S. House and Senate, following the recent pattern, were made by convention. The two exceptions were Republican primaries held to renominate Senator John Warner and Representative Herbert H. Bateman. Both legislators chose a primary in order to avoid what promised to be difficult

Republican conventions dominated by delegates more conservative than themselves. Both Warner and Bateman easily won their primaries and general elections.[22]

In Connecticut all six Democratic House candidates and five Republicans were nominated by party convention. In Utah three of the six congressional nominations, including the nominations of both running incumbents, were by convention.

In Arkansas there were three party conventions held to nominate substitutes for candidates previously nominated by primary. On June 15, Arkansas Republicans nominated Representative Tim Hutchinson for the U.S. Senate, in place of Lt. Governor Mike Huckabee, who had resigned the nomination in anticipation of becoming governor. In November, Tim Hutchinson became the first Republican Senator from Arkansas since Reconstruction. At a more contentious gathering, third district Republicans selected Asa Hutchinson to succeed his brother in the U.S. House.[23] Democrats in the third district also held a convention to nominate a substitute candidate. In November, Asa Hutchinson defeated Democrat Ann Henry.

Party Committee

Nomination of major party candidates by party committee is infrequent, and is most often used to replace a candidate selected in the primary who has subsequently withdrawn or died. A committee is also used for original nomination when the primary has not nominated a qualified candidate.

Generally, candidates chosen to replace incumbents do well in November. The one such case in 1996 was highly unusual, however. In Oregon, first-term Representative Wes Cooley won the Republican primary in the second district. But after the filing deadline for the primary, it became apparent that Cooley had lied about his military record and wedding date. Republican leaders—national, state, and local—urged Cooley to resign the nomination. Reluctantly he did, and local political leaders then chose Cooley's predecessor, Robert F. Smith, as the Republican nominee.[24] Smith won comfortably in November.

Candidates chosen by party committee to substitute for a House aspirant or to fill a nomination left vacant in the primary usually fare poorly in the general election. This was true in 1996 as the three original party committee nominees received between 21.6 percent and 30.0 percent of the two-party vote.

Write-in Nominees

A write-in nominee is a candidate who wins the party primary but does not appear on the ballot. Rarely are major party congressional candidates nominated as write-ins. In 1996, there were two such nominations for Democratic House candidates, in the first district of Arizona and the eighth district of Illinois. Write-in candidates may be selected with exceedingly few votes. The Arizona nominee received 1,942 write-ins and the Illinois nominee but 75. Generally, write-in nominees do poorly in November. In 1996, the Arizona nominee received 36.7 percent, and the Illinois nominee 39.8 percent, of the two-party vote.

Self-nominated Candidates: Louisiana and Texas

Candidates entered in the Louisiana unified primary, as described above, are actually the functional equivalent of self-nominated candidates in a general election. In 1996, self-nominated Democrats entered five district primaries and self-nominated Republicans entered six district primaries.

Outside of Louisiana, self-nomination has not been an ordinary method of major party nomination. However, in 1996, due to judicial invalidation of the regular primary in 13 Texas congressional districts, Democratic and Republican candidates in the November 5 special election were "self-nominated." Candidates were free to file for this general election up to August 30.[25]

DISTRICTS CONCEDED BY THE PARTIES

In 1996, both major parties nominated candidates for all of the Senate elections. But in House races, Democrats did not field a candidate for ten seats and Republicans were without a candidate in eight districts. For the second congressional election year in a row, Democrats conceded more seats than Republicans. This is a major reversal in party coverage of congressional districts. Democrats had long offered more candidates than the Republicans.[26]

One consistency, though, is that most conceded seats continue to be in the South. In 1996, the ten districts without a Democratic candidate were in Florida (3 seats), Kentucky (1), Louisiana (2), South Carolina (2), Texas (1), and Virginia (1). Republicans did not field candidates in districts in Georgia, Louisiana, Illinois (2), Massachusetts, Ohio, and West Virginia (2).

The recent surge in Republican coverage of the congressional districts must surely have contributed to their 1994 and 1996 electoral success. The current situation, however, contrasts with the 1896–1930 era. During this earlier period of Republican ascendance in Congress, the Democratic party offered more complete candidate coverage of congressional districts.[27]

CONGRESSIONAL CANDIDATES

We now examine the number and career status of candidates in congressional primaries. The career status of the candidates is classified as incumbent, current office-holder, or non-office-holder.[28] This scheme builds on earlier studies.[29] Less systematically, we highlight celebrity candidates. For each party we look at seats with and without an incumbent. For seats with running incumbents, we also contrast the incumbent party primary and the challenging party primary.

SENATE SEATS WITH AN ENTERED INCUMBENT

The number of candidates running for an occupied U.S. Senate seat is quite small, and the number running in the party of the incumbent is further attenuated. In 1996, the forty major party nominations for these 20 seats attracted a total of 86 candidates, 44 Democrats and 42 Republicans (table 2.3). In the party primaries with an incumbent, there were 35 candidates, including the 20 incumbents. There were 51 candidates in the primaries of the challenging major party.

Numbers alone do not constitute a formidable challenger pool. In Alaska, seven Democrats entered the primary to select a challenger to Republican Senator Ted Stevens. Yet, Joelle Hall, the State Democratic Party Executive Director, called the field of candidates "disappointing."[30] Hall turned out to be prescient, for the eventual party nominee received only 11.9 percent of the two-party vote. For this reason, we turn our attention to the career status of the candidates.

Table 2.3: Candidate Pool for Congressional Seats, 1996[a]

		Seats with an Incumbent			
			Number of Candidates in Primary of:		
Type of Incumbent	Number of Seats	Incumbent Party		Challenging Party	
Democratic					
Senator	7	11	(0)[b]	18	(5)
Republican					
Senator	13	24	(1)	33	(4)
Democratic					
Representative	149	209	(8)	282	(21)
Republican					
Representative	192	260	(2)	314	(41)
		Seats without Incumbent			
			Number of Candidates in Primary of:		
Outgoing Incumbent	Number of Seats	Incumbent Party		Challenging Party	
Democratic					
Senator	7	19	(10)	27	(11)
Republican					
Senator	5	23	(9)	15	(4)
Democratic					
Representative	29	149	(47)	101	(10)
Republican					
Representative	18	83	(29)	44	(9)

[a]The Senate analysis excludes the unified primary in Louisiana and the short-term contest in Kansas. Convention nominations are tabulated as one-candidate primaries. The House analysis excludes districts in Louisiana and Texas with unified primaries; districts in which one or more nominations were decided by a method other than a primary; and the Vermont seat which has a Socialist incumbent.
[b]The figures in parentheses are the number of office-holding candidates other than the incumbent.

Only ten office-holders sought incumbent senate seats, and but one of these ten challengers, a state representative from South Carolina, was a candidate in the incumbent senator's own party primary. Republican Strom Thurmond beat this challenger by better than two to one.

The Iowa senate seat retained by Democrat Tom Harkin attracted three Republicans, a state senator, and a state representative, and U.S. Representative Jim Ross Lightfoot, who won the primary. The Texas seat retained by Republican Phil Gramm attracted four Democrats, including two members of the U.S. House. However, in a story which made the front page of the *New York Times*, both representatives were eventually defeated by Victor M. Morales, a $36,000 a year civics teacher.[31]

In South Dakota, Democratic U.S. Representative Tim Johnson won an uncontested primary and then defeated Republican Senator Larry Pressler in the general election. In Massachusetts, Republican Governor William Weld was unopposed in the primary, but he lost to Democratic Senator John Kerry in November. In Montana, Lt. Governor Dennis Rehberg defeated two candidates in the Republican primary, but he lost the general election to Senator Max Baucus.

The remaining office-holder seeking an incumbent seat was Don McCorkell, a Democratic state representative in Oklahoma. McCorkell lost the primary to Professor Jim Boren, who enjoyed wide name recognition because his cousin David Boren had held the contested Senate seat from 1979 until his resignation in 1994.[32] In November, Jim Boren lost to Republican incumbent James M. Inhofe.

HOUSE SEATS WITH AN ENTERED INCUMBENT

Many of the patterns concerning candidate numbers and career status in Senate primaries are evident in House contests. In 1996, there were 341 congressional districts with an incumbent running for another term in which a primary was the only means of nomination used. These potential 682 major party nominations drew a total of 1,065 candidates, 523 Democrats and 542 Republicans (table 2.3). In the party of the incumbent there was a total of 469 candidates (including 341 incumbents), and in the primaries of the challenging party there were 596 candidates.

There were very few current office-holders among the challengers. This was particularly so in the party primary of the incumbent member of Congress. Republican incumbents drew only two office-holders as opponents, and Democratic incumbents drew only eight office-holding opponents in their own primaries, including three in a safe Democratic district in Detroit to oppose losing incumbent Barbara-Rose Collins. The five other Democratic incumbents with an office-holding challenger were successful. In the most covered of these campaigns, in Georgia, Representative Cynthia McKinney, an African-American, defeated three white candidates, including a state senator, in a district with a new white majority due to recent redistricting.[33]

In challenging party primaries there were 41 Democratic and 21 Republican office-holders, including 33 state legislators. Office-holding candidates won 30 Democratic and 13 Republican nominations, and in November eight of them, six Democrats and two Republicans, beat the opposing party incumbent. The most familiar of these successful nominees was Democrat Dennis J. Kucinich, a state senator in 1996 when he defeated Republican Martin R. Hoke, but best known for his stint as mayor of Cleveland in the late 1970s.

In challenging party primaries, non-office-holders were by far the largest group of candidates, and they won 156 Democratic nominations to oppose Republican incumbents and 129 Republican nominations to oppose Democratic incumbents. In November, 10 of these Democrats, but none of these Republicans, won. In these districts, no challengers entered the remaining 7 Republican and 6 Democratic primaries, and nominees were not selected.

Democratic Representative Carolyn McCarthy, a nurse when elected to Congress in 1996, was the least politically experienced of the elected non-office-holders. Her political career was instigated by the murder of her husband and maiming of her son in a shooting spree on a Long Island Railroad commuter train. After the tragedy, McCarthy advocated gun control and she was very disappointed with her representative's views on this issue. When McCarthy decided to run for Congress, local Republican leaders did not support her plans, but she was eagerly courted by local and national Democrats. In September she won an uncontested primary and in November she defeated Representative Dan Frisa.[34]

Senate Seats Without an Entered Incumbent

In 1996, 13 Senators retired and this resulted in a like number of senate seats without an entered incumbent. In the twelve states with party primaries, there were 84 candidates for these seats, 34 Democrats and 50 Republicans.[35] The 84 candidates were evenly divided between the defending and challenging parties (table 2.3). The average number of major party candidates running for an open senate seat was 7.0, and it was 4.3 for seats with an entered incumbent.

A larger contrast between open senate seats and those with an incumbent, however, is the career status of the candidates. In the senate races without an entered incumbent, 34 of the 84 entered candidates, 40.5 percent, were current office-holders. By contrast, in the 20 senate races with an incumbent only 10 of 66 challengers, 15.2 percent, were in office. The largest gap was in incumbent parties; in seats with an incumbent senator, only 1 of 15 challengers was an office-holder, but in seats with a retiring incumbent, 19 of 42 candidates held office.

Elected officials dominated in the open senate primaries, winning nine Republican and eight Democratic nominations. These nominees were U.S. Representatives (7), state senators (3), state attorney generals (2), state treasurers (2), a governor, a state secretary of state, and a state representative. In November, these nominees won 10 of the 12 open senate seats.

Non-office-holders won seven open senate seat nominations, but only two of this group won the general election: Republicans Susan Collins of Maine and Chuck Hagel of Nebraska. Both of these new senators had extensive political experience, but neither had been elected before to public office.

HOUSE SEATS WITHOUT AN ENTERED INCUMBENT

In the major party primaries for the 47 open seats exclusively using the primary, there were 377 candidates (table 2.3). These candidates were almost evenly divided between the Democratic party (193) and the Republican party (184). There were 232 candidates in the primaries of the incumbent party, and 145 candidates in the challenging party primaries. Whereas the open House seats averaged 8.0 candidates, only 3.1 candidates entered major party primaries in districts with an incumbent.

Both political parties had willing candidates for all open congressional seats, and the field of candidates swelled for a dominant party primary. In each of the 94 party primaries in the open districts there was at least one candidate, and in 81 primaries more than one. But a few districts skewed the average number of candidates. In an overwhelmingly Democratic district centered on west Baltimore, a record 27 Democratic hopefuls vied in the Democratic primary.[36] A traditionally Republican district, the seventh district of Indiana, attracted the largest GOP field, 15 candidates.

There were ample office-holders among the congressional candidates in the open districts and they tended to concentrate in the party of the outgoing incumbent. As with the senate races, the contrast between the incumbent and open seats was greater with respect to the number of office-holding candidates than it was to the total number of candidates. In open House seats, office-holders composed 25.2 percent, 95 of 377, of the candidate pool. By contrast, in the 341 incumbent House seats, only 72 of 724 challengers, 9.9 percent, were office-holders.

In the open races, the contrast between the candidate pools of the incumbent and challenging party primaries, however, was much greater in House races than it was for the Senate. In the open House races the pool of office-holders was much larger in the incumbent party, probably because there are many more elected officials in locally dominant parties. In the 29 open Democratic seats, there were 47 Democratic and ten Republican office-holders, and in the 18 open Republican seats, there were 29 Republican and nine Democratic officials. These 95 office-holders were from a variety of state, county, and municipal posts, and included 52 state legislators. There were office-holders in both party primaries in only 11 of the 47 open districts.

In the 29 Democratic open seats, the 47 Democratic office-holders won 19 nominations and 16 general elections, and the 102 non-office-holders won 10 nominations and five general elections. The ten Republican office-holders won six nominations and three general elections, while the 91 non-office-holding Republicans won 23 nominations and five general elections.

In the 18 Republican open seats, the 29 Republican office-holders won ten nominations and eight general elections, and Republican non-office-holders won eight nominations and six general elections. One of these winning non-office-holders was Jim Ryun of Kansas, who in the 1960s was the world record-holder for the one-mile run and an Olympic athlete. The nine Democratic officials won six nominations and two general elections. The 35 non-office-holding Democrats won twelve nominations and one general election. Independent candidate Jo Ann Emerson, the widow of Missouri Republican Representative Bill Emerson, won the remaining Republican district. Emerson was forced to run as an independent because her husband died after the filing deadline, but she joined the new Congress as a Republican.

Overall, in both Senate and House primaries, incumbents did very well and only infrequently were they challenged by office-holders in their primary or in the opposition party primary. Office-holders were much more successful in primaries and general elections than non-office-holders. In open districts, party success increased with previous control of the district and candidate quality.

ELECTORAL PATTERNS IN CONGRESSIONAL PRIMARIES

Competition, turnout, and incumbency performance in the 1996 congressional primaries are the concern of this section of the chapter.

CONTESTED AND UNCONTESTED PRIMARIES

U.S. House

In 1996, only 39.7 percent, 307 of 774, of the House primaries were contested. Specifically, the proportion of House primaries contested, controlling for party and incumbency, was:

	Democratic		*Republican*	
Without incumbent	46.8%	$\frac{110}{235}$	56.8%	$\frac{109}{192}$
With one incumbent	27.2%	$\frac{41}{151}$	24.0%	$\frac{47}{196}$

Incumbency considerably diminished the frequency of contests in House primaries, especially in Republican primaries. The electoral strength of incumbents deterred many potential challengers from entering into a primary fray.

In each of the 18 election years between 1956 and 1990, Democratic primaries, both with and without an incumbent, were contested more often than Republican primaries.[37] However, in 1992 and 1994, in primaries without an incumbent, Republican contests were slightly more frequent. In 1996, this pattern continued, and the gap between the parties widened considerably, a difference caused by the large drop in Democratic contests. There has been a marked trend toward contests in southern nonincumbent Republican primaries. In 1996, 69.0 percent of these primaries were contested, compared to only 27.2 percent between 1956 and 1974.[38] By contrast, in 1996, 49.2 percent of the southern Democratic nonincumbent primaries were contested, a decline from the 66.7 percent contested rate for 1956–1974.

Another contributing factor to the rise of contested Republican primaries is that party's recently enhanced electoral prospects. In both Democratic and Republican primaries—when there is not an entered incumbent—the likelihood of a public contest increased with a rise in the party's November prospects, measured as the party general election vote. Thus there were 19 districts in which a nonincumbent of either party won with 60 percent or more of the two-party vote, and in all these districts the winner had survived a contested primary. By contrast, party primaries were contested less than 30 percent of the time in districts in which the party received less than 30 percent of the two-party vote. In all regions of the United States, enhanced electoral prospects led to more frequent contests.

Among primaries with an incumbent, there was a contest about one-fourth of the time. The presence of an incumbent eliminated the positive relationship between November prospects and primary contests.

The traditional party battle within each of the sections is of some importance in explaining the frequency of contests.[39] Rarely were incumbents of a weak sectional party challenged in the primary—southern Republicans (4 of 51 contested); Plains states Democrats (0 of 7); and Mountain Democrats (0 of 3). The Atlantic, which traditionally has few contests, was the only region in 1996 with more frequent contests in primaries with an incumbent. And the Border states and Midwest were the only sections above the national contesting rate for all four types of House primaries. Surprisingly there were no challenges to any of the ten Republican incumbents in the Plains.

U.S. Senate

In 1996, 71.0 percent, 44 of 62, U.S. Senate primaries were contested. This is a marked contrast with the House figure of 39.7 percent, and is to be expected given the longer term of office for senators and their more diverse and larger constituencies. (In addition there were contents in both primaries for the remaining two years of Robert Dole's vacated Senate seat.) The proportion of each type of U.S. Senate primary contested was:

	Democratic		Republican	
Without incumbent	75.0%	$\underline{18}$	88.9%	$\underline{16}$
		24		18
With incumbent	28.6%	$\underline{2}$	61.5%	$\underline{8}$
		7		13

Overall, the Senate primaries followed patterns similar to the House primaries: more contests in primaries without an incumbent, more contests in Republican primaries after controlling for incumbency, and a recent spurt in southern Republican contests. In these basic respects Senate primaries were consistent with—but always with more frequent contests than—the House primaries.

The overwhelming number, 34 of 42, of Senate primaries without an incumbent were contested. The distribution of the uncontested primaries reflected traditional party strengths and the stature of the eventual nominees. The two uncontested Republican primaries were in strongly Democratic West Virginia and Massachusetts, where the Republican nominee was Governor William Weld. Three of the six uncontested Democratic primaries were in the traditionally Republican Plains states of Kansas, Nebraska, and South Dakota. Furthermore, the Democratic nominee in Nebraska was Governor Ben Nelson, and the South Dakota Democratic nominee was Tim Johnson, elected to the at-large congressional district since 1986. Another uncontested Democratic primary was in strongly Republican Idaho. The sixth uncontested primary was in New Jersey, where Democratic Representative Robert G. Torricelli was the nominee.

Primaries with a senate incumbent were less likely to be contested. Only 2 of 7 Democratic senators, John D. Rockefeller IV of West Virginia and Paul Wellstone of Minnesota, were challenged in the primary. Among Republicans, though, eight of thirteen incumbents were challenged. In the southern and border states, seven of eight Republican senators had primary competition. Only Jesse Helms of North Carolina was not challenged. However, outside of the South only one senator, Ted Stevens of Alaska, was challenged, while four were renominated in an uncontested primary. (The newly appointed Republican Senator from Kansas, Sheila Frahm, was also challenged in the primary.)

Voter Turnout

An Overview of Participation Levels

In order to measure voter turnout in the 1996 congressional primaries, we selected the 74 congressional districts and 15 states (not including the short-term Kansas senate race) with simultaneously contested Democratic and Republican primaries. The numbers voting were then compared to the voting age population and the number of general election voters in these districts and states.

The central finding of this analysis is that turnout levels in congressional primaries were quite low. In more than one-half of the House districts and states the turnout for congressional primaries was less than 20 percent of the voting age population. In no district and in only one state did primary turnout exceed 35 percent of the voting age population.

Turnout in congressional primaries was also low in comparison to voter participation in subsequent general elections. In 59 of 74 House districts with two contested primaries, turnout in the primaries was less than half of the general election figure. For the senate seats, turnout in the primaries attracted more than half of the general election vote in only two of 15 states.

The Distribution of Voters Between Party Primaries

The nomination contests that we are studying take place, of course, within the confines of a political battlefield defined by the skirmishes of the two major parties.[40] A party's congressional nomination gains importance directly with the stature of the party among the electorate as a whole. The stronger a party is among the voters in a district, the more that party's primary becomes the real focus of electoral decision. Popular interest, it follows, should thus center upon the primary of the stronger political party.

This speculation is confirmed by an analysis of the 74 House districts and 15 states with a pair of contested primaries in 1996. Voter participation in the Democratic or Republican primaries resembled the November vote split. As the November percentage of the Democratic party rose, so did the percentage of primary voters participating in the Democratic primary. Thus the Democrats received between 30.0 percent and 39.9 percent of the November vote in 11 districts, and in those districts the average Democratic percentage of the primary vote was 34.4. percent. In four House districts, the Democrats received 70.0 percent to 79.9 percent of the November vote, and in those districts they received an average of 76.3 percent of the primary vote.

In senate races, also, there is often a correspondence between the distribution of voters on primary day and election day. In Alaska, for example, the Democrats received 10.3 percent of the two–party primary turnout, and in November they received 11.9 percent of the two-party vote. Meanwhile, in Rhode Island, the Democrats received 82.1 percent of the primary vote, and 64.4 percent of the two–party November vote.

The distribution of voters on primary day, however, is more likely than the November election to reflect the traditional political pattern of a state or district. This is evident in the just–noted Rhode Island senate race in which the traditionally strong Democratic party drew a higher proportion of primary voters than November voters. This proposition is also illustrated by the voting pattern contrasts in the first and ninth congressional districts of Tennessee. The first district in the eastern end of the state has traditionally been a "one–party" or "safe" Republican constituency. In 1996, the Democrats received 33.3 percent of the two-party vote, but only 14.5 percent of the primary voters. On the other had, the ninth district in the southwest corner of the state, encompassing Memphis, has traditionally been a Democratic stronghold. In 1996, Democrats received 62.1 percent of the two-party vote, but 89.6 percent of the primary voters. In both districts, the dominant party had a stronger hold on voters on primary day than on election day. These districts thus support V. O. Key Jr.'s proposition that there is a "tendency for popular interest to concentrate in the primary of the stronger party."[41]

MARGINS OF VICTORY

Primaries with an Incumbent

Competitive levels in congressional primaries with an incumbent are extremely low. Most of these primaries are uncontested, and those with a public contest are rarely decided by a close margin. In 1996, no senate incumbent won with less than 60 percent of the leading two-candidate vote, and six of the ten contested Senate primaries were won with 80 percent or more of this vote. (The short-term Kansas primary is excluded from these figures.)

Of the 347 House incumbents in party primaries, only two lost, and only six more won with less than 60 percent of the leading two-candidate vote. Forty-six of 88 contested House primaries were won by the incumbent with 80 percent or more of the two-candidate vote.

An examination of the losing and closely contested incumbent races suggests some of the factors that lead to incumbency weakness in congressional primaries. In Detroit, Democratic Representative Barbara-Rose Collins, weakened by ethical problems, largely stemming from campaign finance, lost to state representative Carolyn Cheeks Kilpatrick, a well-respected challenger.[42] Three of the six representatives winning by a small margin—Republicans Joseph McDade (53.3 percent) and Bill Goodling (54.9 percent) of Pennsylvania, and Republican Jay Kim (58.2 percent) of California—were also hurt by charges of wrongdoing.[43] In addition, and in contrast to the California challenger, the Pennsylvania challengers in these two primaries were credited with strong campaigns.[44]

In Texas, Republican Representative Greg Laughlin—who switched from the Democrats to the Republican party in June 1995—failed to win the nomination of his new party. Laughlin lost to Ron Paul, a Republican U.S. representative in the 1970s and 1980s from a partially overlapping district, who enjoyed high name recognition and "ran an aggressive and well-funded campaign." Paul charged that Laughlin was not a true Republican or conservative.[45]

Political ideology also played a role in three of the close incumbent wins. In Albany, New York Democratic Representative Michael R. McNulty was held to 57.0 percent of the vote by a challenger who argued that McNulty was too conservative, pointing out that McNulty supported the Republican Contract with America 63 percent of the time. In the Hudson Valley of New York, Republican incumbent Sue W. Kelly won 55.8 percent of the two-leading candidate vote, as a former Representative from an adjoining district, Joseph J. DioGuardi, attacked her for being too liberal on social issues, especially for being too permissive on abortion. In San Diego, Democratic Representative Bob Filner was held to 54.5 percent of the vote, as he was attacked for being too liberal. In these three cases, also, the challenger campaigns were high profile.[46]

Only rarely do congressional incumbents lose primaries. One exception to this general proposition is the poor fate of appointed U.S. Senators.[47] In 1996, the hazards facing appointed senators continued as Senator Sheila Frahm of Kansas, appointed to the Senate to replace Robert Dole on May 24, 1996, was defeated in the Republican primary on August 6 by U.S. Representative Sam Brownback, who then went on to win the remaining two years of Dole's term.

Primaries Without an Incumbent

Levels of competition were higher in primaries without an incumbent than they were in primaries with an incumbent. Primaries without an incumbent were more often contested; and contested primaries were more often won with a smaller percentage of the vote.

In the absence of an incumbent, many of the contested primaries were won by a small margin. In House primaries, the winning margin was less than 60 percent in 40 of 110 Democratic contests and 42 of 109 Republican contests. In Senate primaries, five of 18 Democratic contests and six of 16 Republican contests were won with less than 60 percent of the vote.

House primaries without an incumbent were rarely won with more than 80 percent of the two-leading candidate vote. In House primaries only 15 of 110 Democratic contests and 13 of 109 Republican contests were won this overwhelmingly. Senate outcomes were more frequently one-sided, as eight of 34 contested Senate primaries were won with at least 80 percent.

CONCLUSION

The major party nominating process is the crucial first step in the election of members of Congress. Once the party nominations have been decided, the quest for office and the realistic alternatives presented to voters are ordinarily limited to the two major party nominees. In the American political system, to paraphrase V. O. Key Jr., a good deal of politics is intraparty, rather than interparty.[48] Congress is a national legislature with local roots, and the constituency-based nomination process is an integral link between the two Congresses: the one in Washington, D.C. and the one in the districts. [49]

NOTES

1.   Frederick W. Dallinger, *Nominations for Elective Office in the United States* (New York: Longmans, Green, 1897), 3.

2.   V. O. Key Jr., *Politics, Parties, and Pressure Groups*, 5th ed. (New York: Crowell, 1964), 375.

3.   The major source for 1996 nomination methods and final results in primaries is Richard M. Scammon, Alice V. McGillivray, and Rhodes Cook, *America Votes 22: 1996* (Washington, DC: Congressional Quarterly Inc., 1998). This handbook was supplemented by *CQWR*, 1996; Philip D. Duncan and Christine C. Lawrence, *Politics in America 1998* (Washington, DC: Congressional Quarterly Inc., 1997); and Michael Barone and Grant Ujifusa, *The Almanac of American Politics 1998* (Washington, DC: National Journal Inc., 1997).

4.   *The Book of the States, 1996–1997* (Lexington, KY: Council of State Governments, 1996), 157–158; and Karen M. Markin, *Ballot Access 2: For Congressional Candidates* (Washington, DC: National Clearinghouse on Election Administration, Federal Election Commission, 1995).

5.   Maureen Moakley, "Political Parties in Rhode Island: Back to the Future," in *Parties and Politics in the New England States*, ed. Jerome M. Mileur (Amherst, MA: Polity Publications, 1997), 95–112, quote 109.

6.   Joseph A. Kunkel III, "Party Endorsement and Incumbency in Minnesota Legislative Nominations," *Legislative Studies Quarterly* 13 (May 1988): 211–223.

7.   This classification of state primary systems is from the state reports in *America Votes 22: 1996*.

8.   *Tashjian v. Republican Party of Connecticut* 107 S. Ct. 544 (1986).

9.   League of Women Voters Education Fund, *Vote! The First Steps* (Washington, DC, 1996). This paragraph does not include the three unified primary states.

10.   James A. Palmer, Edward D. Feigenbaum, and David T. Skelton, *Election Case Law 97* (Washington, DC: Federal Election Commission, 1997), 82–83, 99–100, 234.

11.   *Ballot Access News*, May 4, 1995; April 3, 1996; May 28, 1996; July 20, 1996; and August 12, 1996; Ronald D. Elving, "Court Lets Decision Stand on Alaska's Open Primary," *CQWR*, May 17, 1997, 1156.

12.   Marc Birtel, "Ballot: 'Jungle Primaries' Adopted... Reclassifying Lions Rejected," *CQWR*, March 30, 1996, 902–903; Michael Ross, "California Voters Adopt an Anti-party 'Open' Primary," *Party Developments*, June 1996, 5–6.

13.   Michael Barone and Grant Ujifusa, *The Almanac of American Politics 1982* (Washington, DC: Barone and Co., 1981), 426; Jack Bass and Walter DeVries, *The Transformation of Southern Politics* (New York: Meridian, 1976, 1977), 181.

14.   Gregory L. Giroux, "Louisiana: Primary Statute Struck Down," *CQWR*, December 6, 1997, 3041; "States Cannot Change November Election Date for Federal Offices," *Party Developments*, February 1998, 24.

15.   *Book of the States*, 157–158; Markin, *Ballot Access 2*.

16.   Warden Moxley, "Southern Primaries," in *Guide to U.S. Elections, 1789–1974* (Washington, DC: Congressional Quarterly Inc., 1975), 889–993; and Charles S. Bullock III and Loch K. Johnson, *Runoff Elections in the United States* (Chapel Hill: University of North Carolina Press, 1992), 1–8.

17.   V. O. Key Jr., *Southern Politics in State and Nation* (New York: Knopf, 1949), 422; Cortez A. M. Ewing, *Primary Elections in the South: A Study in Uniparty Politics* (Norman: University of Oklahoma Press, 1953), 6–7.

18.   Bullock and Johnson, *Runoff Elections*, 37.

19.   Bullock and Johnson, 50.

20.   Bullock and Johnson, 66.

21.   Key, *Southern Politics*, 438–442.

22.   Alan Greenblatt, "It Will Be Warner vs. Warner as Incumbent Beats Miller," *CQWR*, June 15, 1996, 1707; *Almanac of American Politics 1998*, 1440, 1446.

23.   *Almanac of American Politics 1998*, 114, 122.

24.   Robert Marshall Wells, "Smith May Try to Reclaim 2nd as Cooley Ends His Bid," *CQWR*, August 10, 1996, 2271; *Almanac of American Politics 1998*, 1185–1186.

25.   Juliana Gruenwald, "Panel Redraws Texas Map, Sets Election Date," *CQWR*, August 10, 1996, 2270; and idem, "New Districts to Stay in Place; Tougher Races for Candidates," *CQWR*, September 7, 1996, 2542.

26.   Also see Peverill Squire, "Competition and Uncontested Seats in U.S. House Elections," *Legislative Studies Quarterly* 14 (May 1989): 281–295; and Gary C. Jacobson, *The Electoral Origins of Divided Government: Competition in U.S. House Elections, 1946–1988* (Boulder, CO: Westview Press, 1990), 46–50.

27.   Cortez A. M. Ewing, *Congressional Elections, 1896–1944: The Sectional Basis of Political Democracy in the House of Representatives* (Norman: University of Oklahoma Press, 1947), 55–57.

28.   The career status of candidates is based on the listings and campaign narratives in *CQWR*, 1996; *Almanac of American Politics 1998*; and *Politics in America 1998*.

29.   The methodology used here is an adaptation of analyses in David T. Canon, *Actors, Athletes, and Astronauts: Political Amateurs in the United States Congress* (Chicago: University of Chicago Press, 1990), 74–87; Gary C. Jacobson, *The Politics of Congressional Elections*, 4th ed. (New York: Longman, 1997),

34–37; and Gary C. Jacobson and Samuel Kernell, *Strategy and Choice in Congressional Elections* (New Haven: Yale University Press, 1981), 19–34.

30.   *CQWR*, June 1, 1996, 1554.

31.   Sam Howe Verhovek, "Running on Dare, Teacher Wins Senate Primary," *NYT*, April 11, 1996, Al, B8.

32.   Alan Greenblatt, "Republicans Inhofe, Stevens Easily Win Renomination," *CQWR*, August 31, 1996, 2482.

33.   Deborah Kalb, "Redistricting Leaves McKinney Fighting the Pack in the 4th," *CQWR*, June 29, 1996, 1815–1816.

34.   *Politics in America 1998*, 972–973; *Almanac of American Politics 1998*, 979–980.

35.   The thirteenth open senate seat was in Louisiana, where a unified party primary attracted 15 candidates: six Republicans, four Democrats, and five independents.

36.   Deborah Kalb, "32 Candidates Try to be Heard in Race for Maryland 7th," *CQWR*, February 24, 1996, 451–453.

37.   For presentation of the 1956 to 1974 data, see Harvey L. Schantz, "Contested and Uncontested Primaries for the U.S. House," *Legislative Studies Quarterly 5* (November 1980): 545–562.

38.   Schantz, 552–553.

39.   Schantz, 551–552.

40.   V. O. Key Jr., *American States Politics: An Introduction* (New York: Knopf, 1956), 97–100.

41.   Key, *American State Politics*, 100.

42.   *Almanac of American Politics, 1998*, 766; Robert Marshall Wells, "Collins Loses to Kilpatrick," *CQWR*, August 10, 1996, 2264.

43.   In 1998, Kim, confined to two months of "home detention," for ten campaign finance misdemeanors, lost his primary. See Marc Birtel, "Rep. Kim Must Remain East for Most of Campaign," *CQWR*, April 4, 1998, 902.

44.   *Politics in America 1998*, 206, 1247, 1273.

45.   *Politics in America 1998*, 1401; Juliana Gruenwald, "Bryant, Laughlin Foiled by Unlikely Opponents,"*CQWR*, April 13, 1996, 999–1000, quote 1000.

46.   *Almanac of American Politics 1998*, 1018, 1023; *Politics in America 1998*, 231–232, 1018, 1023–24; and Ronald D. Elving, "Incumbent Filner Battling Challenger in Primary," *CQWR*, March 23, 1996, 814–816.

47.   William D. Morris and Roger H. Marz, "Treadmill to Oblivion: The Fate of Appointed Senators," *Publius* 11 (Winter 1981): 65–80.

48.   Key, *Politics, Parties, and Pressure Groups*, 435.

49.   Roger H. Davidson and Walter J. Oleszek, *Congress and Its Members*, 7th ed. (Washington, DC: CQ Press, 2000).

CHAPTER 3

The Presidential Campaign and Vote in 1996

Job Ratings of Presidents—and Success or Failure at the Polls

MILTON C. CUMMINGS JR.

In an election year that some commentators asserted produced the dullest and least exciting presidential campaign in many decades, there were nonetheless a number of noteworthy features in the final voting returns. President Bill Clinton, the Democratic nominee, won a decisive victory over former Senator Bob Dole, his Republican opponent, and Ross Perot, the candidate of the Reform Party. Clinton carried thirty-one of the fifty states and the District of Columbia, and won 379 electoral votes to 159 for Dole. Clinton's victory marked the first time since 1936 that a Democratic president had been elected to a second full term. And he was only the fourth Democratic president in history—along with Franklin Roosevelt, Woodrow Wilson, and Andrew Jackson—to win two consecutive presidential terms.[1]

Clinton's vote went up between 1992 and 1996; but the vote for the other presidential candidate who ran in both years, Ross Perot, dropped sharply, from 18.9 percent in 1992 to 8.4 percent four years later. Even so, Perot's 1996 presidential showing was the sixth largest vote percentage polled by a third-party or independent presidential candidate since the Civil War. In addition, though little noted, there was another sign in 1996 that many voters were not wedded firmly to the two major parties. Between 1992 and 1996, the vote for minor-party candidates for president other than Perot more than doubled.[2] Those "other" minor-party tallies included close to 700,000 votes for Ralph Nader on the Green Party ticket, and nearly half a million votes for Harry Browne on the Libertarian ticket.

The 1996 voting for Congress also produced an outcome that would have a powerful impact on relations between the president and Congress for at least the next two years. The Republican party suffered a moderate net loss of seats in the House of Representatives and gained strength in the Senate. But the election left the Republicans with clear majorities in both houses of Congress, and Clinton continued to face a Congress controlled by the opposition party after his second inauguration.

The presidential election results were:

	Popular Vote	Electoral Vote	Popular Vote Percentage
Bill Clinton (D)	47,402,357	379	49.2%
Bob Dole (R)	39,198,755	159	40.7%
Ross Perot (RP)	8,085,402	0	8.4%
Others	1,591,358	0	1.7%
Totals	96,277,872	538	100.0%

THE AMERICAN ELECTORATE OF 1996

The size of the electorate that turned out to vote dropped sharply between 1992 and 1996. About 96.3 million people went to the polls in 1996—eight million fewer than had voted four years earlier. Moreover, since the number of Americans who were of voting age increased between 1992 and 1996, this drop in the actual vote also produced the largest four-year drop in the percentage turnout since the wartime election of 1944. The 1996 turnout—just 49.0 percent—was the nation's lowest since 1924.[3]

This decline in the number of Americans who voted for president took place in every major region of the country and in almost every one of the fifty states. (Only two states with small populations, Idaho and Wyoming, were exceptions.) In addition, the actual drop in the number of voting Americans in some of the large states was enormous. In New York the total vote was down by 610,000; in Pennsylvania the drop was 453,000; and in Illinois it was 749,000. In California alone, 1,112,000 fewer people voted for president in 1996 than had voted in 1992.

In some respects, however, the men and women who voted in 1996 did not differ greatly from the active electorates in other recent presidential elections. By their own report, the ratios between Protestants and Catholics (54 percent to 29 percent) and between Democrats and Republicans (39 percent to 35 percent) remained about what they had been four years earlier.[4] A solid majority (66 percent) had family incomes of $30,000 per year or more. And more than half (52 percent) of those who went to the polls were women—a trend that first began to assert itself in the 1960s.

One sign of change in the active electorate that is likely to continue in the near future did turn up in 1996. The ethnic and racial composition of America's voters became somewhat more diverse in 1996. In 1996, as before, a very large majority of those who voted (83 percent) were white—compared to 10 percent who were African-American and 5 percent who identified themselves as Hispanic. Nevertheless, compared with 1992, the white share of the electorate was down by four percentage points in 1996, while the African-American and the Hispanic percentages both increased. If present population trends hold, Hispanic Americans are destined to become the nation's largest ethnic minority group in the twenty-first century.

Two other changes in the active electorate between 1992 and 1996 also should be noted. There was a noticeable jump (from 19 percent to 23 percent) in the share of the total vote that was cast by members of union households in 1996—a trend that worked to President Clinton's advantage. And, in 1996, the percentage of the voters who were under 30 went down by five points, from 22 percent to 17 percent, while the proportion of the electorate who had reached or passed age 60 went up from 16 percent to 24 percent. Compared with 1992, it was a markedly older group of voters who went to the polls in 1996.

PRELUDE TO 1996—1993, 1994, AND 1995

President Clinton began his presidency in 1993 with the broad approval that the American public usually gives a new president at the start of the first term.[5] After his first few days in office, the Gallup poll reported that 58 percent of the public approved of the job Clinton was doing as president, and only 20 percent disapproved (See table 3.1). Over the next nineteen months, however, his popularity plummeted, so that by September 1994—shortly after his major proposal for health-care legislation had been rejected by Congress—only 39 percent of the public approved of Clinton's job performance; a full 54 percent disapproved. Two months after that came the Republican electoral sweep in the congressional elections of 1994, which produced GOP majorities in both the U.S. House and the U.S. Senate.

The Democratic defeat that year was especially dramatic in the House of Representatives, which the Democrats had controlled for forty consecutive years. No other elected institution of the national government—not the presidency, not the U.S. Senate—had ever been controlled that long by one party. Now the Republicans and the new Speaker of the House, the outspoken Newt Gingrich of Georgia, were firmly in control.

Among Democrats, Clinton himself received much of the blame for their party's electoral catastrophe. As Gerald Pomper has written, in addition to losing the midterm elections, the Clinton record of his first two years included "the defeat of ambitious programs such as health-care reform, a cascade of investigations and allegations about his personal conduct, foreign policy embarrassments, and an often maladroit administration of the executive branch."[6]

During the winter of 1994–1995, there was widespread speculation among politicians and in the press that one or more prominent congressional Democrats might challenge Clinton for the Democratic nomination in 1996, just as President Jimmy Carter had been challenged in 1980.

Table 3.1: President Clinton's Job Rating, 1993–1996*

Date of Interviews	Approve (%)	Disapprove (%)	No Opinion (%)
Clinton Elected with 43% of the Vote, November 1992			
Clinton Inaugurated, January 1993			
January 24–26, 1993	58	20	22
April 22–24, 1993	55	37	8
"Travelgate," "$200 haircut," several presidential			
nominations encounter difficulties with Senate,			
David Gergen joins White House, May 1993			
June 5–6, 1993	37	49	14
September 13–15, 1993	46	43	11
Clinton announces health care proposal in			
speech to Congress, September 1993			
September 24–26, 1993	56	36	8
November 19–21, 1993	48	43	9
Clinton's second State of the Union address, January 1994			
January 28–30, 1994	58	35	7
April 22–24, 1994	48	44	8
Health care reform dies, September 1994			
September 6–7, 1994	39	54	7
Midterm elections—Republicans capture the House and Senate,			
November 1994			
December 28–30, 1994	40	52	8
Oklahoma City bombing, April 1995			
April 21–24, 1995	51	39	10
September 14–17, 1995	44	44	12
November 17–18, 1995	53	38	9
January 5–7, 1996	42	49	9
Government shutdown ends, Clinton's fourth			
State of the Union address, January 1996			
January 26–29, 1996	52	42	6
April 25–28, 1996	56	37	7
July 18–21, 1996	57	35	8
Republican and Democratic Conventions, August 1996			
September 7–9, 1996	60	31	9
October 1–2, 1996	58	34	8
October 26–29, 1996	54	36	10

*Responses to the question: "Do you approve or disapprove of the way Bill Clinton is handling his job as president?"

Source: Data provided by the Gallup poll.

Public attention focused on the efforts of Speaker Gingrich and the fresh-man Republicans to push their ambitious and conservative program, the Contract with America, through Congress. At one point President Clinton even felt the need to remind journalists that he was still relevant to the gov-erning process: "The Constitution gives me relevance, the power of our ideas gives me relevance."[7]

Amid the Democrats' gloom, however, there remained two factors that should have given Clinton's partisans some hope for the future. The presi-dent's public approval ratings were often low during his first two years in office, and certainly they were too low to serve as a basis for reelection to a second term. Yet even so, he nearly always retained the support of a solid core of about 40 percent of the electorate (table 3.1). Even during his worst periods in 1993 and 1994, Clinton's job ratings in the Gallup poll never went as low as did those of his three immediate predecessors—Jimmy Carter, George Bush, and even that formidable vote-getter, Ronald Reagan.

Carter's approval rating fell to 21 percent in July 1980, as he was preparing for his ultimately unsuccessful fall reelection campaign. Bush reached a low point of 29 percent in early August 1992, again just a few weeks before the fall presidential campaign. And Reagan's approval ratings stood at 35 percent in January, 1983, shortly after the 1982 recession reached bottom. In that January 1983 Gallup poll, 56 percent of the pub-lic "disapproved" of "the way Ronald Reagan is handling his job as President."[8]

A second factor that some Democratic electoral strategists noted is that despite the Republicans' great midterm election victory in 1994, there was no net realignment of the nation's voters in terms of partisan identification. The ratio between Democrats and Republicans in the electorate at large remained unchanged. According to the Gallup Poll, the distribution of the electorate in 1995 was Democrats 38 percent; Republicans 29 percent; and independents 33 percent.[9] This meant that among prospective voters, Democratic identifiers continued to outnumber Republican identifiers by a moderate margin going into the 1996 election year; and in fact, the exit polls suggest, about four million more Democrats than Republicans voted in November 1996. The Republican party made large gains in terms of party identification in the mid-1980s, sharply narrowing their disadvan-tage in numbers compared with the Democrats. But the GOP did not con-tinue to gain ground in the party identification figures in the first half of the 1990s.

Moreover, even before his party's drubbing in the 1994 elections, Clinton began to take steps to try to improve both the perceived perfor-mance and the actual performance of his administration. He started by making key changes in his White House staff. In June 1994, the president announced that his longtime friend Thomas F. (Mack) McLarty would be replaced as the White House Chief of Staff by Leon E. Panetta, director of the Office of Management and Budget and a former member of Congress from California. Panetta had served in the House of Representatives for sixteen years and—unlike McLarty—had broad knowledge of the Washington political world. After Panetta took charge as chief of staff, the morale and performance of the White House staff appeared to improve. Clinton also brought in State Department spokesman Michael McCurry to be his White House press secretary, replacing Dee Dee Myers. McCurry proved skillful in handling the daily White House press briefings and in dealing with the news media.

Slowly, the president's job-approval ratings began to rise. When a federal office building was bombed in Oklahoma City in April 1995, killing 169 people, the nation was shocked and looked to Washington for reassurance. Clinton and the federal government responded decisively to the tragedy. In the aftermath, Clinton's standing in the polls went up. As John Tierney has noted, some of Clinton's post-1994 foreign policy actions also seemed to help his popularity. He also appeared to gain greater approval by taking more moderate positions on a broad range of issues. The Democratic president was moving to "the center."[10]

Much of the national political debate in 1995 focused on the attempts of Republicans in Congress to pass their legislative program, and Clinton's efforts to block or modify the Republican proposals. During Clinton's first two years in office, when the Democrats controlled Congress, the president did not veto a single bill. In Clinton's second two years in office, with a Republican Congress, he exercised his veto fifteen times.[11]

In December 1995, Republican leaders tried to force Clinton to approve their budget bill by withholding funds to run the federal government. The result was a government shutdown. In November, and again in December–January, many government agencies were closed for days. It was a defining event in Clinton's first term. The public appeared to blame the Republicans in Congress more than they blamed the president for the impasse; when the confrontation was over, the president's job-approval rating had increased to 52 percent in the Gallup poll taken at the end of January 1996. During the rest of the year, through the November election, President Clinton's job rating never dropped below 52 percent (table 3.1).

This surge in the president's popularity had other effects on the 1996 campaign. Clinton was able to avoid a potentially divisive fight within his own party for the nomination; he was the first incumbent Democratic president since Franklin Roosevelt not to have a significant challenge for renomination. And by early 1996 Clinton had moved ahead of all of his potential Republican opponents in the polls. It was a lead that the president never relinquished.

1996: THE GENERAL ELECTION CAMPAIGN

August 1996 was the month during which the three most visible presidential candidates were formally nominated. Dole was formally chosen by the Republicans on August 14; Perot easily won his party's nomination by a margin of two to one over the former governor of Colorado, Richard Lamm, on August 17; and Clinton was renominated by the Democratic National Convention on August 28.

One other minor-party candidate received a fair amount of media attention—Ralph Nader of the Green party. In the spring of 1996, polls showed that about five percent of the public said that they would vote for Nader, a well–known consumer advocate. Many Democratic political leaders initially worried about the Nader candidacy, because they feared that most of his support would come from Democratic voters who would otherwise vote for Bill Clinton. During the summer and fall of 1996, however, Nader's support faded.

Both the Republicans and the Democrats appeared to gain a surge in popular appeal from their national conventions—the so-called "convention bounce." Dole's choice of Jack Kemp as his candidate for vice president also was initially well received both by the public and by Republican activists. Nevertheless, after the Democratic convention, a new Gallup poll reported that President Clinton and his running-mate, Vice President Al Gore, held a 55 percent to 34 percent advantage over Dole and Kemp going into the final two months of the campaign (See table 3.2).

As the last phase of the campaign got underway, it was clear that Clinton was continuing to benefit from good news about the American economy. Price inflation and unemployment were remarkably low: inflation was running at 3.0 percent and unemployment was 5.4 percent.[12]

In many voters' minds, however, there were continuing questions about the Whitewater affair and the controversy over Clinton's business dealings in the 1980s in Arkansas. Nevertheless, the main drama during September centered around plans for the upcoming televised presidential and vice-presidential debates.

On September 10, Ross Perot selected the author and economist, Pat Choate, as his vice-presidential running-mate. On September 17, though, the bipartisan Commission on Presidential Debates decided to exclude Perot and Choate from the televised debates, on the grounds that only Clinton and Dole had a realistic chance of winning the election. Perot filed a lawsuit against the debates commission in the District of Columbia Federal District Court, but about one week before the first debate, Judge Thomas F. Hogan ruled against him.

The Clinton and Dole campaigns agreed to schedule two presidential debates, without Perot, on October 6 and October 16, and one vice-presidential debate on October 9. Millions of Americans watched the debates, although the audiences were smaller than they had been four years earlier.

Table 3.2: Voter Support for Clinton, Dole, and Perot: The Gallup Poll's Three-Way Trial Heats Between February 1995 and Election Eve 1996

Date of Interviews	For Clinton %	For Dole %	For Perot %	For Others, No Opinion %
February 3–5, 1995*	45	51		4
April 17–19, 1995	40	37	18	5
August 4–7, 1995	39	35	23	3
Government shutdown ends, January 6				
January 12–15, 1996	43	39	16	2
Clinton's fourth State of the Union address, January 23				
January 26–29, 1996*	54	42		4
March 8–10, 1996	47	34	17	2
Dole clinches Republican nomination, March 26				
April 9–10, 1996	49	35	15	1
July 25–28, 1996	50	35	10	5
Republican Convention, August 12–15				
August 16–18, 1996	48	41	7	4
Democratic Convention, August 26–29				
September 9–11, 1996	55	34	5	6
October 3–4, 1996	51	39	5	5
October 5–6, 1996	55	35	5	5
Presidential and vice-presidential debates, October 6–16				
October 17–18, 1996	55	32	8	5
October 20–21, 1996	54	35	6	5
October 30–31, 1996	52	34	10	4
Final Poll	52	41	7	0
Election Results	49	41	8	2

*Perot's name not included in poll questions.

Source: Data provided by the Gallup poll.

In their first debate, in Hartford, Connecticut, Clinton and Dole sparred over the economy, education, Medicare, and tax cuts. Dole accused Clinton of being "a liberal," but Clinton retorted, "That's what their party always drags out when they get in a tight race."[13] Polls indicated that viewers preferred Clinton's performance—51 percent thought that Clinton had "won" the debate, compared with 32 percent who said that Dole had won.[14]

In another relatively low-key debate on October 9, the vice-presidential candidates, Gore and Kemp, faced off. Once again the Democrats scored a debate victory. Polls showed that the voters thought that Gore had "won" the debate, 57 percent to 28 percent.[15]

The days leading into the final presidential debate brought good news and bad news for the Democratic camp. On October 13, the Dow Jones industrials stock market index broke the 6,000 barrier, an event that the Democratic party seized upon as another sign that the economy was doing well. But the Clinton administration's moments of success often seemed to be followed by troubles, and this time the difficulty involved campaign finance. The Republicans began to attack Clinton and the Democrats for accepting contributions of $485,000 to the Democratic National Committee from the members of an Indonesian banking family and for taking other contributions from foreign sources.

The final presidential debate took place on October 16 in San Diego, California; and this time Dole sharply attacked Clinton over what Dole said were the administration's ethical problems and "scandals." For the most part Clinton ignored his rival's attacks. Once again, he led in the post-debate polls, 59 percent to 29 percent.[16] Dole had been counting on the debates to enable him to catch up with Clinton. But the debates had failed to narrow the gap.

There were now just nineteen days left before election day. On October 23, Dole sent his campaign manager Scott Reed to Dallas to ask Ross Perot to drop his presidential bid and endorse the GOP ticket. However, Perot declared that he was in the race to the finish.

In the final days of the campaign, Clinton urged people to turn out and vote. He also made campaign stops that he hoped would benefit Democratic congressional candidates. Dole launched a dramatic last-minute push to mobilize support—a seventeen-stop, ninety-six-hour sprint during which he campaigned almost around the clock. Perot's campaign finale, on election eve, consisted of four thirty-minute "infomercials" in which he sharply attacked the Clinton presidency. Perot suggested that Clinton, if reelected, would spend much of his second term answering charges of corruption and scandal in his administration. The final polls indicated that there had been some narrowing of Clinton's lead. But all of the major national polls still had Clinton ahead.

On election day, it was sunny or partly sunny over much of the nation, with high temperatures in the 60s as far north as Nebraska, Illinois, Ohio, and Maryland. There were showers, however, in the states around the Great Lakes. Despite the generally favorable weather, the turnout was low. For the first time in seventy-two years, there were more nonvoters than voters in a presidential election. When the votes were counted, Clinton had won by a margin of 8.5 percentage points over Dole and by about 8.2 million popular votes.

NOVEMBER 5, 1996—THE PATTERN OF THE VOTE

On election day, 47.4 million people cast their ballots for Clinton and almost 39.2 million voted for Dole. Perot polled nearly 8.1 million votes, a sharp drop from the 19.7 million votes he received in 1992, but still an unusually strong showing for an independent candidate. In the electoral college, because Perot did not win the popular vote in any state, all of the electoral votes went to Clinton and Dole. The Democratic nominee received 379 of the nation's 538 electoral college votes; and Dole won 159.

Because the presidential popular vote was split three ways, in twenty-six states no presidential candidate won a majority of the total vote. Of these states that were won by popular-vote pluralities, Dole carried thirteen, and Clinton carried thirteen. On the other hand, in the twenty-four states that were won with more than 50 percent of the total popular vote, Clinton was the decisive winner. Dole won clear majorities in six states, most with small populations—Alabama, Alaska, Idaho, Kansas, Nebraska, and Utah. These states gave the former Kansas senator 32 electoral votes. Clinton, by contrast, carried eighteen states with a popular-vote majority. These states, and the District of Columbia, gave Clinton a total of 230 electoral votes— just 40 short of the number needed for an electoral college majority. Aside from this overall verdict, there were many noteworthy features in the November 5, 1996 vote.

THE NATIONAL VOTE

1. About 96.3 million voters went to the polls. As has been pointed out, the number of people who voted for president was down by more than eight million from 1992, and the percentage turnout— 49.0 percent—was the nation's lowest since 1924.
2. President Clinton's share of the total popular vote—49.2 percent— was substantially higher than the 43.0 percent that he received in 1992. But he remained one of eleven American presidents to be elected with less than 50 percent of the vote. He was also one of only three presidents to win two terms while receiving less than half the vote each time. The other two presidents who won two terms without polling at least 50 percent of the vote were Grover Cleveland, in 1884 and 1892, and Woodrow Wilson, in 1912 and 1916.

3. In the total popular vote for president, Clinton ran 8.5 percentage points ahead of Dole. However, in the voting dynamics that determined the crucial outcome in the electoral college, the popular vote for the two major-party candidates, Clinton defeated Dole by 9.4 percentage points—54.7 percent to 45.3 percent. Clinton's 9.4 point lead in the *two-party* vote came close to Franklin Roosevelt's two-party vote lead over Wendell Willkie in 1940 (55.0 percent to 45.0 percent). It also somewhat bettered the two-party vote lead that George Bush had over Michael Dukakis in 1988—53.9 percent to 46.1 percent.

THE PEROT FACTOR

1. As has been noted, the 8.1 million votes (8.4 percent) polled by Ross Perot was the sixth largest percentage received by a minor-party or independent presidential candidate since the Civil War. Even so, in raw numbers, Perot's 1996 vote was down by 11.6 million from what it had been in 1992.
2. It is probable that many 1992 Perot voters did not vote in 1996; in the 1996 exit polls, only 12 percent of the 1996 voters said that they had supported Perot in 1992, but Perot's actual share of the 1992 vote was almost 19 percent.[17]
3. The exit polls suggest that more than seven million 1992 Perot voters did go to the polls again in 1996. Among these former Perot voters, about a third (33 percent) voted for Perot a second time. But about two-thirds of the 1992 Perot supporters voted for one of the two major-party candidates in 1996. Furthermore, this sizable group of voters went for Dole over Clinton by a margin of two to one, 44 percent to 22 percent.
4. Despite their drop in numbers from 1992, the eight million Perot supporters in 1996 remained a huge bloc of voters who could be "up for grabs" in the next presidential election, in the year 2000. Much depends on whether Perot chooses to run again in 2000, and whether the Reform party runs another presidential candidate if Perot drops out.

SECTIONAL PATTERNS

1. In the presidential vote, as in 1992, the most Democratic region was the Northeast, where Clinton outpolled Dole by 56 percent to 35 percent. Along the East Coast, for example, Clinton carried every state from Maryland to the Canadian border—a feat that not even Franklin D. Roosevelt had been able to achieve. Clinton, in fact, swept the eastern seaboard—from the District of Columbia to Maine—twice, in 1996 and in 1992.

2. In the Midwest, the outcome was closer. There, Clinton ran ahead of Dole 48 percent to 41 percent—very close to the division of the vote in the country as a whole.[18]

3. Next to the Northeast, the Democrats' most solid regional stronghold was the group of Pacific Coast states of California, Oregon, and Washington with their seventy-two electoral votes. In this section of the country, Clinton led Dole by a decisive margin, 53 percent to 34 percent.

4. With Clinton and Gore as their nominees, the Democrats in 1996, as in 1992, were running the first all-southern major-party presidential ticket since Andrew Jackson and John C. Calhoun ran together in 1828. In 1996, the Clinton–Gore ticket again made inroads into previous Republican strength in presidential voting in the South. By the narrowest of margins—about 24,200 votes out of more than 26 million votes cast—Clinton and Gore won the popular vote in the South.[19] It was the first time since 1976, when the Democrats nominated Jimmy Carter of Georgia for president, that the Democrats had held their own or ran ahead in the popular vote in the South. The Democrats' popular vote in the South allowed them to carry four states—Arkansas, Florida, Louisiana, and Tennessee—of the former Confederacy.

5. Nevertheless, the South remained a very important sectional base for the Republican party in presidential voting. In the eleven states of the former Confederacy, Dole won a solid majority of the electoral votes and, as noted, ran almost even with Clinton in the popular vote—46.1 percent to 46.2 percent. In the rest of the country, Clinton led Dole by a sizable margin—50.4 percent to 38.7 percent.

6. In the Rocky Mountain states, a region where Ronald Reagan carried most of the states by landslide margins in the 1980s, Dole ran ahead of Clinton in 1996—by 47 percent to 43 percent. Perot won 9.6 percent of the vote in the Rocky Mountain states, a big drop from his showing in 1992 when he polled nearly one vote in every four in the region. Nevertheless, among the eight states in the Rocky Mountain region Clinton was the winner in three—New Mexico, Nevada, and Arizona. No Democrat had carried Arizona since Harry Truman won there in 1948.

7. The Clinton tide ran strongly in the East, Midwest, and the Pacific Coast region. It also enabled Clinton to carry at least some states in most major sections of the country. However, there were important centers of Dole strength in four areas—most of the Southeast, Indiana, a string of six states in the center of the country running from Texas to the Canadian border, and five of the eight Rocky Mountain states.

8. In the popular vote New England was the strongest Democratic section and the Rocky Mountain region was the best area for the Republicans. There were greater sectional differences in the popular vote and popular vote swing in 1996 than in 1992. This rise in sectionalism, according to Harvey Schantz, "is mainly a reflection of the increased individuality of the Middle Atlantic states and especially New England. The Mountain states were also quite distant from the national vote distribution in 1996." [20]

SOCIAL GROUPS

1. As in 1992, Clinton did well with some traditionally Democratic groups among which Reagan had made heavy inroads in the 1980s. Among members of union households, Clinton led 59 percent to 30 percent.[21] Clinton also did well among two groups that had remained Democratic in the 1980s and in 1992: Clinton was backed by 84 percent of African-American voters and by 78 percent of Jewish voters.

2. Hispanic Americans, who voted 62 percent to 24 percent for Clinton over Bush in 1992, were even more pro-Clinton four years later as they backed Clinton over Dole by more than three to one— 72 percent to 21 percent. Hispanic Americans were also one of the few major groups in the United States whose voting turnout increased in 1996. Close to five million Hispanic Americans went to the polls in 1996 (compared with four million in 1992); and voting shifts toward Clinton in Hispanic American neighborhoods were a key factor in President Clinton's victories in Florida and Arizona.[22]

3. The contribution made by African-American voters to the Democratic presidential victory was particularly noteworthy. One in every ten Americans who went to the polls was African-American. This large group voted 84 percent for Clinton, and only 12 percent for Dole. The exit polls suggested that African Americans gave Clinton a margin of about 6.9 million votes, or most of his 8.2 million margin of victory.

4. The state of the economy was strongly reflected in the returns. One third of the voters (33 percent) reported that their family's financial situation was better in 1996 than it had been in 1992. Among that large group of voters, Clinton led Dole by 66 percent to 26 percent. There was a smaller group of voters (20 percent), however, who said that their family's financial situation was worse in 1996 than in 1992. Those voters opted for Dole over Clinton, 57 percent to 27 percent.

5. Clinton made gains in 1996 in one group that had been a key component of the Roosevelt New Deal coalition but which had been

less strongly Democratic in recent years—Roman Catholics. Nearly three voters in every ten (29 percent) were Roman Catholic; and they supported Clinton over Dole 53 percent to 37 percent. Among Protestants, by contrast, Dole had a moderate lead over Clinton, 47 percent to 43 percent. One source of Clinton's stronger showing among Catholics in 1996 was undoubtedly the surge of support the president received from Hispanic American voters.

6. Another aspect of the voters' religious identifications left a deep imprint on the returns. In 1996 voters who were interviewed as they left the polls were asked whether they considered themselves members of the "Religious Right." Seventeen percent said "yes"; 80 percent said "no." Among the self-identified members of the Religious Right, Dole led Clinton by a decisive margin—65 percent to 26 percent. Among the larger group who did not consider themselves adherents of the Religious Right, Clinton ran well ahead of Dole, by a margin of 54 percent to 35 percent.

7. In discussions of American politics in recent years, the voting preferences of members of the "Religious Right" have, quite correctly, received a great deal of attention. The 1996 exit polls suggest, however, that when examining the voters' religious preferences, there are two other groups in American society that should be looked at for their impact on American presidential elections. In 1996, some 87 percent of the voters said that they were Protestants, Catholics, or Jews. But another six percent said that they belonged to "other religions," and seven percent said that they had no religion. These latter two groups together accounted for 13 percent of the American electorate—and they were a cluster of voters three-fourths the size of the self-identified Religious Right. In 1996, adherents of other religions and those professing no religion voted heavily for Clinton, giving the president close to 60 percent of their votes compared with 23 percent for Dole.

8. Perhaps the most striking feature of all in the 1996 election was the "gender gap": the tendency of men and women to vote differently in the presidential race. Among male voters, Clinton and Dole polled an almost equal share of the vote. Men voted 44 percent for Dole; 43 percent for Clinton; and 10 percent for Perot. Among women, however, the president led Dole by sixteen percentage points—54 percent to 38 percent; with 7 percent for Perot. If all the voters had voted the way that American women cast their ballots in 1996, Clinton would have won the election by more than 15 million votes, instead of by 8.2 million.

PARTY LOYALTY AND DEFECTION

1. Despite the Clinton victory, the major change in party identification that took place in the mid-1980s was once again strongly evident in the returns. Among those who voted, self-described Democrats outnumbered Republicans by only a moderate margin—39 percent to 35 percent. This moderate margin was certainly helpful to Clinton, because it meant that there were probably about four million more Democrats than Republicans at the polls. But it was a major change from the large advantage the Democratic party used to have in the number of party identifiers. As recently as 1980 (and in spite of Ronald Reagan's presidential victory that year), the exit polls suggested that 43 percent of the voters considered themselves Democrats, compared with 28 percent who said they were Republicans.[23] By the second half of the 1980s, however, the Democratic party had clearly lost the large lead in party identification that it had enjoyed for more than four decades.

2. Nevertheless, although the number of Republican identifiers had grown substantially since the early 1980s, Dole suffered some significant defections among Republican voters in 1996. Eighty percent of the Republicans supported their party's presidential ticket in 1996; but 13 percent voted for Clinton and 6 percent defected to Perot.[24] Clinton did slightly better than Dole in holding his party's identifiers, winning 84 percent of the votes of Democrats, while losing 10 percent to Dole and 5 percent to Perot. It was only the second time since the Johnson landslide over Goldwater in 1964 that the Democrats mobilized a higher percentage of their partisans than did the Republicans. Clinton also had greater success with Democratic voters than Bush had in mobilizing the Republicans in 1992.[25]

3. Clinton also out-polled the Republican ticket among voters who considered themselves independents, as he had in 1992. His lead over Dole among independents was eight points (43 percent to 35 percent)—about what his lead was among the electorate as a whole.

4. In 1996 Ross Perot showed some strength among all three types of voters—Democrats, Republicans, and independents. He won the support of 5 percent of the Democrats and 6 percent of the Republicans. Among independents, the Perot share rose to 17 percent.

CONTROL OF GOVERNMENT

1. Despite the Democratic presidential victory for Bill Clinton, in many of the contests for public offices other than the presidency, Republican candidates did well in 1996. The election left the Republican party in control of both the U. S. Senate and the House of Representatives, and it also left the GOP with a strong lead in the nation's governorships.

2. In a close, hard-fought battle, the Republicans won the important contest for control of the House of Representatives. The Democrats made a modest net gain of seats to bring the House membership to 207 Democrats and 227 Republicans, and one independent member. The Republicans' overall majority in the House was the narrowest House majority held by either party since 1954, and it narrowed further in the midterm election of 1998, as the partisan split in the new 106th Congress was 223 Republicans, 211 Democrats, and one independent.

3. In the Senate, the Republicans gained two seats, increasing their margin of control. The new Senate had 55 Republicans and 45 Democrats. The election left the new Senate Majority Leader Trent Lott of Mississippi, former Senator Dole's successor, with the largest Republican Senate majority since 1929. The partisan division of seats was not changed in the 1998 midterm election. In 2000, 19 Republican seats and 14 Democratic seats will be up for election.

4. Perhaps the most important point of all about the 1996 election was that for two years, at least, there would continue to be divided government in Washington. The Democratic party was in control of the presidency; the Republicans controlled both houses of Congress. The situation reminded some observers of the electoral outcome of 1972, when President Richard Nixon and an opposition Democratic Congress were both reelected just as the Watergate scandal began to unfold. At the very least, the 1996 electoral verdict meant that during a period when an almost unprecedented series of investigations of the president were underway, the chairs of congressional committees who might have to act on the results of those investigations were members of the opposition party. The 1996 election results were thus an invitation to struggle between the executive and the legislative branches of the government. On the other hand, given the closeness of the balance of political forces left by the returns, the outcome also gave leaders in both parties reasons for caution, and even for a measure of cooperation. How the Democratic president and the Republican

congressional leaders shared their power would go a long way toward determining how their parties would fare in future elections.

EXPLAINING THE PRESIDENTIAL ELECTION OUTCOME OF 1996: "IT'S THE PRESIDENT'S JOB RATING. . . ."

Throughout nearly all of the 1996 campaign year—from March 1996 to the end of October—President Clinton maintained a lead of at least 12 percentage points over his Republican opponent, Robert Dole, in the Gallup poll. The only exception occurred in a single poll taken in August, immediately following the Republican National Convention. In that one poll, Dole cut the Clinton lead to seven percent (table 3.2).

Journalists who were following the presidential campaign found it a frustrating contest to cover because they thought it was so difficult to make it interesting for their readers. Republican activists who worked in the Dole campaign were also frustrated because they could never seem to close the gap between their presidential ticket and the Democrats. As the chairman of the Republican National Committee, Haley Barbour, put it after the election was over, "We started (presidential) polling in April, and we never measured Dole above 41 percent in a single survey, even during the [GOP] convention.[26] Two political scientists who studied the 1996 campaign, Paul S. Herrnson and Clyde Wilcox, called their analysis "A Tale of a Campaign That Didn't Seem to Matter."[27] Until the last few days of the campaign, the incessant poll results hardly seemed to move at all. Then, in the final week, Clinton's lead over Dole narrowed a bit, but not enough to make the election close.

After the election, there was some discussion of whether, with different candidates and different campaign strategies, the Republican party could have made the outcome different. At the very least, it is fair to say, for the Republicans to have won in 1996 would have been very, very hard. The fact is that Clinton probably won the November 1996 election sometime between early 1995 and the spring of 1996. It was during this period that the way the American people viewed Clinton's job performance as president moved from clearly negative to clearly positive.

This movement of opinion can be traced in table 3.1, which sets forth the responses of the American public to the question: "Do you approve or disapprove of the way Bill Clinton is handling his job as president?" A similar question has been asked concerning the president's job performance for every president since Franklin Roosevelt. As the poll numbers in table 3.1 make clear, Clinton's job rating at the end of 1994 was not good—40 percent of the American public approved of the job he was doing, 52 percent disapproved.

In April 1995, following the administration's firm response to the Oklahoma City bombing tragedy, the president's poll ratings moved into positive territory (51 percent approving, versus 39 percent disapproving).

During the next nine months, the president's approval ratings sometimes sagged again, most notably at the beginning of January 1996, in the middle of the government shutdown confrontation with the Republican Congress. However, other polls taken at the time suggest that more of the public blamed Republican congressional leaders than blamed Clinton for that impasse.[28] And when the confrontation over the government shutdown was over, President Clinton soon began to enjoy the highest job ratings he had had in two years. Moreover, although his job rating slipped a little just before the November election, his approval ratings remained strongly tilted toward the positive side. Looking at President Clinton's job ratings during his first four years as president, the overall pattern is clear. It was almost as though the collective judgment of the American public was: first two years, job performance "poor"; last two years, job performance "pretty good."

As the final set of poll numbers in table 3.1 indicates, President Clinton went into the last week of the 1996 election campaign with an approval rating of 54 percent. In an election in which the vote for minor-party presidential candidates reached 10 percent, Clinton did not get 54 percent of the total vote. (His share of the total was 49.2 percent.) Clinton did, however, get 54.7 percent of the two-party vote.

For other presidents, also, there has been a fairly close relationship between the way the American public rated the president's job performance and the verdict of the voters when the president sought reelection. During the second half of the twentieth century, eight American presidents have fought election campaigns as an incumbent attempting to be returned to the White House. Two of those presidential candidates, Lyndon Johnson and Gerald Ford, had ascended to the presidency through the death or resignation of the previous president. The other six presidents seeking reelection—Eisenhower, Nixon, Carter, Reagan, Bush, and Clinton—had been elected to a first term.

In table 3.3, the job approval ratings of these eight presidents as they approached election day are set forth. The percentage of the total vote these presidents received and the election outcome are also listed. Five presidents—Eisenhower, Johnson, Nixon, Reagan, and Clinton—had positive approval ratings (above 50 percent) as they attempted to win another term in the White House. All five were returned to office. On the other hand, three incumbent presidents approaching election day clearly were in trouble with the voters, with mediocre job ratings (Ford, 45 percent approval), or very low ratings (Carter, 37 percent; and Bush, 36 percent). All three of those presidents were defeated for reelection.

Table 3.3: Presidents Seeking Reelection; Their Job Ratings; and the Outcome of the Presidential Election: Presidential Approval Ratings in an Election Year and the President's Share of the November Presidential Vote, 1956–1996

Election Year	President Seeking Reelection	Date of Job Rating Interviews	President's Job Rating* % Who Approve	% Who Disapprove	President's % of Total Vote in November	Outcome of the Election
1956	Eisenhower	(08/03–08/56)	67%	20%	57.4%	PRESIDENT REELECTED
1964	Johnson	(06/04–09/64)	74	13	61.1	PRESIDENT REELECTED
1972	Nixon	(mid–June, 72)	59	30	60.7	PRESIDENT REELECTED
1976	Ford	(06/11–14/76)	45	40	48.0	PRESIDENT DEFEATED
1980	Carter	(Sept., 80)	37	55	41.0	PRESIDENT DEFEATED
1984	Reagan	(10/26–29/84)	58	33	58.8	PRESIDENT REELECTED
1992	Bush	(09/21–24/92)	36	54	37.4	PRESIDENT DEFEATED
1996	Clinton	(10/26–29/96)	54	36	49.2**	PRESIDENT REELECTED

*Responses were to the question: "Do you approve or disapprove of the way _____ is handling his job as president?"

**In 1996 Clinton polled 54.7% of the two-party vote.

Source: The Gallup poll presidential approval ratings are drawn from the following sources: George H. Gallup, *The Gallup Poll: Public Opinion, 1935-1971* (New York: Random House, 1972), 1441, 1885 (data for 1956 and 1964); *Gallup Opinion Index*, October–November, Report No. 182, 19 (data for 1972); *Gallup Opinion Index*, July, 1976, Report No. 132, 2 (data for 1976); *Gallup Opinion Index*, October–November, Report No. 182, 13 (data for 1980); *Gallup Report*, December, 1984, Report No. 231, 11 (data for 1984); *The Gallup Poll Monthly*, September, 1992, 39 (data for 1992); and the Gallup Web Site, on May 8, 1997, *http://www.gallup.com/ratings/(data for 1996).*

In 1996, President Clinton's overall favorable job rating undoubtedly stemmed from a complex blend of factors and public motivations—from favorable evaluations of the state of the economy, to positive voter responses to Clinton's skills as a campaigner. But a president who had 54 percent of the American public who approved of the job he was doing as chief executive was going to be extremely hard to beat.

CONCLUSION

The preceding discussion may help to explain why President Clinton coasted to a relatively easy reelection victory in 1996. But it still leaves unanswered two major questions. What was the fundamental nature of the verdict handed down by the American electorate in 1996? And, amid the large number of elections that make up the total "population of elections,"[29] how is the 1996 election to be classified?

One famous typology of elections that might shed light on the nature of the electoral verdict in 1996 was put forward many years ago. V. O. Key Jr. once classified presidential elections into three broad types: (1) Votes of Lack of Confidence; (2) Reaffirmations of Support by Votes of Confidence; and (3) Realignments. The 1996 presidential election appears to be a reaffirmation of support by a vote of confidence. In this type of election, as defined by Key, "substantially the same coalition of voters prevails as provided the majority in the preceding election. Such an election may be regarded as a vote of confidence in the general course of action the Administration has followed."[30]

As we have seen, there were interesting nuances in the vote patterns of 1996 that reflected some change from 1992 to 1996 in the social and geographical groupings that produced a victory for Clinton in both election years. On the other hand, the most striking aspect of Clinton's two elections was the similarity of the voting coalitions that put him into power two times. In 1996, the fundamental character of the electoral verdict was a reaffirmation of support, however qualified, for the Clinton administration. The election returned Clinton and the Democratic party to power in the executive branch, and it gave them four more years to take on the risks of governing. Four years later, to be sure, Clinton would not be running again. But how well his administration was perceived as managing the government would go a considerable way toward determining whether the Democratic party would receive another reaffirmation of support at the presidential level—or a "Vote of No Confidence"—in the election of 2000.

NOTES

1.   Gerald M. Pomper, "The Presidential Election," in *The Election of 1996: Reports and Interpretations,* ed. Pomper (Chatham, NJ: Chatham House, 1997), 173.

2.   All 1996 election returns are from Richard M. Scammon, Alice V. McGillivray, and Rhodes Cook, *America Votes 22* (Washington, DC: Congressional Quarterly Inc., 1998).

3.   Richard M. Scammon and Alice V. McGillivray, *America Votes 20* (Washington, DC: Congressional Quarterly Inc., 1993), 9; and Scammon, McGillivray, and Cook, *America Votes 22,* 1.

4.   The composition of the electorate is based on the Voter News Service exit poll available at *www.cnn.com/ALLPOLITICS/1996 polls.* For a comparison to the electorate of 1992, see Milton C. Cummings Jr., "Political Change Since the New Deal: The 1992 Presidential Election in Historical Perspective," in *American Presidential Elections: Process, Policy, and Political Change,* ed. Harvey L. Schantz (Albany: State University of New York Press, 1996), 51–53.

5.   This narrative account of Clinton's first three years in office and the 1996 campaign and vote draws heavily on Milton C. Cummings Jr. and David Wise, *Democracy Under Pressure: An Introduction to the American Political System,* 8th ed. (Fort Worth: Harcourt Brace College Publishers, 1997), 405–420.

6.   Pomper, "The Presidential Election," 173.

7.   George J. Church, "The Democrats: The Learning Curve," *Time,* September 2, 1996, 33.

8.   Responses to the question: "Do you approve or disapprove of the way _____ is handling his job as President?" *Gallup Opinion Index,* Report No. 180, August 1980, 26; *Gallup Report,* December 1983, No. 219, 18; and data provided for 1992 by the Gallup Poll.

9.   Data supplied by the Gallup Poll.

10.   See John T. Tierney, "The Context: Policies and Politics, 1993–1996," in *America's Choice: The Election of 1996,* ed. William Crotty and Jerome M. Mileur, (Guilford, CT: Dushkin/McGraw-Hill, 1997), 24–25.

11.   Church, "The Democrats," 32.

12.   U.S. Bureau of Labor Statistics.

13.   "A Closer Look at the Debate," *USA,* October 7, 1996, A13.

14.   Susan Page, "Debaters Clash Over Vision, Rivals Cite Fundamental Differences," *USA,* October 7, 1996, A1.

15.   *www.allpolitics.com,* October 9, 1996.

16.   Bill Nichols, "Dole on Offense in Debate," *USA,* October 17, 1996, A1.

17.   This section is based on the Voter News Service Exit Poll available at *www.cnn.com/ALLPOLITICS/1996polls.*

18.   The Midwest includes the five Great Lakes states of Illinois, Indiana, Michigan, Ohio, and Wisconsin, the Prairie states of Kansas, Nebraska, South Dakota, and North Dakota, along with Minnesota, Iowa, and Missouri.

19.   The South, as here defined, includes the eleven states of the former Confederacy—Alabama, Arkansas, Florida, Georgia, Louisiana, Mississippi, North Carolina, South Carolina, Tennessee, Texas, and Virginia.

20.   Harvey L. Schantz, "An Update on Sectional Voting: The 1996 Presidential Election," *Party Developments*, September 1997, 21–22.

21.   This section is based on the Voter News Service exit poll.

22.   B. Drummond Ayres Jr., "The Expanding Hispanic Vote Shakes Republican Strongholds," *NYT*, November 10, 1996, Section 1, 27.

23.   The party identification data cited for 1980 came from exit polls of 12,782 voters conducted by CBS News and the *NYT*; reported in *NJ*, November 8, 1980, 1878.

24.   This section is based on the VNS exit poll.

25.   See Cummings, "Political Change Since the New Deal," 78.

26.   Quoted in Larry J. Sabato, "The November Vote—A Status Quo Election," in *Toward the Millennium: The Elections of 1996,* ed. Larry J. Sabato, (Boston: Allyn and Bacon, 1997), 155.

27.   Paul S. Herrnson and Clyde Wilcox, "The 1996 Presidential Election: A Tale of a Campaign That Didn't Seem to Matter," in *Toward the Millennium,* 121–142.

28.   George Hager, "Republicans Throw in Towel on Seven-Year Deal," *CQWR*, January 27, 1996, 213–216, esp. 215.

29.   The phrase "population of elections" is V. O. Key's. See Key, "The Politically Relevant in Surveys," *Public Opinion Quarterly* 24 (Spring 1960): 54–61, at 55.

30.   V. O. Key Jr., *Politics, Parties, and Pressure Groups,* 5th ed. (New York: Crowell, 1964), 522–536, quote 526.

CHAPTER 4

Strategic Partisan Decisions and Blunted National Outcomes
The 1996 Senate Election Campaign and Vote

DOUGLAS B. HARRIS

INTRODUCTION

The elections for Senate seemed to be the bright spot for the Republican party in the otherwise troubled 1996 elections. Where Republican presidential nominee Bob Dole lost decisively to President Bill Clinton and where Republicans lost seats in the House of Representatives, Republicans actually extended the number of Senate seats they held. Senate Republicans were able to capitalize on an extraordinary number of opportunities in an otherwise unfavorable political climate, picking up two Senate seats. Put in the context of the other national election outcomes, the Republican gains in the Senate are impressive indeed.

However, when one views the great many opportunities Senate Republicans squandered and how short they fell of their earlier stated hope of a filibuster-proof majority, it seems Republicans were lucky to have extended their Senate majority at all. A tide of anti-Republican sentiment—blunted only in the last weeks of the campaign by growing evidence of campaign finance irregularities by the Democratic party and some backlash against the activities of organized labor on behalf of Democratic candidates—kept Republicans from capitalizing as well as they might have on a host of remarkable opportunities for gains in Senate seats.

THE OUTCOMES OF THE 1996 SENATE ELECTIONS

Thirty-five Senate seats were determined during the 1995–1996 election cycle. Thirty-three of those seats were scheduled to be up for election in 1996 and the resignations of Senators Bob Packwood (R-OR) and Bob Dole (R-KS) increased that number to thirty-five. Packwood's Oregon Senate seat was filled in a January 1996 special election. The net outcome of these races was a one seat increase for Senate Republicans. In the November elections (excluding the race to succeed Packwood),

Republicans achieved a net gain of two seats. Republicans endured the defeat of one Senate incumbent, but were able to pick up three seats previously held by Democrats in open Senate races.

THE NATIONAL VOTE

In the thirty-three states that had Senate races, 51,291,071 votes were cast. Over 25.3 million (49.4 percent) of those votes were for Republicans while just over 24.5 million (47.8 percent) were for Democrats.[1] Despite the narrow vote margin in terms of votes cast, Republicans won nearly two-thirds of the Senate races. Of course, the apportionment of Senate seats based on states rather than population explains a great deal of the disparity between votes and seats in Senate elections.

THE RACES

The relatively little partisan turnover in the 1996 elections that saw Republicans extending their Senate majority from 53 to 55 seats masks the fact that with few exceptions the 1996 Senate elections were quite competitive. There were a handful of races, however, in which returning Senate incumbents fended off challengers handily. Incumbent Senators Ted Stevens (R-AK), Joseph Biden (D-DE), Thad Cochran (R-MS), Pete Domenici (R-NM), Fred Thompson (R-TN), and John D. Rockefeller IV (D-WV) all won reelection with over 60 percent of the two–party vote. And several other Senate incumbents—Larry Craig (R-ID), Mitch McConnell (R-KY), Carl Levin (D-MI), and James Inhofe (R-OK)—had little trouble winning reelection.

Despite these convincing victories by incumbents, the 1996 Senate elections were remarkably competitive. In Georgia, Secretary of State Max Cleland defeated Republican Guy Millner by 30,024 votes, 1.3 percent of the total vote. In Louisiana, Democratic State Treasurer Mary Landrieu secured victory over Republican Louis Jenkins with a margin of only 5,788 votes, or 0.3 percent of the total vote. And in New Hampshire, former Democratic Representative Dick Swett failed to unseat incumbent Republican Senator Robert Smith; Smith bested Swett by less than 15,000 votes, little more than 3.0 percent of the total vote. In fact, the New Hampshire race was so close that on election night several news organizations as well as the Democratic Senatorial Campaign Committee (DSCC) projected that Swett had unseated Smith only to have to retract hours later, announcing Smith's narrow reelection victory. A DSCC fax sent out on election night proclaimed: "For the first time in 20 years, New Hampshire will be sending a Democrat to the United States Senate with former Rep. Dick Swett's victory ... over GOP Sen. Bob Smith ... Smith was unable to defend his record as an ineffective legislator who did not represent the interests of average New Hampshire citizens."[2] In all, 26 of the 34 Senate elections were won with less than 60 percent of the vote. And of those 26, sixteen were won with less than 55 percent of the vote. In 1996, over three-fourths of the races were competitive.

REPUBLICAN GAINS

The net outcome of these largely close Senate races was that Senate Republicans, who had won a majority in the 1994 elections, were able to extend that majority by two seats. As in recent years, in 1996 the South was of particular importance in Republican gains. Of the three Republican victories for Senate seats previously held by Democrats, two were in southern states. Four key retirements by southern Democratic Senators J. Bennett Johnston (D-LA), Howell Heflin (D-AL), David Pryor (D-AR), and Sam Nunn (D-GA) forced Democrats to defend these vacated seats in the increasingly Republican South. Democrats lost the seats vacated by Heflin and Pryor to Alabama Republican Jeff Sessions and Arkansas Republican Tim Hutchinson. Moreover, Democrats were barely able to hold onto the Senate seats vacated by Johnston and Nunn, as Democratic candidates Mary Landrieu of Louisiana and Max Cleland of Georgia won the two closest 1996 Senate races. Landrieu won with 50.2 percent of the vote while Cleland won with only 50.7 percent of the two-party vote. The closeness of their races should not diminish the significant accomplishments of Landrieu and Cleland, who became only the second and third non-incumbent Democratic Senate candidates since 1978 to have succeeded another southern Democrat to the Senate (the other was Louisiana Democratic Senator John B. Breaux, who won a 1986 election to succeed retiring Senator Russell B. Long to the Senate).[3]

Nevertheless, had it not been for Republican gains of two southern Senate seats previously held by Democrats, there would have been no net change in Senate seats, as the Republican gain in Nebraska was cancelled by the Democratic gain in South Dakota. Ultimately, the South was crucial in the extension of the Republican Senate majority.

THE SETTING: STRATEGIC DECISIONS AND THE
ESTABLISHMENT OF OPPORTUNITIES

In elections, the public does not make choices that translate unencumbered into electoral victories or governing mandates. Different institutional structures—from the Constitutional requirements of equal apportionment of Senate seats to states and staggered terms, to the strategic decisions of incumbents (to seek reelection or retire) and potential challengers (to run or not to run)—channel the effects voters have on individual Senate races and the national verdict.

THE LUCK OF THE DRAW: WHICH STATES HAVE SENATE RACES IN 1996?

In their study of Senate elections, Alan I. Abramowitz and Jeffrey A. Segal wrote: "The more seats the president's party must defend of the thirty-three or thirty-four Senate seats at stake in a given year, the more seats it can expect to lose."[4] Strictly speaking, Republicans had more to lose in the Senate races of 1996. Of the thirty-four Senate seats to be filled in the November 1996 elections, nineteen were held by Republicans and fifteen were held by Democrats. This, however, is the only point at which Democrats had an advantage over Republicans.

First of all, the fact that Republicans had 19 seats up indicates that many of those states electing senators were Republican states more generally. In 1996, Republican presidential candidate Robert Dole won 19 states while President Bill Clinton won 31 states in his victorious reelection effort. Moreover, Clinton won 49.2 percent of the total popular vote to Dole's 40.7 percent. But for many reasons, Clinton's strength at the top of the ticket did not translate into Democratic strength for other offices. Weak political parties and candidate-centered elections lead the list of possible explanations for a lack of presidential coattails. Another explanation, however, is just as important in identifying why Republicans ran so well in Senate elections despite the overall weakness of Dole's showing in the presidential race: of the 33 states that had Senate races in 1996, a disproportionate number were states in which Dole won. Of the 19 states that Dole won, 16 of them were states that had a total of 17 Senate races (table 4.1). And of the 31 states won by President Clinton, only 17 had Senate races in 1996. Thus, although Clinton won 31 states, the 34 Senate races in November 1996 were split evenly between states won by Clinton and states won by Dole.

Moreover, a sizable proportion of the states that had Senate races in 1996 were never won by Clinton (table 4.1). Thirteen states with fourteen Senate races in 1996 voted for President George Bush in 1992 and Dole in 1996. Only three states that had been won by both Bush and Dole had no Senate race in 1996. Where there were 29 states that President Clinton won in both 1992 and 1996, twelve of those 29 had no Senate seats up in 1996. And Democrats were disadvantaged in 1996 among the five states that voted for Clinton in only one of his two presidential elections. There were only two states Clinton won in 1996 that he had failed to capture in 1992; neither of those states had a Senate seat up in 1996. There were three states (Colorado, Georgia, and Montana) that Clinton won in 1992 but lost in 1996; all three elected senators in 1996. Bill Clinton's national electoral strength did not translate well into Senate races because, in part, Clinton was not particularly strong in half of the states which had Senate races.

Table 4.1: States with 1996 Senate Elections by Presidential Performance in 1992 and 1996

	States won by		
Bush 1992 and Dole 1996	Clinton 1992 and Dole 1996	Bush 1992 and Clinton 1996	Clinton 1992 and Clinton 1996
	1996 Senate Race		
14 (13 states)	*3 states*	*0 states*	*17 states*
Alabama, Alaska, Idaho, Kansas (2), Mississippi, Nebraska, North Carolina, Oklahoma, South Carolina, South Dakota, Texas, Virginia, Wyoming	Colorado, Georgia, Montana		Arkansas, Delaware, Illinois, Iowa, Kentucky, Louisiana, Maine, Massachusetts, Michigan, Minnesota, New Hampshire, New Jersey, New Mexico, Oregon, Rhode Island, Tennessee, West Virginia
	No Senate Race		
3 states	*0 states*	*2 states*	*12 states*
Indiana, North Dakota, Utah		Arizona, Florida	California, Connecticut, Hawaii, Maryland, Missouri, Nevada, New York, Ohio, Pennsylvania, Vermont, Washington, Wisconsin

THE VALUE OF INCUMBENCY

Despite a handful of incumbent losses in House races, 1996, like many previous national election years, might well have been dubbed "the year of the incumbent." Where incumbents typically fare better in House races than in Senate races, 1996 proved a good year for incumbent senators as well as House members. Of the twenty incumbent senators seeking reelection, nineteen were successful. Thus, the percentage of incumbents winning the general election was 95.0 percent.[5] Only twice in post-war Senate elections has the Senate incumbent reelection rate been higher; in 1960 when 96.6 percent of incumbents seeking reelection won, and 1990 when 96.9 percent of incumbents seeking reelection were successful.[6]

The only incumbent to lose the general election was Republican Senator Larry Pressler of South Dakota who was unseated by that state's only House member for the last ten years, Democrat Tim Johnson. Pressler, Chairman of the Senate Committee on Commerce, Science and Transportation, had hoped to capitalize on a significant fundraising advantage. Pressler's committee had overseen the overhaul of a telecommunications law that attracted the interest of many telecommunications corporations that contributed significantly to members of Congress, particularly members of the Committee on Commerce, Science and Transportation. In the 1995–1996 election cycle, Pressler raised and spent $1.49 for every dollar raised and spent by Johnson.

But where Pressler's position helped him secure a considerable fundraising advantage over his formidable challenger, it also opened the incumbent to criticism. In particular, Johnson questioned Pressler's sources of campaign funds by tying donations to the telecommunications bill; Johnson said, "He's taken over $400,000 in contributions from telecommunications companies. You don't have to be a hopeless cynic to think there's a tie-in here."[7] Also, Pressler's support of the elimination of federal funding for public broadcasting was an issue Johnson and other Democrats raised to arouse the party faithful and persuade moderate voters. In March 1996, DSCC Chairman Kerrey predicted that Pressler's criticism of public television would cost him in the November elections; Kerrey said, "The long-standing critic of Big Bird is going to get the big bird."[8]

Although Pressler enjoyed many of the advantages of incumbency, Johnson's victory should not have been a great surprise. As the only House member representing South Dakota, Johnson had represented the same constituency as Senator Pressler for the last ten years. And Johnson had typically garnered a higher percentage of the South Dakota electorate in his statewide races than had Pressler in his Senate races. Of course, this may partly be due to the fact that—as senator—Pressler consistently had drawn better challengers. Nevertheless, Johnson had proven himself popular with the constituency he shared with Pressler. In fact, in 1990—the one election in which they ran simultaneously—Johnson received 67.6 percent of the vote, while Pressler received only 53.8 percent of the vote.

The case of Johnson versus Pressler is very much an example of an exception that proves a rule. Even in the one race in which a Senate incumbent was defeated in pursuit of reelection, that senator lost to another incumbent—a House member—who represented the same constituency. Where Abramowitz and Segal's general point—that the more seats a president's party must defend the more it will likely lose—is sound, evidence from 1996 and some general lessons on the value of incumbency in congressional elections suggest that we should take into account the number of each party's incumbents seeking reelection that year as well. Where Republicans had 19 seats at stake and Democrats had only 15, that advantage was quickly negated by the fact that Republicans had 13 of 19 incumbent Senators running for reelection while Democrats had only 7 of 15 incumbent Senators returning. This left Republicans the task of protecting only six open Senate seats while Democrats had to protect eight open seats. Democrats were able to defend all of their incumbents, but only five of their eight open seats. Republicans, on the other hand, were successful in defending all six of their open seats and twelve of their thirteen returning incumbent Senators. The value of incumbency aided Republicans in protecting the lion's share of their seats in play, while Democrats had to defend more than half of their seats up in 1996 without a returning incumbent.

EARLY EXPECTATIONS AND CANDIDATES' STRATEGIC DECISIONS: WHAT A DIFFERENCE A YEAR MAKES

In an era in which congressional elections are largely candidate-centered, a political party's electoral prospects are governed primarily by its ability to recruit strong candidates. Although such recruitment activity is weak in the United States compared to similar activity in other industrialized democracies, the electoral prospects of Democrats and Republicans at a given time can do much to encourage strong candidates to run under the party's label. Gary Jacobson argued that "when the partisan outlook is gloomy, shrewd and ambitious politicians figure that the normally long odds against defeating an incumbent are even worse than usual and wait for a better day. . . . Politicians of the other party, sensing that electoral tides are moving in their direction, view the chances of winning as better than usual, so more and better candidates compete for the nomination to challenge incumbents."[9] And party prospects also affect whether or not a party's incumbents decide to retire or run for another term in the legislature. Evidence from House elections is telling in this regard. Michael K. Moore and John R. Hibbing, studying retirements from the House from the 1960s through 1992, found that "retirements generally occur on the basis of rational calculation concerning advancement potential, *chances of securing reelection*, and perhaps financial considerations."[10] And if, as Jacobson suggested, challengers and other elites make their strategic decisions based in part on partisan and national factors, then it is likely that congressional incumbents take these into account when assessing their reelection prospects, and consequently when making their decisions whether or not to retire.

The strategic decisions of candidates to emerge or wait, to seek reelection or retire, establish parameters for party success in elections. And—given candidate registration deadlines, the need to raise campaign funds, and the dictates of campaigning more generally—those strategic decisions are necessarily made generally about a year before the election. Hence, the national and partisan conditions that affect politicians' strategic decisions in 1995 are likely to affect electoral outcomes in 1996. And in contemporary politics, what a difference a year can make.

The 1996 election cycle saw more incumbent senators retire than any post-war election. Eight incumbent Democratic senators and five incumbent Republican senators announced that they would not seek reelection in 1996. The previous post-war high was the 1978 figure of ten retirements.[11]

Coupled with the summer 1995 resignation of Senator Bob Packwood (R-OR) and the midterm retirement of Republican presidential nominee Bob Dole, the 1996 elections would necessarily produce a large freshman class in the Senate. Again, many of the decisions that would subsequently affect the outcomes of the 1996 elections were made in 1995. In fact, all of the thirteen Senate retirements were announced by January 1996. Moreover, Senate retirements in the 1995–1996 election cycle seem to support the hypothesis that retirements from Congress are influenced by a candidate's assessment of his or her party's prospects in the ensuing election. In fact, in the first six months after the Republican victories in the 1994 elections, five Democratic senators announced their retirement from the chamber; and the remaining three retiring Democratic senators announced between August and October 1995. But as political conditions changed and public sentiment toward the Republican revolution became more negative in late 1995, partially as a result of the government shutdowns, Republican—not Democratic—senators began announcing that they would not seek reelection. Although Senator Hank Brown (R-CO) had announced his retirement in December of 1994, the remaining four Republican senators who retired in 1996 all announced their plans between November 1995 and January 1996.

The 13 retirements, along with an additional open seat in Kansas caused by an incumbent primary loss, contributed significantly to the overall competitiveness of the 1996 Senate elections. According to reporter David E. Rosenbaum, the fourteen open seats in the November elections were "by far the highest since the Constitution was changed early in this century and states began electing senators by popular vote rather than by votes of the state legislature. The previous record was 10 open seats in 1978. As a consequence, the Senate contests included some of the most expensive and bitter ones ever."[12]

Electoral Opportunities: Many for Republicans, Few for Democrats

Thus, although Republicans had more seats to defend in the 1996 elections than did Democrats, securing the return of most of their incumbents significantly mitigated Republican exposure. Republicans had to protect two open seats in states that Clinton won in 1992 and would win in 1996 as well (Maine and Oregon). Democrats also had to defend two open seats in states that voted Republican in the presidential elections of both 1992 and 1996 (Alabama and Nebraska). Republicans were successful in protecting both, while Democrats lost both that they had to protect. And of the four seats Republicans had to defend in states won by Clinton in both elections (Kentucky, New Hampshire, New Mexico, and Tennessee), all four were won by popular Republican Senate incumbents. Except for the total number of seats to defend, Republicans enjoyed advantages in almost all of the critical institutional factors that would influence the national verdict for Senate seats in 1996. Thus, even if Republicans had a difficult time in the presidential race, they were confident that the opportunities open to them would compensate for any unexpected losses. National Republican

Senatorial Committee (NRSC) Chairman Senator Alfonse D'Amato said, "Notwithstanding the top of the ticket, we are going to hold the majority. Even if we lose one or two Republican seats . . . On balance, we have more Democratic seats in play than Republican seats."[13]

CAPITALIZING ON OPPORTUNITIES: PARTIES, CANDIDATES, AND CAMPAIGNS

With all of their opportunities, early in the 1995–1996 election cycle Republicans had been discussing the potential of the 1996 Senate elections to produce a filibuster-proof majority in the Senate. The sixty seats needed for such a majority seemed plausible in November 1995. With the 1994 election still in recent memory and with the political effects of the federal government shutdowns still in doubt, Republicans were confident in their prospects in the 1996 Senate elections. This feeling coupled with the not–coincidental record number of Democratic senators retiring made it seem likely that Republicans would take full advantage of their considerable opportunities. Republican pollster Ed Goeas did not question whether Republicans would maintain their Senate majority but, rather, he pondered by how much they might extend that majority: "Are we going to come in at 58, 60, 61?"[14]

EARLY RETURNS: OREGON REPLACES PACKWOOD—WITH A DEMOCRAT

The first test of Republican strength was a special election in Oregon to replace Republican Senator Robert Packwood, who had resigned in the wake of scandal. Political observers and politicians often look to special elections as predictors of success in the November elections to follow. In January 1996, voters in Oregon participated in both an electoral experiment and the selection of their senator. In both the December primary elections for the Democratic and Republican nominations for Senate as well as the subsequent general election, Oregon voters made their selections by mail.

On December 4, Gordon Smith, the president of the Oregon Senate, won the Republican nomination while Representative Ron Wyden beat U.S. House colleague Peter DeFazio for the Democratic nomination. On the night that each won his party's nomination, Smith and Wyden invoked both national and statewide issues in setting the tone for the general election campaign. Smith painted Wyden as a tax-and-spend liberal, saying, "It's hard to think of a tax Ron hasn't voted for."[15] In addition, Smith poked fun at a misstep Wyden made in his primary campaign. When asked in a televised interview if he could quote the prices of milk and bread in Oregon, Wyden failed. On primary election night—when it was clear that he would face off against Wyden—Smith said, "Real Oregonians have real problems and buy real products. And they know what they cost."[16]

For his part, Wyden hoped to tie Smith to an increasingly unpopular national Republican party. Wyden linked Smith to the "Newt Gingrich Congressional majority," saying that "the choice in this election . . . is between mainstream values and extreme values."[17] Wyden, like many Democrats in both House and Senate campaigns in 1996, persisted in this throughout the race. In one televised debate Smith bristled at what was likely an effective campaign strategy; Smith told Wyden, "If you want to run against Newt Gingrich, you'd better move to Georgia."[18] Wyden's strategy of nationalizing the Oregon election was successful, as his campaign was likely the beneficiary of good timing and strong voter sentiment against national Republicans as a result of the federal budget standoff and the government shutdowns.[19] A poll of Oregon voters conducted in late January revealed that Oregon voters clearly reacted more positively to national Democrats than Republicans in the wake of the government shutdowns. And, in the end, Wyden won by less than 20,000 votes.

Parties successful in a special election are likely to suggest that that particular election is an indicator of how the party will do in the following November elections. By contrast, officials and activists of the losing party will likely emphasize the unique aspects of the special election and discount it as a bellwether for November. Despite the fact that Wyden won by only one percent, probably aided by the high levels of turnout fostered by the mail-in balloting system, Democrats were quick to point to the possibility of a national trend. One Oregon Democratic pollster said, "The Oregon election shows the bloom is off the rose [for Republicans]. . . . It does not mean the Democrats are going to sweep the races, but it does mean Republicans will have to make more of a statement about the environment than (just saying) we're overregulated."[20] And House minority leader Richard Gephardt (D-MO) said of Wyden's victory: "To say that this election doesn't have national implications is like saying that an elephant doesn't have ears."[21]

A signal of a national Democratic trend or not, the Oregon race—by virtue of its mail-in character—did provide some hope for those who believe that more voter participation and more candidate and campaign contact with voters, by means other than television, are good for representative democracy. Record high turnout and some return to traditional campaigning marked this new voting method.[22]

The election of Ron Wyden to the Senate in the January 1996 Oregon special election made the Republican's hope for a filibuster-proof Senate majority more distant by one critical seat. The significance of Wyden's capturing the seat previously held by Republican Packwood was not lost on Republican officials and campaign operatives. Republican pollster Ed Goeas said, "I think the wind went out of that sail [the filibuster-proof majority] when the special election in Oregon went by the wayside."[23]

PARTY ACTIVITIES AND PARTY STRATEGIES

Candidate Recruitment and Quality

Although political parties have little control over the selection of candidates who will run under the party's label in contemporary candidate-centered elections, they can engage in some activities that can encourage candidates to run. Party recruitment efforts were likely of unusual importance in the 1996 Senate elections given the record number of open seats. Because Democrats had considerably less money than Republicans and they had to field so many non-incumbent candidates, the DSCC hoped to recruit many candidates who would be able to get along without much financial assistance from the party. To meet this objective, DSCC Chairman Senator Bob Kerrey (D-NE) recruited many Democratic candidates with business backgrounds and considerable personal wealth. Dubbed "Kerrey's Merry Millionaires," these candidates included several entrepreneurs and business executives (Mark Warner of Virginia, Tom Bruggere of Oregon, Walt Minnick of Idaho, and Elliot Close of South Carolina) and a millionaire physician and pharmaceutical executive (Charlie Sanders of North Carolina).[24] Note, however, that none of these candidates was victorious in his Senate bid; Sanders of North Carolina did not even make it to the general election. Democratic recruitment efforts were more successful with professional politicians as candidates for the Senate. In Illinois, DSCC Chairman Kerrey unsuccessfully tried to entice William Daley, lawyer and brother of Chicago's Mayor Daley, to succeed Senator Paul Simon as the Democratic candidate for Senate in Illinois. Instead, the Democrats slated Representative Richard Durbin for the Senate and he won in November.

On the Republican side, the NRSC had considerably more resources than the DSCC and thus did not have to rely so heavily on wealthy political novices. In fact, when it came to those crucial and highly competitive open seats, neither party had much trouble recruiting professional politicians to take a shot at the Senate race. In the fourteen open seats, Republicans ran twelve candidates with prior political experience, including five House members or former House members, four state legislators, an attorney general, a state treasurer, and a state cabinet official. In those same fourteen open seat races, Democrats ran eleven candidates with prior political experience, including four House members or former House members (including one who had also been governor), one (additional) governor, one state legislator, an attorney general, two state secretaries of state, and two state treasurers.

Party Money

Contemporary parties are also active in fundraising and contributions to candidates. The DSCC and NRSC spent nearly $100 million in the 1995–1996 election cycle with the NRSC's $66.1 million more than doubling DSCC disbursements of $30.8 million.[25] Direct contributions to candidates remained only a small portion of party spending while more and more dollars were allocated to party development and overhead expenses. Although Democrats languished behind Republicans in fundraising, in the last weeks of the 1996 election cycle, some corporate and trade group donors increased giving to Democrats as it became increasingly possible that Democrats could regain control of the House and possibly the Senate. Steve Jarding, the DSCC communications director, said, "They're coming back because it looks like we can win some of these seats. They're hedging their bets."[26] Despite the Democrats' fundraising disadvantage, both national parties remained active and strong in the 1996 Senate elections.

Moreover, a Supreme Court ruling in the summer of 1996 had an impact on party spending in the 1996 election cycle as well. On June 26, 1996, the U.S. Supreme Court, in *Colorado Republican Federal Campaign Committee v. Federal Election Commission,* opened up a new area of political party campaign spending, allowing parties to now make "independent expenditures" in elections for national office.[27] In 1996, all independent expenditures (IEs) made by the national parties were made by the two senatorial campaign committees; neither national committee nor neither House campaign committee made any. Moreover, the Republicans' considerable fundraising advantage made this new avenue of party spending particularly helpful to the GOP effort to extend their majority in the Senate. In 1996, the Democratic senatorial campaign committee had independent expenditures of $1,452,507 and the Republican committee's expenditures were $9,438,331.[28]

When the Court handed down the *Colorado Republican* decision, there was considerable confusion among both politicians and commentators regarding the impact the decision would have on the 1996 elections. Not surprisingly, the parties' respective responses to the decision were made in light of their perceptions of the impact the decision would have on their competitiveness. The day after the Court announced its decision, the NRSC began planning for a new subdivision in order to both coordinate party independent expenditures as well as to demonstrate the "independence" of the new IE unit from ongoing NRSC activities that had already been "coordinated" with candidates. The IE subdivision "was located in a building separate from the NRSC headquarters, and was staffed by employees relatively far removed from prior NRSC coordinated activity with particular Senate candidates. While funding the independent expenditures unit, the NRSC steadfastly denied any control or advance knowledge of the unit's spending decisions."[29] Democrats—who had supported IEs in principle by submitting an amicus brief in the *Colorado Republican* case—tried to diminish Republicans' considerable advantage in 1996 IEs by asking the Federal Election Commission (FEC) to issue an advisory opinion on whether parties could, as a practical matter, engage in *independent* expenditures given the fact that prior to the Court's decision parties and candidates had been coordinating their activities. This was less of an attempt by Democrats to clarify the practical application of the new decision than it was an attempt to have the FEC rule on Republican IEs.[30] The FEC General Counsel proposed an advisory opinion that would have halted Republican and Democratic IE activity in 1996, but the FEC failed to pass it.

Left unregulated, both parties engaged in IE spending in Senate races. As expected and noted, Republicans outspent Democrats in IEs by over a six to one margin. In fact, the over $1.4 million in IEs Republicans made in the Louisiana Senate race nearly equaled all of the Democratic IEs combined. Over 55 percent of Republican IEs, over $5.2 million, were made in the six open seats they had to defend and the three open seats picked up from Democrats and "81.1% of all Republican IEs were spent in the 14 open Senate races" of 1996.[31]

NRSC independent expenditures were an important component in Republican success in the 1996 Senate elections. If the goal of the NRSC and Republicans generally was to win the battle of the open seats and to protect incumbents in trouble, IEs were an important resource on both fronts. "Republican IEs in open seats and in. . .three close races where Republicans sought to protect their incumbents [Smith in New Hampshire; Helms in North Carolina; and Pressler in South Dakota] amounted to 95.0% of all Republican independent expenditures."[32] Both parties, though Republicans far more than Democrats, exploited this new avenue of campaign spending in strategic ways, as IEs were added to the increasingly significant arsenal of national party spending opportunities.

CANDIDATE-CENTERED SENATE ELECTIONS

Despite these national party activities, congressional races, particularly Senate races, are elections that have very individualistic characteristics. Though parties can help themselves through candidate recruitment and financial assistance, most Senate races have distinctive aspects. In 1996, for example:

> *In Massachusetts, popular Republican Governor William Weld challenged incumbent Democratic Senator John Kerry in a race that was characterized by voluntary spending limits and primarily (if not exclusively) genteel, intellectual debates on issues.

> *In Louisiana, State Treasurer Mary Landrieu had to overcome a significant rift with several African-American Louisiana Democratic leaders in her successful quest to defeat Republican state legislator Woody Jenkins.

*In Minnesota, former Republican Senator Rudy Boschwitz unsuccessfully attempted to avenge his 1990 defeat at the hands of Paul Wellstone.

*Nebraska's popular Democratic Governor Ben Nelson was upset by a late media blitz by the campaign of his Republican opponent Chuck Hagel. Hagel spent over $210,000 in personal money as well as almost $250,000 in campaign money to fund the media blitz. The NRSC also chipped in over $325,000.[33]

*And in New Jersey, Republican Representative Dick Zimmer lost to Democratic Representative Robert Torricelli in what was described by many as one of the least civil campaigns in memory.

Altogether, major party candidates for the Senate raised about $226.7 million in the 1995–1996 election cycle. In both parties, incumbent candidates raised the most money. On average, Democratic incumbents raised $5,015,685 and Republican incumbents had receipts of $3,536,845. In open seats, Democratic candidates averaged $2,839,688 and Republican candidates took in $3,442,813. In both parties, challengers had the lowest average receipts, $2,515,975 for the Democrats and $2,992,036 for the Republicans.[34] Winning candidates had considerable financial advantages over their opponents. Only five losers raised more money than their winning opponents in the 1995–1996 election cycle.[35] Losers, on average, spent 79 cents for every dollar spent by their victorious opponents. And when the five losers who spent more than their opposition are removed from the analysis, the average loser spent 58 cents for every dollar spent by the winner in that race.

INCUMBENT-CENTEREDNESS AND PARTISAN TRENDS IN OPEN SEATS

Despite the individual nature of many of these elections, the national outcomes of Senate elections, if not always the individual races themselves, are best understood from a perspective that places primary emphasis on party activities and partisanship. This is mainly due to the influence of national parties and political conditions on state candidates and campaigns.

National Themes

Candidates from both parties invoked national themes in their individual races. Democrats did their best to tie their Republican opponents, incumbents and non-incumbents alike, to some of the perceived ideological excesses of the Republican congressional majority. Democrats made charges of "extremism" on Medicare, the government shutdowns, and other issues. And they attempted to tie even Senate candidates, some of whom were not even in Washington for the 104th Congress, to House Speaker Newt Gingrich. This tactic was used even in Massachusetts where

Senator John Kerry highlighted a long-standing association between his opponent, the very moderate Republican Governor Weld, and Gingrich. Kerry called Weld "one of Newt's lieutenants," and recalled for voters Weld's 1995 reference to Gingrich as an "ideological soulmate." Only days before the election, Weld conceded that Kerry's strategy could be effective; he said, "If it's me and [Kerry], I win. If it's a nationalized race, if it's Kerry versus Gingrich in people's minds, then I'm a goner."[36]

Republicans, on the other hand, made frequent use of the word "liberal" to describe their Democratic opponents. The relatively consistent use of this strategy was not an accident. A chief architect of this strategy, consultant Arthur J. Finkelstein, worked not only as a strategist for the NRSC, but Republican Senate candidates were encouraged by NRSC Chairman D'Amato to hire Finkelstein personally as well; six Republican Senate candidates did hire Finkelstein (Rudy Boschwitz, MN; Nancy Mayer, RI; Raymond Clatworthy, DE; Dick Zimmer, NJ; Robert Smith, NH; and Larry Pressler, SD). Finkelstein's strategy was to call all Democrats "liberals." According to Democratic strategist Mandy Grunwald: "Essentially he has dictated the message strategy for the Republican party. I don't know a Senate race in the country where the Republican message isn't charging liberal, liberal, liberal."[37] In some races, "liberal" became part of the Democratic candidate's name:

*Rhode Island: "Liberal Jack Reed opposes the balanced budget amendment."

*Minnesota: "Ultraliberal Paul Wellstone voted for the largest tax increase in American history."

*New Jersey: "Tell liberal Bob Torricelli to stop raising your taxes."[38]

In the races where that was not the case, "liberal" was used nevertheless. In Ray Clatworthy's attempt to unseat Delaware Senator Joseph Biden, the NRSC issued a press release which claimed that "Ray Clatworthy is closing the gap on Joe Biden because he is . . . focusing on the differences between his commonsense conservatism and Joe Biden's extremely liberal voting record."[39] And in New Hampshire, Senator Robert Smith ran ads which called former Representative Dick Swett "too liberal for New Hampshire."

The day after the election, the DSCC quickly pointed out that Finkelstein's strategy had been unsuccessful, as the only one of Finkelstein's six candidates to win was New Hampshire's Smith who only narrowly avoided defeat in his reelection bid. And Senator Larry Pressler, Finkelstein's other incumbent client, was not as lucky as Smith. Pressler's campaign had called Representative Tim Johnson "surprisingly liberal." For his part, Johnson claimed that South Dakotans, who had elected him to the House five times, knew that he was "Just solid, like South Dakota."

Presidential Vote and Senate Vote

The large number of open seats in 1996 likely enhanced the importance of partisanship in the national outcomes of the Senate elections. Studies of House elections are useful in explaining the importance of national and state-specific factors in the 1996 Senate elections. Abramowitz and Segal's suggestion (that the more Senate seats a president's party must defend in an election, the more seats the president's party will lose) has its correlate in the study of House elections in the "exposure model" which predicts the net partisan change in outcomes of House races on the basis of how many seats a party already has in the House. If a party has many seats above an equilibrium point, it is likely to lose seats. If it currently has fewer seats than its equilibrium, it will likely gain seats.[40]

Although the exposure thesis predicts the broad contours of outcomes in House elections, it is improved considerably when one factors in the decisions of incumbents to run for reelection or retire.[41] Not only does the exposure model fare better, but by implication it also seems that national factors better explain seat swings when there are many open seats. In fact, a study of presidential coattails in House elections finds that "presidential coattails are, on average, nearly two times stronger in open than in defended seats."[42]

Additionally, it should be noted that scholars James Campbell and Joe Sumners have found that "given the prominence of Senate elections, . . . presidential coattails for Senate candidates are about half as long as those provided to House candidates."[43] Nevertheless, Campbell and Sumners found that "even in the recent period of weakened mass partisanship and this rise of more highly financed Senate contests, presidential candidates have coattails that affect the Senate vote."[44] Moreover, it is likely that other (non-presidential) national and partisan factors affect the Senate vote as well. This is probably even more the case when the intervening variable of an incumbent running for reelection is removed.

Given these scholarly findings, we would expect national factors—coattails, national partisanship, and national issues—to be more pronounced in open seats than in seats with an entered incumbent. This proposition is supported by simple correlations of a state's vote for Clinton with the state's vote for the Democratic Senate candidate. There are significant differences in the relationship between the presidential vote and Senate vote in open seats and in seats with incumbents running. The correlation of the presidential vote to the Senate vote was much stronger in open seat races (r=.84, n=14), than in elections where an incumbent was running (r=.59, n=20). When no incumbent was running, the Democratic vote for President and Senate were strongly correlated, but when an incumbent was running, the strength of that relationship diminished.

Thus, a party can mitigate the potential losses in a difficult election year by persuading its incumbents to run for reelection, thus blunting the effects of national tides on the outcome in that individual race. This likely bene-fited Republicans in 1996. In many of the states where Bill Clinton was popular and Republicans were vulnerable, Republicans had popular incumbents in place seeking reelection. Democrats, on the other hand, had a difficult time retaining incumbents in Alabama and Nebraska, for exam-ple. Republican presidential candidates carried both of those states in 1992 and 1996, but incumbents Howell Heflin and Jim Exon did not seek reelec-tion and therefore were not poised to blunt the Republican trends in their states.

CONCLUSIONS

Scholarly attention to Senate elections—like attention to the Senate more generally—is scant compared to studies of House elections. Comprehensive evaluations of the national outcomes of Senate elections are rare indeed. But Senate elections have important national and partisan consequences, both on election night and for the subsequent six years of governance. In the 1996 Senate elections, the advantages Democrats enjoyed in November 1996 were mitigated and the Republicans' disadvantages alleviated by the strategic decisions candidates of both parties made as early as 1995. Republicans' advantages in the seats to be protected, incumbents returning, fundraising, as well as strategic disbursements, allowed Republicans to blunt the effects of an albeit small Democratic tide in 1996.

Democratic failure to gain Senate seats in an otherwise Democratic year continues a pattern whereby Republicans have made significant gains in the Senate since the 1960s. From the 1958 to the 1968 elections, Democrats held at least 60 Senate seats (they held as many as 68 after the 1964 elec-tions). Throughout the 1970s, Democrats won smaller Senate majorities. But in 1980 Republicans gained twelve Senate seats and won a majority for the first time since the election of 1952. In 1986, however, Democrats once again gained control of the Senate. Republicans gained a Senate majority once again, though, in 1994.

Since 1960, Democratic strength has eroded in the South and the West.[45] Immediately after the election of 1960, Democrats held all twenty-two southern Senate seats and twenty of the West's twenty-six Senate seats. Twelve years later, by contrast, in the aftermath of the 1972 election, the Democrats held only fifteen of those southern seats and fifteen of those western seats. And in 1980, when Democrats lost control of the Senate, it was in large part due to Republican gains in the South and West. Democrats only had twelve of the South's twenty-two seats in 1980; and they held onto only nine of the West's twenty-six seats. While Democratic losses in the West seem to have leveled, the 1996 election showed further erosion of Democratic strength in the South: Democrats held only seven of the South's twenty-two Senate seats in 1997–1998. The two seats Republicans picked up in 1996 equal the two they picked up in Alabama and Arkansas. From 1980 to 1996, there was stability in the partisan competition for Senate seats in the Northeast, the Border states, and the West, and Democrats gained in the Central states. However, these trends do not offset Republican gains in the South. There are forty-eight Senate seats in the twenty-four states of the South and West. Democrats controlled forty-two of those seats in 1961 (and that represented nearly two-thirds of the Senate Democratic party at that time). But after the 1996 election, Democrats held only seventeen of those seats (a little over a third of the Senate Democratic party).

Democrats could conceivably regain a Senate majority without recouping southern and western losses, but that would require winning more seats in one or all of the three other regions than they have in more than thirty years. Overall trends currently favor Republicans; they are now the party of the South and the West by nearly two-to-one. And nearly half the Senate seats are in the South and West. In 1998, though, the Democrats gained an eighth southern seat in North Carolina, as Democrat John Edwards defeated Republican incumbent Lauch Faircloth. However, there was no net partisan change in 1998, as the GOP held 55 seats and the Democrats 45 seats during 1999–2000.

NOTES

1.   Election returns throughout this chapter are from Richard M. Scammon, Alice V. McGillivray, and Rhodes Cook, *America Votes 22* (Washington, DC: Congressional Quarterly Inc., 1998).

2.   Quoted in "Elections '96; Washington Insight," *Los Angeles Times*, November 7, 1996, A16.

3.   Alan Greenblatt and Robert Marshall Wells, "Parties Aim to Dominate Senate, But Big Gains Look Unlikely," *CQWR*, September 21, 1996, 2682–92, 2683.

4.   Alan I. Abramowitz and Jeffrey A. Segal, *Senate Elections* (Ann Arbor: University of Michigan Press, 1992), 94.

5.   This figure drops to 90.5 percent if one counts Senator Sheila Frahm's (R–KS) unsuccessful attempt to win the Republican nomination. Frahm had been appointed to fill the vacancy left by Senator Robert Dole's resignation from the Senate; she was defeated by Representative Sam Brownback in the Republican primary.

6.   For 1946–1994 data, see Harold W. Stanley and Richard G. Niemi, *Vital Statistics on American Politics*, 5th ed. (Washington, DC: CQ Press, 1995), 190–191.

7.   William M. Welch, "Two Incumbents Vie in South Dakota," *USA*, November 1, 1996, A11.

8.   Quoted in Chris Black, "Kerrey Speaks Mind on Republican Rivals," *Boston Globe*, March 9, 1996, 3.

9. Gary C. Jacobson, *The Politics of Congressional Elections*, 3rd ed. (New York: HarperCollins, 1992), 164; also see Jacobson and Samuel Kernell, *Strategy and Choice in Congressional Elections*, 2nd ed. (New Haven: Yale University Press, 1983).

10. Michael K. Moore and John R. Hibbing, "Is Serving in Congress Fun Again? Voluntary Retirements from the House Since the 1970s," *AJPS* 36 (August 1992): 824–8, 827. Emphasis added.

11. Stanley and Niemi, *Vital Statistics*, 190–191.

12. David E. Rosenbaum, "Two Parties Battling for Control of Senate in Most Competitive Lineup of Races in Years," *NYT*, November 6, 1996, B5.

13. Quoted in Elaine S. Povich, "On the Edge of their Seats: In Senate, Power Hangs in Balance," *Newsday*, September 23, 1996, A4.

14. Quoted in Juliana Gruenwald, "Sizing Up the Senate; Parties Aim at Magic Numbers in Senate Elections," *Minneapolis Star Tribune*, December 26, 1995, 7A.

15. Quoted in "Two Advance in Race to Succeed Packwood," *NYT*, December 7, 1995, B16.

16. "Two Advance in Race to Succeed Packwood," B16.

17. Quoted in "Two Advance in Race to Succeed Packwood," B16.

18. William Claiborne, "Democrats Win Oregon Senate Race; Observers Say Result Could Be Bellwether," *WP*, January 21, 1996.

19. "Oregon Voters in Poll Blame GOP for Budget Standoff," *USA*, January 31, 1996.

20. Quoted in Lynne K. Varner, "Wyden Win in Oregon Heartens Democrats—Is Victory Start of a Trend or a One-Time Thing?" *The Seattle Times*, February 5, 1996.

21. Quoted in Timothy Egan, "Oregon's Mail-In Election Brings Cheer to Democrats," *NYT*, February 1, 1996, A1, A19.

22. Robert Marshall Wells, "Wyden, Smith in Tight Race for Packwood Seat," *CQWR*, January 20, 1996, 155–56.

23. Quoted in Greenblatt and Wells, "Parties Aim to Dominate Senate,", 2682.

24. See "Kerrey Senate Campaign Strategy Didn't Pan Out on Election Day," *Omaha World Herald*, November 15, 1996, 24. See also Robert Marshall Wells and Jonathan D. Salant, "Wealthy Democrats Are Tapped to Challenge GOP Senators," *CQWR*, February 24, 1996, 443–7.

25. Federal Election Commission.

26. Quoted in Ruth Marcus, "GOP Keeps Fund-Raising Lead Despite Trade Groups' Shift in Giving," *WP*, November 3, 1996, A31.

27. See John P. Forren and Douglas B. Harris, "Misconceptions of Party in *Colorado Republican Federal Campaign Committee v. FEC*," paper prepared for delivery at the 1997 Annual Meeting of the Midwest Political Science Association, Chicago, Ill. Much of the discussion below is taken from this paper.

28. Federal Election Commission.

29.   Forren and Harris, "Misconceptions of Party," 23. See also Ruth Marcus, "Reinterpreting the Rules," *WP*, October 26, 1996.

30.   "Democrats Seek to Foil Republican Spending Plans with FEC Advisory Opinion," *Political Finance and Lobby Reporter*, July 24, 1996.

31.   Forren and Harris, "Misconceptions of Party," 27–28.

32.   Forren and Harris, "Misconceptions of Party," 28.

33.   Jonathan D. Salant, "Late Spending Won Senate Seat for Hagel," *CQWR*, December 21, 1996, 3451.

34.   Federal Election Commission. The FEC document had both Republican Sam Brownback and Democrat Jill Docking listed as "challengers" in their Kansas senate race. As no incumbent was running in the general election, their receipts have been subtracted from the "challenger" pools and added to the open seat categories.

35.   They include Republicans Millner (GA) and Pressler (SD), and Democrats Strickland (CO) and Mark Warner (VA). The fifth case is somewhat misleading. In North Carolina, Democrat Harvey Gantt raised $300,000 more than Senator Jesse Helms in the 1995–96 election cycle, but Helms had raised and spent over $6.7 million in the previous two election cycles although he was not up for reelection in either.

36.   See R. W. Apple Jr., "Kerry vs. Weld: An 'Elegant Hammering' of a Race Remains a Tossup," *NYT*, November 3, 1996, Section I, 35; and Frank Phillips, "Weld Ranks 2d Only to Gingrich in Help from GOPAC," *Boston Globe*, August 23, 1996.

37.   Quoted in Howard Kurtz, "GOP Consultant's Strategy: Label Opponents Liberally," *WP*, October 22, 1996, A1.

38.   Kurtz, "GOP Consultant's Strategy."

39.   NRSC press release, October 8, 1996.

40.   See Richard W. Waterman, Bruce I. Oppenheimer, and James A. Stimson, "Sequence and Equilibrium in Congressional Elections: An Integrated Approach," *JOP* 53 (May 1991): 372–93.

41.   Ronald Keith Gaddie, "Congressional Seat Swings: Revisiting Exposure in House Elections," *Political Research Quarterly* 50 (September 1997): 699–710.

42.   Jeffrey J. Mondak, "Presidential Coattails and Open Seats: The District-Level Impact of Heuristic Processing," *APQ* 21 (July 1993): 307–19, 314.

43.   James E. Campbell and Joe A. Sumners, "Presidential Coattails in Senate Elections," *APSR* 84 (June 1990): 513–24, 519.

44.   Campbell and Sumners, "Presidential Coattails," 520.

45.   For our purposes, the South is defined as Alabama, Arkansas, Florida, Georgia, Louisiana, Mississippi, North Carolina, South Carolina, Tennessee, Texas, and Virginia. For later discussion, the West is defined as Alaska, Arizona, California, Colorado, Hawaii, Idaho, Montana, Nevada, New Mexico, Oregon, Utah, Washington, and Wyoming.

CHAPTER 5

Sideshows and Strategic Separations
The Impact of Presidential Year Politics on Congressional Elections

GARRISON NELSON

INTRODUCTION: BENEATH THE STATUS QUO

So identical were the electoral college maps of the 1992 and 1996 presidential elections that analysts were quick to decree that 1996 was a "status quo election."[1] After all, only five states had shifted their party allegiance between the two elections. President Bill Clinton had picked up two states—Florida and Arizona—from his previous showing and lost three others. Both Florida and Arizona were heavily populated with retirees. It was widely asserted in press accounts that Clinton had benefited from the Democratic party's efforts to raise anxiety among senior citizens about the Medicare and social security cuts contemplated by the Republican Congress.[2] Republicans called it a tactic of "Mediscare" and it seemed to have worked in these two states. Three other states that had cast electoral votes for Clinton in 1992—Colorado, Montana, and Georgia—returned to the Republican fold in 1996. But forty-five states and the District of Columbia retained their electoral affiliations from the previous election.

In the elections for Congress as well, continuity seemed to triumph over change. In the Senate, there was a net shift of only two seats as the Republican majority grew from 53 to 55, and only one of twenty Senate incumbents lost, Larry Pressler (Rep-S.D.). In the House, the shift was only nine seats, and the incumbent success rate was 94.4 percent. There is thus little surprise that the 1996 election was dubbed "the status quo election."

That continuity can triumph in a time of national peace and economic prosperity is no surprise. That the election continued divided government in place is perhaps the real story of 1996. Why for the first time in American history was a Democratic president elected simultaneously with a Republican Congress?

It is the major contention of this chapter that the historic linkage between presidential and congressional elections was broken in the 1970s and 1980s by the conscious actions of two key figures—President Richard

M. Nixon and Speaker of the House Thomas P. "Tip" O'Neill Jr. These two men sought to protect their party's control over their respective institutions and believed that the continuing linkage between presidential and congressional elections would jeopardize that control.

THE CONTEXT OF THE 1996 HOUSE ELECTIONS

In the House elections of 1994, history was made. For forty years (1955–1994), the Democrats had controlled the House, the longest single-party control of an elective national institution in American history. The Republicans had become a "permanent minority."[3] In spite of the Republican presidential victories of 1956, 1968, 1972, 1980, 1984, and 1988, House Democrats had held on. In 1972 and 1984, House Democrats retained control of the chamber in the face of 49–state landslide victories by Presidents Nixon and Reagan. Scandals and mismanagement seemed to have little or no impact upon Democratic control of the House. But Congress began to slide precipitously in the estimation of the public. In December of 1965, at the close of the first session of the 89th Congress—the Great Society Congress—62 percent of people polled by Louis Harris and Associates said that Congress was doing a "good job."[4] During the Watergate crisis, the Gallup Poll began its annual "Confidence in Institutions" ratings. Congress scored a 42 percent confidence rating in that initial poll but it slipped steadily to an approval rating of 18 percent in the 1991 through 1994 ratings.[5] Even the long-noted tendency of citizens to differentiate between the positive qualities of their own members of Congress and the negative ones of the institution seemed to collapse. Incumbency that had protected House Democrats fell before the 1994 tide. Thirty-four incumbents lost in 1994 and all were Democrats.[6]

What had happened in 1994 was the nationalization of a congressional election. For years, the prevailing wisdom of House elections was contained in former Speaker Thomas P. "Tip" O'Neill's (Dem-Mass.) pithy aphorism, "All politics is local."[7] Protect your constituents and bring home the bacon and your reelection was guaranteed.

Newt Gingrich (Rep-Ga.) changed that perception. Gingrich, the ostensible leader of the House Republicans in the summer of 1994, worked with a savvy conservative pollster, Frank Luntz, to identify positions that were both popular with the public and which could create a philosophical agenda uniting most House Republicans. Ten proposals were identified and labeled with public-pleasing phrases and named the "Contract with America."[8] Democrats scoffed, calling it the "Contract on America."

Gingrich was triumphant. By nationalizing the election, Gingrich had crafted a strategy to overturn the Democrats' forty-year dynasty. When the results rolled in that evening, Gingrich was decreed to be a genius. Democratic incumbents fell throughout the nation, including scandal-weakened Ways and Means Chair Dan Rostenkowski (Dem-Ill.), and Speaker of the

House Thomas Foley (Dem-Wash.), the first Speaker to lose an election since 1862.

Meanwhile, not a single incumbent Republican governor or member of Congress lost that evening. The pundits were stunned and one of the descriptive terms gaining currency in the weeks following the 1994 election was "tsunami"—a giant tidal wave.[9] So dramatic was the perception of the impact of the 1994 election and new Speaker Gingrich's agenda on American politics that Newt Gingrich was named "Man of the Year" by *Time* magazine for 1995.[10]

Table 5.1: Fifty-Plus House Seat Election Gains and House Party Control in the Twentieth Century

Election Year	Prior Election Majority	Minority	Net Seat Change	Impact on House Party Control
1910	R 219	D 172	D +56	Dems gained control
1912	D 228	R 161	D +63	Dems expanded control
1914	D 291	R 127	R +59	Dems retained control
1920	R 240	D 190	R +61	Reps expanded control
1922	R 301	D 131	D +74	Reps retained control
1930	R 267	D 167	D +53	Dems gained control
1932	D 220	R 214	D +93	Dems expanded control
1938	D 331	R 89	R +75	Dems retained control
1946	D 218	R 208	R +55	Reps gained control
1948	R 245	D 188	D +75	Dems gained control
1958	D 233	R 200	D +54	Dems expanded control
1974	D 239	R 192	D +52	Dems expanded control
1994	D 258	R 176	R +54	Reps gained control

Source: Calculated by author from U.S. Bureau of the Census, *Historical Abstracts of the United States, Colonial Times to 1970*, Bicentennial Edition, Part I (Washington, DC: U.S. Government Printing Office, 1975), 1083-1084; and U.S. Bureau of the Census, *Statistical Abstract of the United States: 1998* (118th ed.) (Washington, DC: U.S. Government Printing Office, 1998), 287, Table no. 466.

In historic terms, the change was less dramatic than it first appeared. This was the thirteenth time in the twentieth century that a fifty-seat or more House gain had taken place (table 5.1). On eight occasions, Democrats had gained fifty-plus seats, while in five years, Republicans benefited. Only five times had party control of the House been affected by a fifty-plus seat shift: three for the Democrats, 1910, 1930, and 1948; and two for the Republicans, 1946 and 1994. On three occasions, the party in power lost fifty-plus seats but retained control of the House: 1914 and 1938 for the Democrats and 1922 for the Republicans. And in five cases, the House majority party expanded its numbers by more than fifty seats: 1912, 1932, 1958, and 1974 for the Democrats and 1920 for the Republicans. In three cases, the magnitude of these expansions presented the gaining party with 90-plus House seat turnarounds within a two-election cycle. The Democrats gained 119 seats in the 1910–12 cycle; the Republicans gained 91 in the 1918–20 cycle; and the Democrats gained 146 in the 1930–32 cycle. These gains are of the magnitude that creates new House majority parties. This was the goal of newly elected Speaker of the House Newt Gingrich: to follow up 1994's gain with a massive seat expansion in 1996 that would consolidate Republican power in the House through the end of the twentieth century and well into the next one.

But a presidential election awaited. Money and talent that might have made the House seat expansion possible would likely be siphoned off for the presidential race. The 1996 presidential contest could be potentially disruptive for the Republican congressional majority.

THE SIDESHOW PROBLEM

American politics are defined by presidential elections. For the most part, midterm congressional elections are treated as referenda on presidential performance and as harbingers of trends for the upcoming presidential elections.[11] Unless midterm elections result in a massive philosophical shift such as the Republican takeover of 1994 or the Democratic Watergate babies of 1974, they tend not to be very memorable in their own right.

Congressional elections in presidential years are even more relegated to the back pages of history, and are often viewed primarily as reflections of presidential politics. For many years, political pundits calculated the size of the coattail effect of successful presidential candidates by measuring the percentage of the president's vote and the percentage of House seats won by his party.[12] It was generally inferred that longer coattails would help the president's legislative agenda and that shorter coattails would limit his legislative effectiveness.

In an important 1966 study, Milton Cummings compared the district-by-district results to assess the separation of the presidential and congressional electoral systems.[13] In the 1970s, Walter Dean Burnham amplified the theme of party decomposition.[14] Presidential and congressional election systems are now somewhat independent entities, and this trend is revealed by examining midterm elections as predictors of presidential elections, split district results for the U.S. House and president, and the incidence of split party control in Washington.

MIDTERM ELECTIONS AS PRESIDENTIAL ELECTION PREDICTORS

For most of a century, the party controlling the House would win the upcoming presidential election. From 1856 through 1944, there were twenty-two presidential elections. The party controlling the House gained the presidential popular vote 21 times (95.5 percent) and the electoral vote 19 times (86.4 percent). In 21 of 22 elections, the popular vote leader in the presidential balloting had been foreshadowed by his party's victory in the midterm House election.

The only genuine exception to this predictive link between midterm House elections and presidential contests in the 1856–1944 era occurred in the 1880 election of Republican James A. Garfield. Apart from Garfield, the other two exceptions to the linkage between the midterm and presidential elections—the Hayes–Tilden contest of 1876 and the first Cleveland–Harrison battle of 1888—proved the rule. The House Democrats had won both the midterm elections of 1874 and 1886 preceding those presidential contests. It was the machinations of the fifteen-member Electoral Commission and its 8–7 Republican split that deprived Governor Samuel Tilden (Dem-N.Y.) of his victory. By counting only the Republican electors from three southern states, the Commission gave former Ohio Governor Rutherford B. Hayes a one-vote win in the electoral college.[15] In the 1888 case, it was the switch of fifty-one electoral votes in the states of New York and Indiana from the Democratic column in 1884 to the Republican one four years later that prevented President Grover Cleveland (Dem-N.Y.) from having his popular vote plurality reflected in an electoral college majority.[16] For almost ninety years, the midterm elections were the best predictor of presidential politics. And then this relationship ended.

THE BEGINNING OF THE DISCONNECTION

In 1946, a war-weary nation disappointed by unfulfilled promises in the aftermath of World War II turned on the Democratic party and ended their control of Congress. For the first time since the election of 1928, Republicans won both the House and the Senate. At last, the Republicans would end the Democrats' sixteen-year grip on the White House. After all, the party that controlled the House following the midterm had gone on to win almost all of the subsequent presidential contests.

Yet when the votes were tallied, President Harry Truman retained the White House and the 1946 House midterm election did not predict the 1948 presidential election. Nor did the 1950 midterm election predict the 1952 Republican victory. The failure of midterm House elections to predict subsequent presidential contests recurred in 1956, 1968, 1972, 1980, 1984, 1988, and 1996. In the thirteen elections from 1948 through 1996, the party that won control of the House in the midterm election has won the subsequent presidential contest only four times—1960, 1964, 1976, and 1992—for a success rate of 30.8 percent.

A THREE-VARIABLE PRESIDENTIAL ELECTION PREDICTIVE MODEL

One simple dimension is obviously insufficient to explain American politics. By adding more variables, preferably those that the key political actors know, predictability may be increased. In table 5.2, a simple three-variable predictive model is used to forecast the presidential elections from 1892 through 1996.[17]Using three readily available cues from the political environment in place at the time of the election, presidential contests were once quite predictable. The three cues were:

1) partisan control of the House following the midterm election;
2) the relative size of the House seat loss for the president's party in the midterm election; and
3) the proportion of governors held by the president's party at the time of the election.

Table 5.2: House and Gubernatorial Pre-Election Presidential Cues, 1892–1996

Midterm House Cues	Number of In-Party Governors		
	Over 55.0 percent	45.0 to 54.9 percent	Under 45.0 percent
In-Party Holds House Seat-swing Under 10 %	T.ROOSEVELT, 1904 TAFT, 1908 HOOVER, 1928 F.ROOSEVELT, 1936 JOHNSON, 1964 *Carter, 1980*	McKINLEY, 1900 Stevenson, 1952	
In-Party Holds House Seat-swing Over 10 %	WILSON, 1916 F.ROOSEVELT, 1940	F.ROOSEVELT, 1944 Humphrey, 1968	COOLIDGE, 1924
Out-Party Holds House Seat-swing Under 10 %		*BUSH, 1988*	Cox, 1920 EISENHOWER, 1956, NIXON, 1972 *Bush, 1992*
Out-Party Holds House Seat-swing Over 10 %		TRUMAN, 1948	Harrison, 1892 Bryan, 1896 Taft, 1912 Hoover, 1932 Nixon, 1960 Ford, 1976 REAGAN, 1984 CLINTON, 1996[a]

Note: Presidential electoral vote winners are CAPITALIZED. Exceptions are in italics.

[a] 1996 Prospects: Out-Party Holds House (-)
   Seat-swing of 21.0 % Over 10 % (-)
   In-Party Governors of 38% Under 45% (-)
   In-Party Nominee an Incumbent (+)

Source: Adapted and updated from W. Ross Brewer and Garrison Nelson, "Election Expectations and Outcomes: A Theory of Nominating Convention Conflict, 1896-1976," in *Public Policy and Public Choice*, ed. Douglas W. Rae and Theodore J. Eismeier, (Beverly Hills, Cal.: Sage Publications, 1979), 151–207.

The expectation was simple. If all three cues were *positive* (the president's party held the House at the midterm; the seat loss was under 10 percent; and 55 percent or more of the governors at election time belonged to the president's party), then the party holding the White House would retain it, regardless of the status of the nominee, be it elected incumbent, a Vice President-successor, or a new nominee. Conversely, if all three cues were *negative* (the president's party lost the House in the midterm; the House seat loss exceeded 10 percent; and less than 45 percent of the governors belonged to the president's party), then the party holding the White House would be voted out of office, regardless of the status of the nominee, be it elected incumbent, a Vice President-successor, or a new nominee. And if the cues were *mixed*, then incumbent presidents would continue in office and non-incumbent nominees of the in-party would be defeated.

As table 5.2 indicates, this three-variable model worked perfectly in twenty-two elections from 1892 to 1976. When all three cues were *positive*, the five pre-1980 in-party nominees were elected: one elected incumbent (Franklin D. Roosevelt, 1936); two successor-Vice Presidents Theodore Roosevelt, 1904, and Lyndon B. Johnson, 1964); and two first-time nominees (William Howard Taft, 1908, and Herbert Hoover, 1928). When all three cues were *negative*, the six pre-1980 in-party nominees were defeated: three elected incumbents (Benjamin Harrison, 1892; William Howard Taft, 1912; and Herbert Hoover, 1932); one successor-Vice President (Gerald Ford, 1976) and two first-time nominees (William Jennings Bryan, 1896, and Richard M. Nixon, 1960). When the cues were *mixed*, only the eight White House incumbent candidates were successful: William McKinley, 1900; Woodrow Wilson, 1916; Calvin Coolidge, 1924; Franklin D. Roosevelt, 1940 and 1944; Harry Truman, 1948; Dwight Eisenhower, 1956; and Richard Nixon, 1972. And all three non-incumbent nominees of the president's party met defeat in mixed circumstances: James Cox, 1920; Adlai Stevenson, 1952; and Hubert Humphrey, 1968.

Here was a simple presidential predictive model based only upon three political cues that worked in twenty-two consecutive elections. Since 1980, however, this model has failed to predict the White House victors in five consecutive elections. President Jimmy Carter's 1980 reelection bid had all three cues in his favor yet he was defeated by 9.7 percent of the vote. The size of Carter's defeat enabled him to pass Martin Van Buren and gain the dubious distinction of the nation's worst defeated Democratic incumbent. In 1984, all three cues were negative, yet President Ronald Reagan swept to a 49-state landslide in spite of them. Four years later, Vice President George H. W. Bush was elected President in spite of the fact that he was a non-incumbent confronting mixed cues. To further confound the model, President Bush lost as an incumbent in 1992 while also facing mixed predictive cues. And in 1996, President Bill Clinton faced a bleak political landscape. Clinton's party did not hold the House; the seat loss for his party in the midterm election was 21 percent; and Democrats only had 19 governors. Yet he won reelection. A predictive model that fails to predict successfully five consecutive times is a model that should be discarded.

SPLIT PARTISAN RESULTS IN CONGRESSIONAL DISTRICTS

In the twelve presidential elections from 1900 through 1944, the mean proportion of congressional districts splitting their partisan results between their own House candidate and presidential nominees was only 11.3 percent. But in the presidential elections from 1948 through 1996, the district differential jumped to 30.5 percent.[18]

The 44.1 percent presidential–House seat differential in 1972 set a high standard for ticket-splitting that was toppled in 1984 by President Reagan's 49-state landslide over former Vice President Walter Mondale. In that year, the presidential–House seat differential rose to 45.0 percent.

Only the nomination of southern presidential candidates by the Democrats—Lyndon Johnson of Texas in 1964; Jimmy Carter of Georgia in 1976 and 1980; and Bill Clinton of Arkansas in 1992 and 1996—has kept the differential relatively low. Four of the five greatest presidential–House seat party differentials were recorded in those years with non-southern Democratic nominees: Hubert Humphrey of Minnesota in 1968 (32.0 percent); George McGovern of South Dakota in 1972 (44.1 percent); Walter Mondale of Minnesota in 1984 (45.0 percent); and Michael Dukakis of Massachusetts in 1988 (34.0 percent). The three southern–born Democratic nominees averaged a 28.9 percent district party differential in their five campaigns, while the four northern–born Democratic nominees averaged a 38.8 percent differential. Not coincidentally, the five southern nominations resulted in four presidential victories for the Democrats while the four northern nominations resulted in none. But the Democrats won control of the House eight times and the Senate six times in those contests regardless of the regional origins of their presidential nominee.

THE GROWTH OF DIVIDED GOVERNMENT

Divided government is neither new nor uncommon: it has occurred in 37 of the 106 Congresses convened in the United States—34.9 percent (table 5.3). Defined simply as one of the three elective national institutions—the presidency, the Senate, and the House of Representatives—organized by a party majority dissimilar from at least one of the other institutions, divided government has been a regular feature of American government. However, the incidence of divided government has varied between political eras. Before 1947, divided government only occurred about one-fourth of the time. However, in the last fifty years, divided government occurred more than 60 percent of the time.

Table 5.3: Congresses With Divided Government by Era, 1789–2001

	Eras							
	1789–1857		1857–1947		1947–2001		Totals	
	N	percent	N	percent	N	percent	N	percent
United government	26	76.5%	33	73.3%	10	37.0%	69	65.1%
President isolated	3	8.8	3	6.7	14	51.9	20	18.9
House isolated	4	11.8	7	15.6	3	11.1	14	13.2
Senate isolated	1	2.9	2	4.4	0	0.0	3	2.8
Totals	34	100.0%	45	100.0%	27	100.0%	106	100.0%

United Government, 1789–2001	69/106	65.1 %
Divided Government, 1789–2001	37/106	34.9 %

Source: See Table 5.1.

It has been within this most recent half-century of American politics that divided government has become the rule and not the exception. However, analysts were slow to discern this change in political life. With the Democratic capture of Congress in 1948, analysts concluded that the two-year period of divided government, was a post-war anomaly. The next time of divided government, under Republican President Dwight Eisenhower, lasted for six years (1955–61) and was explained away with the concept of the deviating election.[19] With Eisenhower retired from public life, the Democratic party with its party-identifier advantage resumed control of American political life. Thus, the election of Senator John F. Kennedy (Dem-Mass.) was seen to be a "reinstating" one.[20]

The four instances of divided outcomes in the eleven elections between 1946 and 1966 (36.4 percent) were now safely explained. But analysts were not prepared for the extraordinary eruption of divided government that appeared in 13 of the 16 Congresses (81.2 percent) elected between 1968 and 1998.

Once again, events have overtaken explanations. The 1968 circumstance was explained away with the George Wallace vote that enabled Nixon to gain an electoral vote majority while white southerners could vote for Wallace's presidential candidacy yet retain Democrats in Congress. Nixon's 1972 victory was contemporaneously attributed to his Southern Strategy and his own non-partisan Committee to Re-elect the President, which de-emphasized his Republican affiliation, thus permitting Democrats to vote for the reelection of Nixon and their own Democratic members of Congress. But in 1988, George Bush won 40 states and the Democrats still retained both houses of Congress. Bush's victory was the fifth for Republicans in the previous six presidential contests, but in none of those elections were they able to end Democratic hegemony over the House. The new explanation was that Americans trust Republican presidents in foreign policy, but wish Democrats to control domestic policy in the House of Representatives.[21]

Once again, anomalous events have taken command. In 1996, President Bill Clinton became the first Democratic presidential nominee ever to win election and have his party gain control of neither chamber of Congress. Back to the drawing board.

SEPARATION AND SURVIVAL I: THE PRESIDENTIAL DISENGAGEMENT OF RICHARD NIXON

The midterm election of 1970 marked an important turning point in American history. Eager to remove liberal Democrats from the U.S. Senate, President Nixon and Vice President Spiro Agnew campaigned from coast to coast.[22] Republicans gained two senate seats, but they also suffered a net loss of eleven governors, including seven incumbents.[23] This was the largest loss of governors for any party since 1938. Nixon and his campaign operatives were fearful that Nixon's fragile electoral coalition would not hold in 1972.

Entering the 1972 election year, Nixon's Republicans confronted a bleak political landscape. The Vietnam War continued to claim American lives. Democrats held a ten-seat margin in the Senate and a 74-seat margin in the House. Nixon's Gallup Poll approval rating was a very modest 49 percent and polls indicated that Democratic party identifiers outnumbered Republican party identifiers 41 percent to 23 percent.[24] To hold the presidency, the Nixon White House developed a three-part strategy.[25] First, run Nixon as the incumbent president, avoid mentioning the Republican party, and do little to help other Republican candidates. Second, appeal to the supporters of Alabama's Governor George Wallace by further soft-pedaling the Republican party's traditional commitment to civil rights and by finding prominent southern Democrats such as Texas Governor John Connally to endorse President Nixon, the so-called Southern Strategy.

Third, use the tactic of divide and conquer among the supporters of the Democrats' three leading moderate contenders: Senators Edmund Muskie of Maine, Hubert Humphrey of Minnesota, and Henry M. "Scoop" Jackson of Washington.[26] This tactic would hurt all three and pave the way for the nomination of a Democratic candidate who was likely to have a political base strong enough to obtain the nomination but too narrow to win election. The likeliest of these candidates was Senator George S. McGovern (Dem-S.D.), an anti-war liberal who had rewritten the party's delegate selection rules. This part of the 1972 strategy eventually led to the Watergate crisis.

In the Congress, Nixon's 1972 strategy of electoral separation had won him few friends. Not many Republican members felt obligated to Nixon for their victories, and to some, he had squandered a great opportunity to gain party control of Congress in pursuit of a personal victory. This lack of

Republican obligation would manifest itself in the House committee votes on impeachment in July 1974.

Nixon's 1972 experiment in consciously separating presidential elections from congressional ones seemed to be bad politics and even worse government. However, it would be tried again. The next time, it would be Democratic congressional leaders who would separate the elections to protect themselves from an unpopular incumbent of their own party.

SEPARATION AND SURVIVAL II: THE CONGRESSIONAL DISENGAGEMENT OF TIP O'NEILL

Congressional Democratic leaders welcomed the 1976 election of Jimmy Carter. Following the election, Democrats held sixty-one seats and a 23-seat margin in the Senate, and 292 seats and a 149-seat margin in the House. Disillusionment with President Carter was slow to develop, but once it did, it was difficult to repair. It became clear that Carter's executive style was to confront the legislature when it failed to deliver on his program. His style had some limited success in one-party Georgia, but it failed miserably in two-party Washington.[27]

President Carter's approval ratings dropped from a high of 75 percent in 1977 to 28 percent in 1979. In July 1980, popular approval of the Carter presidency dropped to 21 percent, the lowest approval rating ever scored by a president in the years since the Gallup Poll had first posed the question in 1938. No previous president had fallen so low, so fast, and so completely.[28]

In an extraordinarily candid poll conducted among 243 members of Congress by *U.S. News and World Report* in 1979, only 10.2 percent of Democrats said that they would be helped by President Carter's "presence at the head of the Democratic national ticket" in 1980. Almost two-fifths of the Democrats (36.7 percent) said that Carter's presence would hurt their campaigns.[29]

Congressional Democrats launched two hardball strategies to get Carter off the 1980 ticket. In the spring of 1979, a six-month investigation was launched to force Carter to answer questions concerning the financing of the 1976 presidential campaign and a number of congressional Democrats urged Massachusetts Senator Ted Kennedy to challenge Carter for the 1980 nomination.[30] But the Kennedy challenge weakened as waves of patriotism induced by the Iran hostage crisis pushed Carter's popularity from 31 percent in October 1979 to 61 percent in December.[31]

Carter's conflicts with Congress worsened as he permitted the Justice Department and the FBI to collaborate on an elaborate sting operation involving agents posing as Arab businesspersons who tried to bribe members of Congress. This operation, known as "Abscam," netted one U.S. Senator and six U.S. Representatives; all but one were Democrats.[32] One month before the convention, the Democratic Senate launched an investigation of Carter's brother, Billy, and his lobbying contract with the Libyan government of Muammar Qaddafi. Despite this investigation, Carter was able to gain renomination with only 64 percent of the delegates, the lowest delegate percentage ever recorded for a renominated Democratic incumbent.[33]

The fears of congressional Democrats that Carter's 1980 candidacy would be costly were partially confirmed as the Senate fell to the Republicans for the first time since the election of 1952. Republicans picked up twelve seats in the Senate and 35 in the House, reducing the Democrats' margin from 119 seats to 51.[34] But the Democrats held onto the House in 1980 because during the 1970s, the House Democrats developed incumbent protection strategies by funding the expansion of constituency operations with more district offices and larger staffs to accommodate the growing casework demands of the voters.[35] The "all politics is local" mindset had sunk in.

The Democrats controlled the House in 1981, but their smaller majority permitted a group of conservative southern Democrats to become the key swing vote in the House. These conservative Democrats provided President Reagan with a number of legislative successes. In fact, Ronald Reagan's success rate with the Congress reached 82 percent for 1981 according to *Congressional Quarterly*.[36] It was the highest success rating for a president with Congress since 1965, the first session of Lyndon Johnson's Great Society 89th Congress.

Reagan's success with the Congress heightened the importance of the 1982 congressional elections. In California, which gained two seats in the 1982 reapportionment, U.S. Representative Phil Burton was instrumental in a successful Democratic gerrymander. As a result, the party split among the California House delegation shifted from 22 Democrats–21 Republicans to 28 Democrats–17 Republicans—a net gain of ten seats.[37]

Tony Coelho was a second California Democrat whose assistance allowed House Democrats to elect majorities in the Reagan years. In 1981, Coelho became chair of the Democratic Congressional Campaign Committee (DCCC), the House party's key fund-raising operation. In this position, Coelho was able to move vast sums of PAC (Political Action Committee) money into the campaign coffers of incumbent House Democrats.[38] To journalist Brooks Jackson, Coelho's policy was "honest graft."[39] But it was successful and the House Democrats survived both the Reagan 49-state landslide of 1984 and the Bush 40-state near-landslide of 1988. Incumbent–focused PAC contributions not only contributed to Democratic control of the House, but it led to overall incumbent reelection rates that averaged 94.8 percent in the six congressional elections between 1980 and 1990.[40]

A third person who helped the House Democrats separate from and survive presidential politics was Christopher Matthews, a speechwriter in the

Carter White House who joined the staff of Tony Coelho in 1981 as a "media consultant."[41] Within months, Matthews was working for Speaker O'Neill. O'Neill was a master of "retail politics" back home in his Massachusetts congressional district and on the floor of the House in dealing with individual members. But in 1981, Speaker O'Neill faced President Ronald Reagan, a master of wholesale politics.

With Matthews's assistance, O'Neill was made over from an out-of-touch Boston Irish pol to the one person standing between Reagan's insensitive Republicans and those Americans who were poor, elderly, unemployed, and of color. House Speaker Thomas P. O'Neill Jr. became simply "Tip" to most Americans and was able to thwart successfully the Reagan agenda. And before O'Neill and Matthews were through, it was Reagan who was seen as out of touch.[42] The Democrats were now able to withstand most of the legislative thrusts of the Reagan White House, and according to *Congressional Quarterly*, the president's success rate with the Congress dropped steadily throughout his term in office.[43]

The presidential–House electoral disconnect of the 1980s was unprecedented. The three Democratic presidential defeats of 1980, 1984, and 1988 had yielded a total of only 20 of 153, or 13.1 percent, of possible state victories (including the District of Columbia) and only 10.8 percent of the total electoral votes. Not even the horrendous consecutive defeat strings suffered by presidential Democrats in the 1896–1908 era and the 1920–1928 era were as one-sided as the 1980–1988 sequence. The Democrats failed to capture a single Congress in those two previous eras. Yet in the 1980–1988 era, the House Democrats won every congressional election and captured 57.9 percent of the House seats in those three presidential debacles. Their continued success was the greatest president–House electoral disconnection in American history. The strategy of separation had worked.

SEPARATION AND SURVIVAL III:
THE DISENGAGEMENT OF PRESIDENT CLINTON, SPEAKER GINGRICH, AND THE REPUBLICAN FRESHMEN

President Clinton faced an uncertain future late in the summer of 1995. The *Cook Political Report* for August 1995 counted only twelve states that Clinton could hope for in 1996: five were listed as "Solid Democratic," five as "Likely Democratic," and two in the "Lean Democratic" column.[44] Taken together, these twelve states provided 105 electoral votes, or 165 fewer than necessary for President Clinton's reelection. Senator Dole's totals from this same report were as follows: "Solid Republican," 12 states with 79 electoral votes; "Likely Republican," 5 states with 72 electoral votes; and "Lean Republican," 10 states with 98 electoral votes. With 14 months to go, Dole had 27 states with 249 electoral votes, only 21 shy of victory. There were 12 "Toss-up" states with 184 electoral votes. President

Clinton had to carry 90 percent of the electoral votes in the toss-up states to win, while Senator Dole needed only 11 percent.

Clinton also confronted a Congress controlled by a powerful and ideologically united Republican majority. Speaker Gingrich and his conservative House loyalists attempted a coup de grace on the weakened Clinton presidency by partially shutting down the federal government twice between November 1995 and January 1996. The closings were intended to make the president accept their budget proposals, which would have altered the federal role substantially. Coming as it did when Gingrich's presidential trial balloons were aloft, this gambit may have been the Speaker's attempt to demonstrate to Washington that he was the more powerful leader of the two. However, at the urging of longtime Gingrich nemesis ex-Representative Leon Panetta (Dem-Cal.), the new White House Chief of Staff, Clinton did not budge. The shutdown tactic backfired, and it was the Gingrich Republicans who suffered the brunt of the criticism.[45] Knowing that they were outmaneuvered, House Republicans backed down and Speaker Gingrich put his presidential aspirations aside. The Speaker threw his support to Dole.

But maintaining divided government for another presidential term may not have seemed an unpleasant situation to the Speaker. Should Dole lose and the Republicans retain control of the House, Gingrich would guarantee his continued preeminence within the Republican party. Should Bob Dole win the presidential election, Speaker Gingrich would have tumbled from 1995's "Man of the Year" to occupying a supporting role. With the national government continuing to be divided between the executive and legislative branches, Gingrich would not have to relinquish that preeminence.

Rationality overcame President Clinton, as well. With his return to office on January 20, 1997, the clock began to tick on his lame duck status. Bill Clinton will be fifty-four years old at the end of his second term. The youngest former president, Teddy Roosevelt, left the White House in 1909, at the age of fifty. In 1912, though, Teddy Roosevelt vigorously sought to regain the presidency.

President Bill Clinton has sought to protect his legacy and to advance his standing among American presidents by vesting himself heavily in the career of Vice President Al Gore. Every major event of the second term has occurred with Vice President Gore at the president's side. To protect the Gore candidacy in 2000 and his own legacy, it was in the interest of President Clinton that the House Democrats not regain power. The ideological aftermath of the 1994 election debacle was that the House's moderate Democrats had suffered disproportionate losses, and in 1995, five conservative southern Democrats crossed the aisle to become Republicans. In the 104th Congress, the Democratic party was much more liberal than the president.[46] And the House Democratic leader Dick Gephardt had sought the presidency in 1988.

A House Democratic majority would have elected Dick Gephardt Speaker and jeopardized both the Gore nomination and the Clinton legacy. To limit the House Democrats and to counter the Gingrich Republicans in his bid for reelection, President Clinton adopted the triangulation strategy outlined for him by Dick Morris. This strategy enabled Clinton to "create a new position, not just in between the old positions of the two parties but above them as well."[47] It made wonderful short-term sense. Polarization had taken hold. The Gingrich–led House Republicans pushed their conservative agenda to the point of closing down the federal government twice in 1995–96 and the Gephardt–led House Democrats seemed locked in the age–old liberal Democratic mindset of raising taxes and increasing welfare entitlements.

Neither position seemed to address the public's needs for positive change while protecting the most vulnerable of the nation's citizens. Triangulation allowed President Clinton to call for an income–limited tax cut and meaningful welfare reform. He would be above the fray and be seen as presidential. Triangulation worked and Bill Clinton became the first Democrat reelected to the presidency since Franklin D. Roosevelt's four consecutive successes from 1932 to 1944.

Within the Congress, much of the partisan rancor subsided in 1996 as many of the House Republican freshmen shifted away from the Contract with America and supported President Clinton's shift to the legislative middle.[48] It was they who had come to understand the virtues of separation and survival. Newt Gingrich may have separated himself and his speakership from the collapse of the Dole candidacy, but many fast-learning Republican freshmen separated themselves from Speaker Gingrich to ensure their own reelection.[49]

For the congressional Democrats, triangulation was an electoral disaster. Throughout much of 1996, columnists contended that the Democrats had an outside chance to recapture the House. But President Clinton kept his distance from them for most of the year. Not until August in a speech before the steelworkers did he make his first call for a Democratic Congress.[50] In spite of the urging of many key supporters that a Democratic Congress would bring an end to the legislative investigations that were plaguing him, the president's White House operatives provided minimal financial assistance from the campaign coffers.[51]

A new round of divided government had been purchased. But what would it mean?

THE CONSEQUENCES OF DIVIDED GOVERNMENT FOR PRESIDENTIAL POPULARITY AND SUCCESS WITH CONGRESS

In his classic book *Presidential Power*, Richard Neustadt argued that in order to gain the power to persuade, presidents must successfully combine public popularity with a solid professional reputation established inside the Beltway of Washington, D.C.[52] Legislative success with the Congress is one way of measuring a president's professional reputation. For without it, how can a president convince others within Washington that he has the power to accomplish anything? Presidential popularity and success with Congress may easily be compared over time. Widely reported sources of these assessments include the Gallup Poll, which has been asking Americans about the job performance of presidents since the second administration of Franklin Roosevelt, and the "presidential support scores" generated by *Congressional Quarterly* to assess the relative legislative success of presidential administrations since 1953.

The annual averages for the public opinion surveys represent twenty (or so) separate estimates of public opinion from samples of randomly selected citizens. The congressional success score is an annual measure of the won–lost record of a president on floor votes in both the House and Senate on which he took a position. The comparison of these data from 1953 through 1998 shows that Congress tends to be more supportive of presidential agenda items than the public is of the president.[53] For every president from Dwight Eisenhower to Bill Clinton (1993–1998), with the exception of George Bush, the mean annual presidential support score exceeded the mean annual approval rating. The largest differential was during the four–year Carter administration from 1977–1980, when the president enjoyed 76.4 percent support in Congress but only 46.3 percent support among the public. During the first six years of the Clinton administration, through the end of 1998, the president had an average CQ support score of 61.4 and a mean Gallup approval rating of 53.2.

These data are most clear when comparing the presidential popularity ratings to a president's legislative success rate in the U.S. House. Historically, most divided government circumstances pit the House against the president and the Reagan–O'Neill and Clinton–Gingrich encounters bear out the contention that these are the federal institutions which are each other's historical enemy. When a president's year in office is added to the equation, the uniqueness of the conflict becomes clearer. Presidential success in the House of Representatives is relatively constant for the first five years of a united government's presidential administration. The first year's average success rate is 85.0 percent in the House, while the fifth year's success rate is 83.5 percent, only 1.5 percent lower. This is not true of divided government presidencies, where success rates start lower at 63.5 percent for the first year and decline to 47.5 percent by the fifth year.

The sixth year appears to be a last gasp of legislative-executive comity. But by the seventh year in office, presidents are more successful with the public than they are with their legislative program. Clearly, the members of Congress are preparing themselves for the next presidential administration.

Furthermore, the slippage among the citizenry is far greater for presidents operating in united government circumstances than in divided ones. The range in popular support from high years (first years) to low years(fourth years) is 24.5 percent (66.3–41.8) for presidents in united circumstances. The range from high years (first years) to low years (sixth years) is less than a third of that—7.8 percent (59.2–51.4)—in divided circumstances. This would appear to be counter-intuitive. Presidents should fare worse with the public when they are confronting a hostile Congress and must defend themselves and their legislative agendas on a daily basis.

But such is not the case. Ironically, presidents do better with the public during divided governments, for Congress is a more disliked institution than the presidency.[54]

Examination of the Gallup approval ratings shows that public approval of presidents in divided years exceeds that of presidents in united years beginning with the third year in office. It is during the year immediately following the first midterm election that separation begins to have its political benefits. All four presidents in this era who have been reelected—Eisenhower, Nixon, Reagan, and Clinton—have had their legislative parties rejected at the first midterm election yet have gone on to win convincing presidential victories. In each case, they exceeded their initial victory percentages. A president confronting a hostile congressional majority can become heroic.

In times of united government, presidents are held accountable for congressional action (and inaction). If the Congress acts carelessly and in haste, the president is blamed for not providing a brake on its recklessness. And if a united government Congress fails to act, it must be due to the inability of the president to provide effective leadership. Such are not the worries of presidents in divided circumstances. In these cases, the president may portray himself as urging a recalcitrant and unresponsive Congress to act, as Harry Truman successfully did with "the do–nothing 80th Congress." Or the divided government president may be portrayed, as was Ronald Reagan, as the protector of the larger public's interest against the narrow and provincial claims of a greedy and rapacious Congress eager to spend taxpayer money to insure their own reelections.

Presidents in late–term divided government conditions often have a positive standing in the eyes of the public, comparable to their early–term "honeymoon" ratings and higher than those for presidents in united government circumstances. For those presidents whose egos need such emotional support, divided government may be the remedy.[55]

DIVIDED GOVERNMENT AND PRESIDENTIAL LEGACIES

What of the long term issues? With reelection at hand, President Clinton fell into the preoccupation of most two-term presidents; what will be the judgment of history on my presidency?

In late 1996, a panel of historians and presidential analysts assessed all of the presidents once again.[56] The early "greatness" line on the Clinton presidency was "low average." Presumably, a successful second term would elevate him another notch. But divided government has its own dynamic. Presidents who face Congresses with hostile majorities may benefit in the short–term public opinion polls but they suffer in scholarly polls.

A voting public that rejects a president's legislative majority has already decreed that this is a person whom they do not wish to see in total control of the national agenda. In the 1996 Schlesinger poll, four presidents were adjudged "below average" and seven were ranked as "failures." These presidents held office for little more than 45 years. Their terms in office coincided with all or some of 24 Congresses, twenty-one of which were elected while they were atop the ticket or held the White House. In only eleven cases were their legislative majorities approved by the American public—52.4 percent. In ten cases of the twenty-one, the public gave these below average and failure presidents no congressional mandates—47.6 percent. The public had spoken long before the historians had.

In the Schlesinger poll, nine presidents were adjudged "great" and "near-great." These presidents held office for almost 69 years. Their terms in office coincided with all or some of 36 Congresses, thirty-four of which were elected while they were atop the ticket or held the White House. In twenty-nine of these thirty-four cases, their legislative majorities were ratified by the American public—85.3 percent. And among the three greatest presidents—Lincoln, Washington, and Franklin Roosevelt—thirteen of their fourteen Congresses were controlled in both chambers by their party's legislative majority—a success rate of 92.9 percent. United governments produce great presidents.

For President Clinton, the verdict may already be in. He may have to spend the remainder of his days in the presidential purgatory of "low average" for his 1996 willingness to encourage divided government's tradeoff of legislative achievement for the short-term benefits of heightened personal popularity. Certainly, had Clinton worked harder to elect a Democratic Congress, he would have avoided the unfortunate set of impeachment votes cast by the Republican House majority in 1998.

Speaker Gingrich made history, becoming the first Republican Speaker in forty years and playing a large role in the electoral upheaval that led to the House Republican majority. He has been decreed one of the nine "Kings of the Hill" along with Henry Clay, Tom Reed, and Sam Rayburn in a recent book about the history of House leadership.[57]

Like Gingrich, Speakers Reed and Rayburn thrived in periods of divided government. Despite his party's pummeling in the press for the 1995–96 government shutdowns, Gingrich's Republicans were able to retain a majority in the House. It was the first time since the election of 1928 that the Republicans had won the House in successive elections. It was a remarkable accomplishment. Gingrich's return to the speakership in 1997, in spite of ethical difficulties and stirrings of revolt within his own ranks, was also unique.

There is an irony here. Both Democratic President Bill Clinton and Republican Speaker Newt Gingrich seemed to benefit from the extension of divided government in 1996. But for both the gain was only short-term. Clinton was almost impeached by the Republican–controlled 105th–106th Congresses. And Gingrich resigned from the House after Republicans suffered losses in the 1998 elections. Speaker Gingrich, however, has earned his historical stripes. Long after the contemporaneous public opinion polls have faded, it will be Speaker Gingrich and not President Clinton who will be seen as having had the greater impact upon the electoral arena and the legislative agenda as Americans closed the last decade of the twentieth century.

CONCLUSION

In addition to the strategic calculations of politicians, a number of structural changes in the American political system have instigated the separation between presidential and congressional politics. These factors include the development of television as the major source of news and campaign information; the increased incumbency advantage in congressional elections; and the political realignment of the South from the Democrats to the Republicans, which began at the presidential level and only slowly moved to congressional voting.

The uniqueness of the 1996 election, however, is not that the results were divided once again, but that the deliberate separation of the presidential and congressional election systems took place in both parties simultaneously and benefited both Speaker Gingrich and President Clinton. Speaker Newt Gingrich, who had postponed his own presidential bid in 1996, seemed determined to insulate the House Republican majority from the potentially negative consequences of ex-Senator Dole's dispirited campaign. On the other side, it was President Clinton who appeared to run away from the congressional Democrats lest his personal popularity be hurt by their low public esteem. This actor-based version of the 1996 election casts President Clinton and Speaker Gingrich as co-stars in the latest divided government drama.

NOTES

1.   Examples of this assessment include Everett C. Ladd, "The Status-Quo Election: An Introduction," *The Public Perspective* 8 (December/January 1997), 4–5; and Larry J. Sabato, "The November Vote—A Status Quo Election," in *Toward the Millennium: The Elections of 1996,* ed. Sabato, (Boston: Allyn and Bacon, 1997), 143–161.

2.   Typical of these stories was Katharine Q. Seelye, "In Blistering Attack, Dole Says Clinton Is Using Scare Tactics," *NYT*, September 27, 1996, A22; and Spencer S. Hsu and Ellen Nakashiuna, "GOP Says Foes Using 'Mediscare,'" *WP*, October 30, 1996, B6.

3.   William F. Connelly Jr. and John J. Pitney Jr., *Congress' Permanent Minority? Republicans in the U.S. House* (Lanham, Md.: Rowman and Littlefield, 1994).

4.   Roger H. Davidson, David M. Kovenock, and Michael K. O'Leary, *Congress in Crisis: Politics and Congressional Reform* (Belmont, Ca.: Wadsworth, 1966), 53, Table 2.5.

5.   Gallup Poll, "Confidence in Institutions," news release, August 15, 1997, 4–5.

6.   Dave Kaplan and Julianna Gruenwald, "The House: Longtime 'Second' Party Scores a Long List of GOP Firsts," *CQWR*, November 12, 1994, 3232–3239.

7.   Speaker O'Neill's phrase, "All Politics is Local" was the title of the opening chapter of his 1987 autobiography, *Man of the House: The Life and Political Memoirs of Speaker Tip O'Neill* (New York: Random House, 1987). The book was written with William Novak. He also used the phrase again in the title of another book, Thomas P. O'Neill Jr., with Gary Hymel, *All Politics is Local and Other Rules of the Game* (New York: Times Books, 1994).

8.   Among some of the titles were: "The American Dream Restoration Act," "The Taking Back Our Streets Act," and "The Family Reinforcement Act," in *Contract With America: The Bold Plan by Rep. Newt Gingrich, Rep. Dick Armey, and the House Republicans to Change the Nation* (New York: Times Books, 1994).

9.   James A. Finefrock, "The Republican Tsunami," *San Francisco Examiner*, December 9, 1994, A–11. Among the more evocative descriptions were "Stampede!," the cover story for *Time*, November 21, 1994, 46–49ff; J. Weisberg, "After the Deluge," *New York*, November 14, 1994, 28ff.; Meg Greenfield, "After the Big One," *Newsweek*, November 21, 1994, 108; and R. Lacayo, "After the Revolution," *Time*, November 28, 1994, 28–33.

10.   "Man of the Year: Newt Gingrich," *Time*, December 25, 1995, 20ff.

11.   Political scientists have tried to dispel this notion; see Lyn Ragsdale, "The Fiction of Congressional Elections as Presidential Events," *APQ* 8 (October 1980): 375–398. However, political writers continue to foster the belief in the linkage. A smattering of midterm election analyses supports this point; see L. Walczak, "How 1986 Changes the Presidential Race," *Business Week*, November 17, 1986, 8; Gus Tyler, "Straws in the American Political Winds," *The New Leader* 73 (November 12–26, 1990): 10–12; M. Kelly, "Why the President is in Trouble," *Reader's Digest,*

November 1994, 85–90; and J. Weisberg, "Why It's Even Worse for Clinton Than You Think," *New York*, November 21, 1994, 41.

12.   The best-known of these efforts is Malcolm Moos, *Politics, Presidents and Coattails* (Baltimore: Johns Hopkins Press, 1952). Not all of Moos's contemporaries shared his belief in the coattail linkage; see Cortez A. M. Ewing, *Congressional Elections, 1896–1944: The Sectional Basis of Political Democracy in the House of Representatives* (Norman: University of Oklahoma Press, 1947).

13.   Milton C. Cummings Jr., *Congressmen and the Electorate: Elections for the U.S. House and the President, 1920–1964* (New York: The Free Press, 1966), esp. 39–47.

14.   Walter Dean Burnham, "Insulation and Responsiveness in Congressional Elections," *Political Science Quarterly* 90 (Fall 1975): 411–435.

15.   See Sidney I. Pomerantz, "Election of 1876," in *History of American Presidential Elections, 1789–1968*, Vol. II, ed. Arthur M. Schlesinger, Jr. and Fred L. Israel, (New York: Chelsea House, 1971), 1379–1487, esp. 1413–1424.

16.   See Robert F. Wesser, "Election of 1888," in Schlesinger and Israel, 1615–1700, esp. 1645–1649.

17.   This model was first presented in W. Ross Brewer and Garrison Nelson, "Election Expectations and Outcomes: A Theory of Nominating Convention Conflict, 1896–1976," in *Public Policy and Public Choice*, ed. Douglas W. Rae and Theodore J. Eismeier (Beverly Hills, Ca.: Sage, 1979), 151–207.

18.   These data are adapted from Harold W. Stanley and Richard G. Niemi, eds., *Vital Statistics on American Politics*, 2nd ed.(Washington, DC: CQ Press, 1990), 133, Table 4–8. Data for the 1992 and 1996 elections came from Clark H. Bensen of POLIDATA, Lake Ridge, VA.

19.   Angus Campbell, Philip E. Converse, Warren E. Miller, and Donald E. Stokes, *The American Voter* (New York: John Wiley, 1960), 531–538.

20.   Philip E. Converse, Angus Campbell, Warren E. Miller, and Donald E. Stokes, "Stability and Change in 1960: A Reinstating Election," *APSR* 55 (June 1961): 269–280.

21.   The most persuasive advocate of this view is Gary C. Jacobson, *The Electoral Origins of Divided Government: Competition in U.S. House Elections, 1946–1988* (Boulder, Colo.: Westview Press, 1990), 112–120.

22.   Rowland Evans Jr. and Robert D. Novak, *Nixon in the White House: The Frustration of Power* (New York: Random House, 1971), 303–346.

23.   "Democrats take 13 Governorships from Republicans," *CQWR*, November 6, 1970, 2748–2749, 2770. Republicans picked up two state governorships, so the net loss was eleven.

24.   George C. Edwards III and Alec M. Gallup, *Presidential Approval: A Sourcebook* (Baltimore: Johns Hopkins University Press, 1990), 61; American National Election Studies, University of Michigan.

25.   Theodore H. White, *The Making of the President, 1972* (New York: Atheneum, 1973), 48–69.

26.   Bob Woodward and Carl Bernstein, *All the President's Men* (New York: Simon and Schuster, 1974), 112–130.

27.   See O'Neill, with Novak, *Man of the House*, 297. See also the observations of Christopher Matthews, who worked for both Carter and O'Neill, *Hardball: How Politics is Played—Told by One Who Knows the Game* (New York: Summit, 1988).

28.   "President Carter's Popularity," *The Gallup Poll* (August 1979), 223–227; "Presidential Popularity: Carter Rating Lowest of Any President Since '38," *Gallup Opinion Index Report* (August 1980), 24–25.

29.   "Congress Tells Carter How He Rates," *U.S. News and World Report*, August 13, 1979, 21–23.

30.   Warden Moxley, "Kennedy Draft: Movement With Precedents," *CQWR*, September 22, 1979, 2041–2048.

31.   "The Carter Presidency: Carter Praised for Personal Qualities; Few Feel History Will Regard Him Outstanding," *The Gallup Report* (January, 1981), 3–4, 56–57.

32.   "Abscam Scandal Clouded Congresses Image," *CQ Almanac 1980* (Washington, DC: Congressional Quarterly Inc., 1981), 513–521.

33.   Data from Richard C. Bain and Judith H. Parris, *Convention Decisions and Voting Records*, 2nd ed. (Washington, D.C.: The Brookings Institution, 1973), Appendix C, 351–417, and updated with "Key Ballots at 1980 Democratic Convention," *CQWR*, August 16, 1980, 2437.

34.   Charles E. Jacob, "The Congressional Elections," in *The Election of 1980: Reports and Interpretations,* ed. Gerald M. Pomper (Chatham, NJ: Chatham House Press, 1981), 119–141. See also the recollections of ex-Speaker Jim Wright, *Balance of Power: Presidents and Congress from the Era of McCarthy to the Age of Gingrich* (Atlanta: Turner Publishing, 1996), 326–340.

35.   David R. Mayhew, *Congress: The Electoral Connection* (New Haven: Yale University Press, 1974); Morris Fiorina, *Congress: Keystone of the Washington Establishment* (New Haven: Yale University Press, 1977); and Richard F. Fenno Jr., *Home Style: House Members in Their Districts* (Boston: Little, Brown, 1978).

36.   Bill Keller, "Voting Record of '81 Shows the Romance and Fidelity of Reagan Honeymoon on Hill," *CQWR*, January 2, 1982, 18.

37.   Alan Ehrenhalt, "Reapportionment and Redistricting," in *The American Elections of 1982,* ed. Thomas E. Mann and Norman J. Ornstein (Washington, DC: American Enterprise Institute, 1983), 48–49, 71. A solid depiction of Burton's efforts may be found in John Jacobs, *A Rage for Justice: The Passion and Politics of Phil Burton* (Berkeley: University of California Press, 1995), 425–440.

38.   Burdett A. Loomis, *The Contemporary Congress*, 2nd ed. (New York: St. Martin's Press, 1998), 68–73.

39.   Brooks Jackson, *Honest Graft: Big Money and the American Political Process* (New York: Knopf, 1988).

40.   Roger H. Davidson and Walter J. Oleszek, *Congress and Its Members*, 6th ed. (Washington, DC: CQ Press, 1998), 62–63, Table 3.1.

41.   Christopher Matthews, *Hardball*, 42.

42.   See O'Neill, with Novak, *Man of the House*, 331.

43.   "Presidential Victories on Votes in Congress, 1953–1988," *Vital Statistics on American Politics*, 248–249, Table 8–11.

44.   The *Cook Political Report*, August 4, 1995, 1.

45.   Gingrich became a lightning rod for popular discontent with Congress; see Marjorie Randon Hershey, "The Congressional Elections," in *The Election of 1996: Reports and Interpretations,* ed. Gerald M. Pomper (Chatham, NJ: Chatham House, 1997), 212–217; and Gary Jacobson, "The 105th Congress: Unprecedented and Unsurprising," in *The Elections of 1996,* ed. Michael Nelson (Washington, D.C.: CQ Press, 1997), 143–166, esp. 144–147.

46.   Richard E. Cohen and William Schneider, "Voting in Unison," *NJ,* January 27, 1996, 179–201; and Dan Carney, "As Hostilities Rage on the Hill, Partisan-Vote Rate Soars," *CQWR,* January 27, 1996, 199–201.

47.   Dick Morris, *Behind the Oval Office: Winning the Presidency in the Nineties* (New York: Random House, 1997), 79–88, quote 80.

48.   The 1996 congressional voting assessments differ from those of 1995; see Richard E. Cohen and William Schneider, "Soft Center," *NJ,* December 14, 1996, 2681–2699; and Rebecca Carr, "GOP's Election-Year Worries Cooled Partisan Rancor," *CQWR,* December 21, 1996, 3432–3435.

49.   Linda Killian, *The Freshmen: What Happened to the Republican Revolution?* (Boulder, Colo.: Westview Press, 1998), 340–353; and Jonathan D. Salant, "Some Republicans Turned Away From Leadership," *CQWR,* December 7, 1996, 3352–3354.

50.   Eric Pianin, "Clinton Makes First Call for Democratic Congress: Speaking to Steelworkers, He Says Control Is Needed to Protect Social Progress," *WP,* August 9, 1996, A12.

51.   Elizabeth Drew, *Whatever It Takes: The Real Struggle for Political Power in America* (New York: Viking, 1997), 167.

52.   Richard E. Neustadt, *Presidential Power: The Politics of Leadership* (New York: John Wiley and Sons, 1960), 33–107.

53.   These calculations are adapted from *Gallup Monthly Index,* data provided by Gallup Poll, and *Vital Statistics on American Politics*, 248–249, as updated with *CQ Almanac*, various years.

54.   Frank Newport, "Small Business And Military Generate Most Confidence in Americans," Gallup Poll, August 15, 1997; and John R. Hibbing and Elizabeth Theiss-Morse, *Congress as Public Enemy* (Cambridge: Cambridge University Press, 1995).

55.   President Clinton would appear to qualify in this category; see Stanley A. Renshon, *High Hopes: The Clinton Presidency and the Politics of Ambition* (New York: New York University Press, 1996); and Michael Kelly, "A Man Who Wants to Be Liked, and Is: William Jefferson Blythe Clinton," *NYT,* November 4, 1992, A1.

56.   Arthur M. Schlesinger Jr. "The Ultimate Approval Rating," *NYT Sunday Magazine,* December 15, 1996, 46–51.

57.   Richard B. Cheney and Lynne V. Cheney, "Speaker Newt," in *Kings of the Hill: Power and Personality in the House of Representatives* (New York: Touchstone, 1996), 190–210.

CHAPTER 6

Clinton's Second Transition
Historic Aspirations Amidst Divided Government

MARGARET JANE WYSZOMIRSKI

Customarily, the study of presidential transitions has defined the subject as a transfer of power and office from one individual to another that occurs in the approximately eleven-week period between the quadrennial November presidential election and inauguration day the following January. In practice, however, transitions extend much farther in time at both ends of the process. Transition planning reaches back into the months before the election and is affected by the tone, content, and results of the campaign. Similarly, transition implementation extends at least through the so-called "honeymoon period" and into the apocryphal first hundred days of the administration. Although a hundred days is an artificial designation, it is a convenient and popularly recognized marker that is commonly used by journalists and scholars.

Transitions require the president-elect to address four primary tasks: (1) assembling an administration, which involves both making personnel appointments and organizing the administration team; (2) setting a policy agenda; (3) determining a political strategy that takes into account both constraints and assets; and (4) balancing continuity and change as manifest in politics, people, and policy.

FOUR TYPES OF TRANSITIONS

The particular character of each of these four tasks varies depending not only on which of four types of transitions is involved but also upon the specific circumstances of the moment. Regular transfers of power can involve one of two partisan casts—an *inter-party transition* or an *intra-party transition*. Historically, inter-party transitions are seen as the archetypal transition and have attracted most scholarly attention. An inter-party transition occurs when a Republican incumbent is succeeded by a Democratic candidate (for example, Clinton succeeding Bush in 1992–93) or the reverse, when a Republican candidate is elected to succeed a Democratic incumbent (for example, Reagan replacing Carter in 1980–81). Inter-party transitions face wholesale personnel demands, the necessity of enunciating a new policy agenda, and the attempt to launch a strategic presidency. Change, rather than continuity, is the emphasis, except in areas that carry a presumption of independence or bipartisanship such as regulatory and judicial appointments or foreign affairs.

Intra-party transitions occur when a new individual is elected to succeed an incumbent from the same party. These have been rarer, especially in the modern presidency (for example, Bush succeeding Reagan in 1988–89). During intra-party transitions, continuity and change are more evenly balanced as the new president—particularly if he is a former vice president—seeks to extend and revise the policies of his predecessor. In intra-party transitions, the president-elect is less pressed to undertake wholesale personnel replacement, and begins to establish a different and independent governance capacity within a continuing partisan context. In cases of both inter- and intra-party transitions, planning for the transition is expected, is connected with campaign management, and has been expanding since the 1960s.

Presidential transitions can also occur outside the normal electoral cycle—occasioned by the death, resignation, or impeachment of an incumbent president. Such *accidental transitions* then elevate the sitting vice president. In the modern era, most such accidental presidents go on to run for election in their own right at the next opportunity, which may be relatively close at hand (for example, Lyndon B. Johnson had about eleven months before he stood for election in 1964) or may be at quite a distance (for example, Harry S Truman served out the remaining three years and nine months of FDR's last term before running for election in 1948). In such unexpected circumstances, the formal transition takes place quickly, while the effective change of administrations takes much longer. In addition, the immediate transition occurs with little pre-planning, and outside of a direct campaign and electoral context. Initially, continuity is the byword, since the new president lacks electoral legitimacy in his own right. Thus, continuity in personnel and policies is, in large part, expected, while much in the political context remains unchanged in the absence of regularly scheduled congressional elections or the legacy of a recent campaign.

A fourth type of presidential transition involves the reelection of an incumbent president for a second term. During this *inter-term transition*, the reelected president undertakes a revision and renewal of his administration and agenda. While the three preceding types of transitions involve a change of executives, this type of transition does not; rather, it marks the shift between the first and second terms of a continuing president. Here, an incumbent president has the opportunity to deal with personnel issues more strategically than a first-term president since he now has fewer demands, fewer vacancies, and more experience both with governance and staff performance. In setting a policy agenda, the reelected president can be less concerned with electoral coalition strategy and strike more of a balance between the unfinished business of the first term and a more emphatic concern with his potential historical record. Likewise, the political experience of the campaign and election brings both new and different considerations: fewer electoral calculations but the specter of becoming a lameduck, a new congressional power configuration, and succession concerns within his own party. Certainly, the school of hard knocks will have produced lessons in policy, governance, and administration, from which the continuing administration may renew and reposition itself for a second chance at a "strategic presidency."

The reelection of William Jefferson Clinton to a second term as president of the United States in 1996 resulted in a transition of the fourth type. The following discussion will focus on the three basic transition concerns: politics, people, and policy as they evolved during the long transition process that runs from the campaign into the election, through inauguration and across the first hundred days of the administration.

POLITICAL CAPITAL AND POLITICAL CONTEXT

Every president-elect comes out of the campaign and election with a set of factors that establish the amount of political capital that he brings to the task of governance. Perhaps most important among these factors are the partisan majorities in each house of Congress, the president's electoral margin of victory, and current public opinion ratings.[1] To this list, James Pfiffner also adds the zeitgeist of the moment. Sometimes, these factors combine to allow an elected official to claim a mandate for his particular policy agenda. Although the term "mandate" is often used loosely and at times wishfully, a mandate seems to require both a clear and substantial electoral margin (for example, of landslide proportions) as well as a clear voter choice among differing policy choices. Campaign victors often seek to claim a mandate in order to accord their policy preferences greater authority and legitimacy by linking them to the will of the people.[2] As we will see, neither President Clinton nor the Republican congressional leadership were in a position following the election of 1996 to claim a mandate for a particular set of policy positions; rather, it might be said that they shared a public invitation to engage in shared governance as a mode of action.

For the reelected President Clinton, the electoral results conferred only limited political capital. He won reelection with 49.2 percent of the popular vote in an election that—at 49 percent—had the lowest turnout of any presidential election since 1924. Thus, he was the plurality choice of a minority of registered voters. This outcome made Clinton the first president since Woodrow Wilson to be elected twice without a majority of the popular vote. And Clinton became the first Democrat ever to win a second term without carrying Congress.[3] Furthermore, Clinton only secured a plurality vote for his reelection despite being an incumbent running during a period of peace and prosperity, against an opponent who ran a weak campaign.[4] However, this performance bettered his record of 1992, when he won only 43 percent of the popular vote. President Clinton ran particularly strongly among Latino voters and among women voters.[5] In addition, Clinton gathered a large electoral college margin, with 379 votes—over a hundred more than the 270 he needed to win. Thus, Clinton gained more political capital from the election of 1996 than he had in 1992, but he was still a plurality president with particular electoral debts to women and minorities, and he did not have much of a coattail effect on Democratic congressional candidates.

Meanwhile, Republican congressional leaders could not claim an electoral mandate, either. Although the 105th Congress became the first consecutive Republican-controlled Congress since the 1920s, the Republicans' majority in the House fell from 236 to 225. Nor was Congress the incumbent safe institution it had been. The 105th Congress included many newcomers: 53 percent (or 232 members) of the House and 40 senators had arrived since 1992.[6] Furthermore, the tenor of the 105th Congress was less revolutionary than its predecessor and was more inclined toward incrementalism. Indeed, many interpreted the joint but conflicting results of the presidential and congressional elections to be a moderating influence upon both Democrats and Republicans.

Both President Clinton and the Congress began their new term with strong standings in the public opinion polls. At his inauguration, the president enjoyed a 58 percent approval rating. Meanwhile, public approval of Congress stood at 45 percent, its highest level since 1991.[7] While these high ratings were accompanied by high hopes for bipartisan cooperation, the public had lower expectations concerning potential progress on a number of particular issues. Thus, the signals seemed to indicate that both the executive and the legislature were expected to avoid partisan bickering while conducting the public's business, but were unlikely to be held to high standards of policy productivity in a divided government situation. Hence the prevalent zeitgeist seems to have been one that encouraged bipartisanship.

During the opening months of 1997, both the president and House Speaker Gingrich faced investigations into questionable practices that diminished their political capital and distracted their attention. Speaker Gingrich faced a House ethics investigation into his use of charitable foundations that violated tax laws because of their close interactions with GOPAC, a political action committee that Gingrich used to build toward the 1994 Republican takeover of Congress. In January, the ethics committee voted to reprimand the Speaker for his conduct and imposed a $300,000 penalty to help offset the cost of the probe.[8] The investigation caused a number of Democrats to call for the Speaker to step down. Although Gingrich succeeded in winning reelection as Speaker, he was a more chastened and weaker Speaker than he had been in the previous Congress. A number of other changes further depleted Gingrich's leadership resources: the new GOP class of 1996–97 was less beholden to the Speaker than the class of 1994–95; many sophomore members recognized that the confrontational strategies of the 104th Congress had damaged the party; and new Republican rules spread committee and subcommittee chairmanships more broadly and vested more agenda power in the chairs than in the previous Congress.[9]

Meanwhile, the president, the Democratic National Committee, and various members of his administration faced investigations of their own concerning fundraising practices. These included allegations that various White House events (coffees, overnight stays in the Lincoln bedroom) were used to solicit political donations; that Vice President Gore had engaged in questionable fundraising practices; and that the Chinese government tried to influence the 1996 election with $2 million of illegal campaign contributions.[10]

Allegations and investigations of political scandals and misbehavior cost both the Democratic administration and the Republican Congress political capital during the first 100 days of 1997, costs that neither party could easily sustain and that put an added premium on efforts at bipartisan cooperation and on identifying points of convergence between the Clinton and the Republican congressional policy agendas. Indeed, in March, House Republican leaders tried to regain their policy focus by announcing a 13-point agenda that had as its highest priority achieving a balanced budget by 2002 and that Gingrich referred to as "laying the base for 21st century conservatism."[11] Meanwhile, President Clinton turned to using executive powers to advance his policy agenda during a period when congressional attention was dominated by campaign financing investigations. Thus, the President announced that the federal government would hire 10,000 welfare recipients as a step forward in welfare reform. He also extended family leave provisions for federal employees so that parents could attend school conferences. And in the face of stalled action on campaign finance reform, President Clinton asked the Federal Election Commission to institute a regulatory ban on one of the most flagrant abuses—soft money.[12]

PEOPLE: STAFFING THE SECOND CLINTON ADMINISTRATION

A second-term president approaches the task of staffing and organizing the administration with a number of advantages he did not have the first time around. To begin with, a second-term president generally has fewer appointments to make, more time to make them, and a more acute appreciation of both the demands of the jobs and the capabilities of the candidates. In addition, the president can choose to use appointment as a tool in coalition-building in Congress, within his own party, or among interest groups. These coalitions may be characterized as political/electoral or policy-oriented. Thomas Weko notes that although traditionally presidents made appointments with an eye toward political/electoral coalition building, since the Nixon presidency, there has been more of an emphasis on using appointments to build policy coalitions.[13] Thus, staffing has become related not only to the political context but to the policy agenda.

As part of the 1992 transition, President-elect Clinton had over 5,800 appointments for which he was legally responsible, including 590 top executive appointments requiring Senate confirmation.[14] Dealing with this personnel task requires a sophisticated White House personnel service and office that for a first-term president must itself be staffed and organized. Establishing an appointment processing system can be one of the first and most visible signs of the shift from a campaign mode to a governance mode. This step is often fraught with tension and jockeying for power among the president's adherents. Furthermore, the president-elect must decide and communicate what criteria will be important in the selection of appointees, how closely he will monitor appointment decisions, and to what extent he will consider the preferences of secretaries-designate. Then specific appointees need to be selected, cleared, and confirmed.

In 1996, as in 1992, President Clinton wanted his administration to reflect the diversity of America, and he preferred announcing appointments in teams and groups rather than individually. He also wanted to avoid some of the missteps of the first term—notably the confusion in vetting potential nominees that had led to controversies, particularly those around the Attorney General position, as well as the slowness of the appointment process and an ambivalence about commissioning an effective White House chief of staff.[15] After running through three personnel directors in the first half of his first term, Clinton finally settled in February 1995 on Robert J. Nash, a long-time Clinton supporter who had been deputy personnel chief for the Clinton I transition. Thus, Nash approached the Clinton II transition with experience and an established and running personnel office, a close working relationship with the president, familiarity with many of the incumbent appointees, and a smaller, more manageable task.[16] The fact that Nash was also an African–American seemed to underline the President's commitment to diversity among his appointees.

Just before Christmas 1996, President Clinton announced the full set of second-term cabinet selections (see table 6.1). Once again, the president underscored his concern with diversity. He said, "I believe that one of my jobs at this moment in history is to demonstrate by the team I put together that no group of people should be excluded from service to our country and that all people are capable of serving. . . ."[17] Given the strength of their electoral support, President Clinton was particularly mindful of securing representation for women, African–Americans, and Hispanics. The official 14-member cabinet included four women, three African–Americans, and one Latino. In a gesture to bipartisanship, the cabinet also included a

Republican, former Maine Senator William S. Cohen, as Secretary of Defense. New appointees were selected to head the following departments: State (Madeleine K. Albright), Defense (William S. Cohen), Commerce (William M. Daley), Labor (Alexis M. Herman), Housing/Urban Affairs (Andrew M. Cuomo), and Transportation (Rodney Slater). Thus, the cabinet was about an even mix of new faces and continuing loyalists, with one Secretary changing his seat from Transportation to Energy (Federico F. Pena). Except for Senator Cohen at Defense, all of the other new faces may have been new to the cabinet, but were experienced administrators elsewhere in the first Clinton administration. With the departure of Henry Cisneros (HUD) and Robert Reich (Labor), two of the most liberal members of the cabinet left the administration.

Table 6.1: Clinton Cabinets I and II

Clinton II Appointee	Cabinet Office	Clinton I Predecessor
MADELEINE K. ALBRIGHT	State	Warren M. Christopher
ROBERT E. RUBIN[a]	Treasury	Robert E. Rubin since 1/95
WILLIAM S. COHEN	Defense	William J. Perry since 2/94
JANET RENO	Attorney-General	Janet Reno
BRUCE BABBITT	Interior	Bruce Babbitt
DAN GLICKMAN	Agriculture	Dan Glickman since 3/95
WILLIAM M. DALEY	Commerce	Mickey Kantor since 4/96
ALEXIS M. HERMAN	Labor	Robert B. Reich
DONNA E. SHALALA	HHS	Donna E. Shalala
ANDREW M. CUOMO	HUD	Henry G. Cisneros
RODNEY SLATER	Transportation	Federico F. Pena
RICHARD W. RILEY	Education	Richard W. Riley
FEDERICO F. PENA[b]	Energy	Hazel R. O'Leary
JESSE BROWN[c]	Veterans Affairs	Jesse Brown

[a] Succeeded by Lawrence H. Summers (confirmed by Senate July 1, 1999).
[b] Succeeded by Bill Richardson (confirmed by Senate July 31, 1998).
[c] Succeeded by Togo G. West Jr. (confirmed by Senate April 28, 1998).

Clinton also made an effort to reshuffle the White House staff at about the same time, in contrast to the first term, when the staff had followed the cabinet selection process and seemed to suffer from relative neglect as a consequence.[18] Almost immediately after the election, it was announced that former deputy White House chief of staff Erskine Bowles would return to the administration to succeed Leon Panetta as chief of staff.[19] Much of the rest of the senior staff, including the national security adviser (Samuel Berger), the National Economic Council director (Gene Sperling), and the U.S. Trade Representative (Charlene Barshefsky) were veterans who had worked their way up during the first term and were "marked less by any stamp of ideology or personality than they are by tempered, tested allegiance to the boss."[20] With the departures of Harold M. Ickes and George Stephanopoulos from the White House staff, the administration lost two more of its most prominent liberal members. Although these cabinet and staff changes gave Clinton an inner circle that was "loyal, tested, trusted, and collegial," some management experts worried that the group might prove too homogenous, with a tendency toward group-think.[21]

Cross-cutting the cabinet and the White House staff were two policy teams: national security and economic policy. By mid-December, the economic team had taken shape. It seemed to put aside the internal battles of the first term between liberal populists who supported social programs and non-ideological pragmatists with an eye on the financial markets. In the second term, three pragmatic investment bankers—Treasury Secretary Robert Rubin, OMB Director Franklin Raines, and White House Chief of Staff Erskine Bowles—assumed the lead. Others in the economic team seemed to be characterized by loyalty, pragmatism, familiarity, and a dedication to consensus. The president said his main criteria in selecting team members was that "he wanted people he had confidence could do the job . . . [and] he wanted people who could work together as a team."[22] The newest member of the economic team, and the last to be appointed, was Janet Yellen, a Berkeley economist who had been a governor of the Federal Reserve for three years. Yellen was selected to chair the Council of Economic Advisers.[23]

One of the president's appointment priorities was reformulating his national security team for a second term. The incumbent Secretary of State, Warren Christopher, as well as the current Secretary of Defense, William Perry, had both indicated that they would be leaving the administration. The first-term National Security Adviser, Anthony Lake, was interested in moving on—most likely to the Central Intelligence Agency. Women's groups were pressing the president to appoint a woman as part of his top national security team.[24] President Clinton was again interested in forming a team whose members would complement each other, work together, be suited to the task of helping him define foreign policy in the post-cold-war era, and fit what would probably be his own more activist approach during a second term.[25] When the president announced his new national security team on December 6, it was notable for the symbolism of including the first female Secretary of State in history (Madeleine Albright) and the first prominent Republican named to a post in his administration (William S. Cohen). As with other White House positions, the deputy national security adviser, Samuel Berger, was promoted to succeed outgoing National Security Adviser Anthony Lake, who was nominated as Director of the CIA.[26] Later, Representative Bill Richardson (D-N. Mex) would be nominated for Ambassador to the United Nations, replacing Madeleine Albright.[27] Thus, except for Defense Secretary-designate Cohen, the rest of the national security team was typical of the general second-term appointment pattern: diverse, tested, team players.

Thus, in many ways, the president succeeded in managing his second–term personnel tasks better than he had the first term. He maintained his commitment to putting together a diverse administration, while acknowledging key constituencies with representative appointments. He retained his emphasis on assembling institutional and policy teams and moved relatively quickly to get cabinet and senior White House staff in position. Like many second-term presidents, he looked inside his administration to find new blood and rewarded tested service with promotions and recalls. In an effort to cultivate better bipartisan working relations with the Republican congressional leadership, he appointed a Republican to an inner cabinet spot and tempered the liberal composition of his advisory circle.

However, not all of his nominees had smooth confirmation processes: after months of rancor, Anthony Lake withdrew his name from consideration to become Director of the CIA, while Alexis Herman, before winning confirmation as Secretary of Labor, endured months of controversy and delay, mostly over her role in White House fundraising activities. Similarly, although the most senior administration positions were filled in a more orderly and timely manner than during his first term, the process of filling subcabinet and ambassadorial appointments was slow. As of mid-April, only 18 names had been sent to the Senate for 130 vacant positions that required confirmation.[28] Seven months into the term, it was reported that 30 percent of the top political jobs in the administration remained unfilled, while another 67 ambassadorships were also vacant.[29] While some of the delay is attributable to a lengthy clearance process and to Senate handling of nominations, in other cases, vacancies seemed to be clustered in departments which had new secretaries and thus were in more of a transition than others. Since this was a second term, the administration was fortunate in that it had deputies and others in place who served in an acting capacity while the appointment process proceeded at its unhurried pace.

POLICY: SETTING A SECOND-TERM AGENDA

Each president-elect moves from the campaign and election through the transition and into governance with a set of ideas and issues that he thinks are important and merit official attention and action. During the campaign, many issues arise and candidates take positions and make pledges on many more concerns than they can possibly address upon taking office. Elective politicians also carefully monitor the public opinion polls, both to see what is important to the citizenry and to assess potential public response to specific policy options. The party platform is a virtual compendium of possible policy concerns for an incoming administration. Events such as the Oklahoma City bombing occur unexpectedly and put additional issues—in this case, domestic terrorism—before the public, eliciting responses from policymakers. Increasingly over the past thirty years, think tanks—both institutional and informal—have sifted through current issues to offer agenda advice to the president-elect.[30] Interest groups formulate their own policy concerns into position papers, seeking promises from candidates as part of the campaign process. In the 1990s, the parties through their congressional leaders have offered policy agendas such as the Republican "Contract with America" in 1994 and the Democrats' "Families First" agenda for 1996.[31] In these various ways, issues become part of the systemic agenda.

During the transition, this broad systemic agenda undergoes a process of winnowing, focusing, and planning as the president-elect seeks to transform a campaign discussion agenda into an institutional action agenda conducive to strategic governance. Deciding upon this action agenda is an important element of launching a "strategic presidency."[32]

Ben Heineman has argued that a president's "first order issues" agenda in domestic affairs should be limited to five or six items.[33] Paul Light's analysis of the domestic agendas of Presidents Kennedy through Carter revealed that each initially focused on only three to seven major issues.[34] Strategic agenda-setting is equally important to second-term presidents for the following four reasons: (1) they may have more latitude to take on issues free from the calculus of reelection concerns; (2) the campaign and current conditions may have given rise to new issues; (3) they are likely to continue to be concerned with issues that they feel were not adequately addressed in the first term; and (4) they are more explicitly concerned with establishing their place in history. In addition, reelected presidents may want to demonstrate that their administrations still retain vigor and vision despite their presumed lameduck status.

It is generally argued that second-term policy successes are most likely in the initial two years, before midterm elections make it difficult for the president to keep control of the agenda.[35] The twin cycles of decreasing policy influence and increasing policy competence, identified by Paul Light, place a premium on the first hundred days of both first-term and second-term presidents. Furthermore, a second-term strategic agenda presents an opportunity to build on his first-term performance.

Developing a Priority Agenda

Selection of priority agenda items reflects the interplay of many factors. The content of a strategic agenda evolves out of the campaign, reflects the legacies of the preceding administration and the preceding Congress, and responds to current events. As such, setting a strategic agenda is an exercise in issue and option definition rather than in issue discovery. Particularly for a second-term president, the issues of a strategic policy agenda are likely to be embedded in his party's platform, in part because a sitting president plays a crucial, even decisive role in its drafting. In addition, key issues may have been incubated in congressional hearings and perhaps proposed but unrealized legislation. Often potential priority issues surface in public opinion polls throughout the campaign and election period.

As the transition continues, the president has three closely sequenced opportunities to enunciate his policy agenda. These opportunities include the inaugural address, the State of the Union address, and the submission of his proposed budget. Thus we can review these five sources to discern the basic outlines of President Clinton's second-term policy agenda: (1) the party platform, (2) public opinion polls, (3) the inaugural address, (4) the State of the Union message, and (5) the fiscal year 1998 budget proposal. Campaign documents and polls help define initial policy goals, but they do not dictate agenda priorities once an administration takes office. A cross-reading of all of these indicators reveals which issues appear repeatedly and prominently as well as the macro-themes and core values that weave through the issue agenda.

The Democratic Platform of 1996

Although the policy significance of party platforms is sometimes dismissed, Gerald Pomper has demonstrated that platforms are important compilations of party positions and promises that indicate issues that are likely to see policy action after a successful election campaign.[36] As Jeff Fishel has noted, campaign platforms and candidate pledges "provide a foundation from which an administration's early policy initiatives emanate."[37] In 1996, this was clearly the case, as an incumbent president seeking reelection, Clinton, exerted considerable influence over platform content. The proceedings of the 1996 Democratic convention emanated a "wave of togetherness," and the platform sailed smoothly through the drafting process and was adopted without debate.[38] Many of the platform's ideas and emphases resurfaced in Clinton's 1996 acceptance speech.[39]

Three of the four major sections of the Democratic platform were organized around the core values emphasized by President Clinton on the campaign trail—opportunity, responsibility, and community.[40] "Opportunity" emphasized economic growth and balancing the budget, education, and what was called economic security (but might, in other years, have been termed social security and welfare). The "Responsibility" section interwove a redefined role for government with a reinvigorated sense of personal responsibility. Thus, it encompassed a range of law and order concerns (crime, community policing, guns, criminal and juvenile justice, drugs, and domestic violence) as well as personal responsibility in many areas (immigration, welfare/work, child support, teen pregnancy, and choice). It also addressed political responsibility with an emphasis on reinventing government and reforming government ethics, lobbying, and campaign finance. The section on "Security, Freedom and Peace" was essentially a statement of national security concerns and positions. Finally, the "Community" section encompassed a catchall set of planks ranging from family issues, urban and housing policies, agriculture, and environmental issues to discrimination and civil rights, and voluntarism.

Public Opinion Polls and Issues

As reflected in polling during the campaign of 1996, "no single issue or problem dominated the minds of American voters."[41] The lack of prominent issues during the campaign coupled with the generally favorable mood of the electorate, especially concerning the state of the economy, were positive electoral factors for the incumbent president.[42] However, these positive factors exerted relatively few demands on the formulation of his second-term agenda.

The 1997 Inaugural Address

Seeking to position himself as the first president of the twenty-first century, President Clinton's second inaugural address repeatedly referred to the new century or the start of the twenty-first century, linked the promise of the future with the historical legacy of the nation, and echoed the bridge metaphor that had been a hallmark of his 1996 convention acceptance speech.[43] Whereas change had been a theme of Clinton's first inaugural address, the second was concerned with realizing the promise of the future by building on strength, prosperity, and power.[44] Much unfinished business remained from the first term: reforming government, politics, and the budget; educational reform and opportunity; improving racial harmony; and assuring societal security.

The inaugural address reiterated the call for a reinvigorated sense of "responsible citizenship" in which government is neither the problem nor the solution but in which the American people are the solution. This "new sense of responsibility" would be manifest in a new spirit of community, and heightened personal responsibility for ourselves, our families, our neighbors, and our nation.

The State of the Union Address

Although much more explicit about offering specific proposals, Clinton's State of the Union address returned to the macro-theme of pursuing our historic role and common future by attending to unfinished business and preparing Americans "for the bold new world of the 21st century."[45] Undergirding this macro-theme were the core values of opportunity, responsibility, and community.

Unfinished business included balancing the budget, renewing democracy through enacting campaign finance reform, and completing the task of welfare reform, particularly by facilitating the move from welfare to work.

Education emerged as the president's "No.1 priority for the next four years." His ten-point action plan emphasized opportunity and preparation for the future. Highlighting the importance of education, the president called it "a critical national security issue for our future" and one where "politics must stop at the schoolhouse door."

"Harness[ing] the powerful forces of science and technology to benefit all Americans" included a smorgasbord of specific items ranging from promoting connection to the Internet and "build[ing] the second generation of the Internet," through support for the space program and for medical research. It also gave a scientific rather than a social welfare cast to a number of health policy proposals.

"Building Stronger Communities" entailed more attention to safer streets, a "full-scale assault on juvenile crime," the "largest anti-drug effort ever," and revival of poor urban and rural neighborhoods. The president also emphasized the importance of service and called for a millennial celebration of "the American spirit in every community, a celebration of our common culture . . . the world's beacon not only of liberty but of creativity. . . ."

Harking back to the Democratic platform's section on "Security, Freedom, and Peace," the president spoke of America's world leadership role as a balance between continuity and change while dealing with a rapidly changing world.

"Strength Through Diversity" returned to an endorsement of the core value of opportunity amidst diversity, calling diversity "our greatest strength," seeking a resolution of "our differences in our faiths, our backgrounds, our politics," and asking all Americans to be "repairers of the breach." Our leadership in the world depends upon remaining "one America."

Rhetorically the theme of America's historic role was prominent: "America is far more than a place; it is an idea—the most powerful idea in the history of nations. . . ." The president struck a purposeful historic parallel to the 1960s when he concluded with the observation that

> Tomorrow there will be just over 1,000 days until the year 2000. One thousand days to prepare our people. One thousand days to work together. One thousand days to build a bridge to a land of new promise.

Thus, the reference to a thousand days conjured up images of John F. Kennedy, while the "bridge" alluded to a key image of the 1996 Democratic convention and campaign, and the "land of new promise" echoed Clinton's inaugural speech linkage between Martin Luther King's "Dream" with the American dream as a land of promise.

The Fiscal Year 1998 Budget Proposal

Shortly after the State of the Union address, President Clinton presented his fiscal year 1998 proposed budget. Continuing the concern for bipartisanship, the fiscal 1998 budget sought to address both presidential and legislative agendas. As such, it was not greeted with the frosty "dead on arrival" reactions that had become typical during years of divided government and that had greeted President Clinton's budget proposals in 1995 and 1996. Rather, Senate Budget Committee Chair Pete V. Domenici called it "a very good starting point," and Senate Majority Leader Trent Lott expressed a hope that negotiations "might produce a balanced budget agreement within six weeks or so."[46] The budget proposed to end deficits by 2002 while increasing spending for education by 13 percent; for combating drugs, juvenile crime, and terrorism by 5 percent; and for job training programs as part of welfare reform by 8.5 percent.[47] The proposal also juggled specific tax and spending cuts. In his emphases on issues like education, health care for uninsured children, budget balancing, welfare reform modifications and implementation, and fighting crime, President Clinton provided more detail and a price tag for issues and programs that he had sketched out in the campaign and the State of the Union address. After the divided government results of the 1996 elections and after the confrontational budget negotiations of 1995 and 1996, both the president and Republican congressional leaders saw that it was in their interests to promote a more cooperative budgetary process; in addition, they felt they were not so far apart on goals.[48]

Ingredients of the Initial Second-term Agenda

During the election and transition period, six priorities, five of which were domestic, emerged as an agenda. These were achieving a balanced budget, continuing the process of welfare reform, a major emphasis on education programs and tax incentives, targeted tax cuts, fighting crime, and forging a new international leadership role for the nation. In what might be regarded as an implicit priority, Clinton also sought to advance health care and social welfare programs, including health insurance for more children and protection for Social Security and Medicare/Medicaid. Repeatedly during the campaign, the transition, and into the first hundred days, these policy priorities appeared and were pushed toward policy action. Furthermore, this agenda was pursued amidst a set of macro-themes: bipartisan consultation, a view toward Clinton's historical legacy, and an emphasis on the core values of responsibility, opportunity, and community.

It is important to note that the five domestic priorities identified above were essentially an institutional agenda that both the president and Congress shared. The Republican leaders in Congress were also concerned with a balanced budget, welfare reform, crime, education, and targeted tax cuts—although the two parties certainly differed as to program specifics and approaches, spending and cutting levels, and preferred policy targets. Similarly, both the Republican leaders and President Clinton understood the political utility of avoiding partisan confrontation and striving for at least the appearance of bipartisan consultation. Both were concerned with their historic roles: Clinton with his administration's legacy and his role as the first president of the twenty-first century; congressional Republicans with establishing new historical patterns in legislative politics and seeking to institutionalize the new conservatism of the "revolution" of 1994.

Similarly, the president and Congress could subscribe to the core values enunciated by Clinton during the election and transition, even as they differed as to the means of realizing these values in practice and in policy. Republicans might prefer less government responsibilities while Clinton might emphasize more responsible and reformed government as well as a stronger sense of responsible citizenship, but both could agree on more personal, family, and community responsibility. The concept of opportunity might take on more of a free enterprise cast among Republicans while suggesting civil rights, diversity, and other social goals for the president. President Clinton might see community in terms of improved racial harmony, revitalizing poor neighborhoods, stronger environmental awareness, and voluntarism. Congressional Republicans, in turn, might find community more in family, family values, and morality.

Thus, despite different interpretive lenses, a governmental policy agenda emerged during the 1996–97 transition. Though some commentators observed that the 1996 election was not particularly concerned with a prospective policy agenda, and even though divided government was retained, both parties and both elected branches of government agreed on a handful of issues that were of first importance. There was also agreement on two cross-cutting themes—bipartisan consultation and an eye towards history—as well as on the importance of three core values—opportunity, responsibility, and community. Such agenda agreement, however, did not indicate like-mindedness. Rather, it was an invitation to debate and negotiate means and methods. Indeed, the initial agenda of the 1997 transition provided an opportunity to pursue common concerns amidst distinct interests and separate visions.

POLICY AND GOVERNANCE: THE FIRST HUNDRED DAYS

As the first hundred days progressed, President Clinton kept refining and adjusting his issue agenda as well as seeking convergence between his agenda and that of the Republican-controlled Congress. Following his inaugural call for bipartisanship, the effort to cultivate such political cooperation followed a bumpy road, but remained a fulcrum point of political strategy among Democrats and Republicans, executive and legislature.[49] In proposing his budget, the president announced that it included items he hoped would appeal to the Republicans, but then rankled them with a highly partisan speech to the Democratic National Committee that "chastised Republicans as fiscally irresponsible and racially divisive."[50]

On February 11, President Clinton met with congressional leaders at their invitation in the President's Room of the Capitol to discuss the prospects of a mutual agenda. The president intended the meeting to "symbolize a new era of constructive engagement" in the spirit of bipartisan interaction.[51] Vice President Gore characterized the discussions as "uniformly excellent" in tone; Republican Senate Leader Trent Lott referred to them as "an overall good session . . . " with the "atmosphere the best" he had experienced in quite some time.[52] White House Press Secretary Michael McCurry reported that President Clinton was "more than satisfied" and "delighted with the tone."[53] As a result, national political leaders agreed to a five-point list of issues on which they hoped to forge agreement and work toward productive policy action. The agenda included (1) a tax credit incentive for employers to hire current welfare recipients as part of the welfare-to-work reforms; (2) exploring tax cuts for individuals within a balanced budget framework; (3) juvenile justice measures; (4) aid for the District of Columbia as a laboratory for urban reform; and (5) education.

Clearly, there was continued resonance with the issue agenda of the campaign, election, and initial transition: bipartisanship, continuing the process of welfare reform, crime and juvenile justice, and the continued presumption of working toward a balanced budget. Also, both branches seemed to agree on the importance of education as a policy priority, even though they differed considerably on what specific measures were to be championed. Notably absent from this mutual agenda were other issues that had been emphasized by the president during the transition: most notably campaign finance reform, but also environmental policy (the Superfund and toxic waste clean-up) and the extension of health care coverage to more children.

By March, some House Republicans—especially sophomore members of the class of 1994—were frustrated by the slower pace of the 105th Congress and complained that Speaker Gingrich was being erratic, unfocused, and ineffectual in setting an agenda or strategy.[54] Partly in response to these sentiments, House Republicans announced a 13-point list of their legislative priorities entitled "Creating a Better America for Ourselves and Our Children."[55] Like the February bipartisan agenda, the House document voiced concern with balancing the budget, cutting taxes, and community renewal in Washington, D.C. Its concern with ensuring "the integrity of American elections" referred to campaign finance reform in the context of criticism of Democratic fund-raising practices and their investigation. Although reminiscent of the 1994 "Contract with America" agenda, "Creating a Better America" was different in notable ways. It was not a campaign document; it was less specific; and it was not targeted to a 100-day timetable but toward the work of an entire congress.

Within the first hundred days, the promise of drafting a bipartisan agreement to balance the budget was realized. On May 2, 1997, President Clinton and Republican congressional leaders announced a "historic agreement" to "produce the first balanced budget in a generation—a feat that has eluded six presidents and 14 Congresses" over nearly 30 years.[56] According to a CQ analysis, congressional Republicans secured "a political trifecta: a balanced budget in five years; significant, permanent tax cuts; and a plan to keep Medicare solvent for another decade."[57] These were all issues high on the Republican policy agenda, and evidence of the Republican impact on changing political dynamics and policy assumptions since the first year of the Clinton presidency.

For President Clinton, the agreement also embodied a number of important agenda items: it was an important step toward a historic achievement since a balanced/surplus budget had not been seen since 1969; in addition, it included a major spending increase for education programs, restored some welfare benefits that had been cut during the initial stage of welfare reform, and included targeted tax cuts and tax credits. In other words, the May 1997 bipartisan, balanced-budget agreement was a win-win situation for both the president and Republican congressional leaders—a package that was also facilitated by unusually robust economic growth that generated unexpected extra revenues. Thus, politics, policy, and economics converged to produce a window of opportunity for a balanced-budget agreement.

Similarly, legislation on juvenile crime issues got off to a propitious start. Previously characterized by bitter partisan feuding, the House Judiciary Subcommittee on Crime began working on a bill (HR 3) that a Justice Department spokesman described as "a genuine effort on the part of many people to try to work collegially and . . . try to define a comfortable middle ground."[58] By May, the House considered a juvenile crime bill that had the makings of a grand compromise between the Clinton White House and congressional Republicans, only to have the plan fall apart under the weight of procedural maneuvering by House Democrats, many of whom were unhappy with the details of the package. Thus, at the end of the first hundred days, crime and juvenile justice policy had suffered a near miss in the House and awaited a second round of negotiating and politicking in the Senate.[59]

President Clinton's educational plan was detailed and complex. It employed program spending as well as tax breaks to accomplish policy ends.[60] In the 104th Congress, education policy had been a battleground, with Republicans calling for the elimination of the Department of Education. Now, in the 105th Congress and Clinton's second term, Republicans wanted to avoid being characterized as "anti-education" but continued to differ from the president substantially with regard to program priorities and approaches. However, in 1997, House Education and the Workforce Committee Chair Bill Goodling (R-Pa.) did not reject the president's education proposals but instead hoped to refashion them. Similarly, Senator Paul Coverdell (R-Ga.), who was developing the Senate Republican education plan, followed up the February bipartisan agenda meeting with discussions with Education Secretary Richard Riley. In other words, the effort at bipartisan consultation seemed to have improved the atmosphere surrounding education policy negotiations.

Although much of the president's education agenda was tied up with the long budget process, within the first hundred days of his second term, many of the president's proposals were in play. By early May, bipartisan agreement to reauthorize the Individuals with Disabilities Education Act (IDEA) had been approved by both the House and Senate and was on its way to a conference committee to resolve minor, technical differences between the two versions.[61] Clearly, IDEA was a piece of the president's education agenda that had particular resonance with his core value of opportunity.

On both Medicare and Social Security, the parties agreed on a goal of guaranteeing financial viability, but differed significantly on what would be needed and preferable options to achieve this goal. With regard to Social Security, even the Advisory Council on Social Security that reported its recommendations on January 6 was divided, displaying a three-way split between maintaining the system and benefits, privatizing a large portion of Social Security investments into private securities, or partially privatizing the system by the creation of individual security accounts.[62] Similarly with regard to Medicare, Republicans called for "structural reforms" while Clinton focused on reducing payments to providers (doctors, hospitals, and HMOs) rather than fundamental program changes.[63] Clearly, these issues were on the governmental agenda, but it would take much more incubation time before a consensus could be forged to support action.

THE TRANSITION OF 1996–97 IN BROAD PERSPECTIVE

Although President Clinton enjoyed progress on many items of his policy agenda, few of these moved to formal and final action. Nevertheless, positive groundwork had been laid in the first hundred days of his second term. Also true to his call for bipartisanship, working relations between Republican leaders in Congress and the White House seemed more congenial and less combative, perhaps in response to the split outcome of the 1996 election. Thus, in 1997, both parties and both branches came to see bipartisan consultation and cautious action as being in their political interests.

Together, President Clinton and the 105th Congress reached a historic balanced-budget agreement and piloted their way through the transition of 1997. An action agenda had been selected from the broader discussion agenda of the campaign and the unfinished work of the previous Congress and administration. The long governance process had been engaged and the groundwork laid for developing consensus on policy options and specifics in a number of issue areas. Thus, this initial agenda-setting of the transition of 1997 was largely a prelude to the intricate process of policy formulation and enactment that lay ahead.

Measured by the standard of FDR's first hundred days of the New Deal in 1933 or by the standard of the first hundred days of the 104th House of Representatives' "Contract with America," Clinton's first hundred days in

1997 did not produce a wealth of newly enacted legislation. Rather, it reopened bipartisan channels of communication and constructive consultation. That it could set a workable bipartisan tone and lay such substantial policy groundwork in such a short period of time was in itself noteworthy. This constructive beginning was even more of an accomplishment given the distractions and partisanship stoked by extensive and ongoing investigations of both the president and the Speaker as well as of the fund-raising practices of both the Democratic and Republican parties during the 1996 campaign. Indeed, in mid-May, at the end of the transition period, a *New York Times* article observed that Clinton had "acted so quickly on the initiatives that his presidential campaign promoted as the central goals of a second term that his supporters and antagonists alike are asking how he will fill his remaining years in office."[64] Thus, it would seem that President Clinton did indeed succeed in getting his second term off to a "strategic presidency" start. Maintaining such momentum and realizing the fruits of seeds planted during the transition, however, would still be subject to partisan tensions.

In comparison to the first-term transition, Clinton's second-term transition was more sure-handed. With the exception of Anthony Lake's ill-fated nomination to head the CIA, cabinet and White House staffing progressed smoothly and for the most part quickly. Many of the new appointees were not really new, but rather promotions, recalls, or relocations of people who had amassed experience in the first term. Since the learning curve for experienced presidential personnel is generally shorter and less steep, the second-term appointees could keep the wheels of government rolling without the significant missteps, miscues, and overreaches of the first term.

Two final observations emerge. First, the political context of divided government, which characterized the start of President Clinton's second term, was quite different than the context of party government that had obtained during 1993. As David Mayhew has demonstrated, divided government does not forestall or minimize the prospect of policy-making productivity.[65] However, divided government may prompt a variation in the tactics and expectations of achieving a strategic presidency, as well as in the character of full-term policy-making cycles.

For example, as the second term began, the president reverted back to his New Democrat character and emphasized the cultivation of a bipartisan consultative style. This tack was in marked contrast to Clinton's 1993 performance, when he moved to the left and attempted to pursue an ambitious policy agenda while relying almost exclusively on Democratic support in Congress, helping prompt a budget stalemate and the health-care reform imbroglio. Stresses within the Democratic party occasioned intramural politics and generated significant enough general discontent to have contributed to the Republican midterm gains of 1994 and the election of the first Republican-controlled Congress in 40 years. Thus, divided government may in some ways present a prospect for a more manageable policy agenda than does party government, particularly for narrowly elected presidents who have short electoral coattails.

In terms of policy agenda, a situation of divided government—especially in which both the president and congressional leaders operate within a macro-theme of bipartisanship—may require that a president be explicit and diligent in looking for points of convergence between his own values and priorities and those of congressional leaders from another party and/or philosophy. If so, then the president may have less latitude in determining his own priority agenda, while being more mindful of bipartisan strategic considerations. Agenda-setting in a situation of divided government may also yield a different cycle of policy activity. Although initial agenda focus and success will remain important, many policy priorities will require more time to gestate, and more work will be needed to align values, assumptions, and preferences as a prelude to coalition-building. Thus, it may be particularly important to outline a full agenda and secure some consensus on basic priorities in principle, while fully expecting a long, perhaps multi-year policy development process. Hence, rather than a steady decline in policy influence as a term progresses, a divided-government president may build toward a more dispersed set of policy windows of opportunity throughout the term and may actually enjoy a series of annual strategic presidency prospects.

If this proves to be the case, then 1997 could be seen as a year in which some groundbreaking agreements were secured (for example, the balanced-budget agreement and NATO expansion), and agenda status for other issues agreed upon (for example, education, continued welfare reform, and juvenile crime) as both executive and legislature sought to fulfill campaign promises and meet electoral expectations. Although 1998 and 1999 held the potential for incremental and cumulative progress on many issues, such potential was significantly diminished by acrimonious campaign financing hearings in Congress, petty scandals that involved various administration officials, the special prosecutor's investigations of the president and first lady, and ultimately the impeachment and Senate trial of President Clinton.

Second, despite being reelected by only a plurality of the popular vote (and with an unusually low turnout rate), working with a Congress led by the opposing party, and experiencing significant turnover in key administrative personnel, Clinton managed to keep the policy spotlight focused on himself (and Vice President Gore), thus generating the impression that the governmental agenda was very much his presidential agenda. Neither cabinet members nor White House advisers evidenced the high visibility and policy image that had been common in other presidencies. Rather than policy formulators and agenda setters, cabinet and White House staff members seemed to function more in the roles of policy spokesmen, implementers, and behind-the-scenes political deal-makers.

A number of elements may have helped cultivate this policy spotlight for President Clinton (and Vice President Gore, who is literally often in the picture, if not at the president's side). Clinton's reputation as a "policy wonk" who is interested in and in command of policy detail and enjoys mastering policy substance may have initially helped position the president as the policy generator of his administration. That both Vice President Gore and First Lady Hillary Rodham Clinton share this "policy wonk" image also has contributed to this reputation. The visibility and degree of policy delegation that has characterized Vice President Gore's leadership of the administration's reinventing government effort and Gore's clear influence in technology and environmental policy issues also helps keep the spotlight on the presidency.

Additionally, President Clinton seems to have adopted his successful and highly personal campaign device of town meetings and policy seminars into the governance arena. For example, in mid-April 1997, the president hosted a White House conference on early childhood development that spoke to Clinton's agenda on programs of early social welfare and making education a top domestic priority.[66] The following week, President Clinton convened a three-day bipartisan summit in Philadelphia co-chaired by former president George Bush and politically popular Colin Powell, and featuring Vice President Gore and former presidents Jimmy Carter and Gerald Ford. Intended to inspire voluntarism nationwide, the Summit for America's Future was particularly focused on reaching at-risk youth and in emphasizing a community service component to "the meaning of citizenship in America."[67] In such cases, the president effectively demonstrates his engagement in policy substance and issue formation, influences which issues reach the public discussion agenda, and secures significant media coverage.

If these propositions concerning President Clinton's second term bear out, then they may have broader implications for our study and understanding of the presidency as it enters the next century as well as for presidential-congressional relations. Meanwhile, this analysis of the inter-term transition of 1996–97 would seem to indicate that second-term transitions merit more attention and exhibit more interesting aspects than might typically be thought when regarded simply as marking the continuation of a previously elected incumbent.

NOTES

1. James P. Pfiffner, *The Strategic Presidency: Hitting the Ground Running*, 2nd ed. (Lawrence: University Press of Kansas, 1996), 111; idem, "Presidential Transitions: Organization, People, and Policy," paper delivered at the 1996 Annual Meeting of the American Political Science Association, San Francisco, 18. Also see Paul Light, *The President's Agenda: Domestic Policy Choice from Kennedy to Carter* (Baltimore: Johns Hopkins University Press, 1982), 26.

2. A. Lane Crothers, "Asserting Dominance: Presidential Transitions from Out-Party to In-Party, 1932–1992," *Polity* 26 (Summer 1994): 811.

3. *NYT*, November 11, 1996.

4. Rhodes Cook, "Even With Higher Vote, Clinton Remains Minority President," *CQWR*, January 18, 1997, 185–188.

5. Voter News Service exit polls for 1996 in "Presidential Election Exit Poll Results," CNN/Time All Politics, 1996, *http://allpolitics.com/elections/natl/.exit.poll/index1* (November 8, 1996).

6. Allan Freedman, "Lawyers Take a Back Seat in the 105th Congress," *CQWR*, January 4, 1997, 27–30.

7. *NYT*, January 20, 1997.

8. Jackie Koszczuk, et al., "Committee Votes for Reprimand, $300,000 Fine for Gingrich," *CQWR*, January 18, 1997, 160–161.

9. Donna Cassata, "Freshmen Bring a Bit Less Fire, More Savvy to Capitol Hill," *CQWR*, January 4, 1997, 25–26.

10. Bob Gravely, "From Arms to Buddhists to Coffee: The ABCs of the Investigations," *CQWR*, April 5, 1997, 797, 800–801.

11. Jackie Koszczuk, "Republicans Set the Stage: Try 104th Agenda Again," *CQWR*, March 8, 1997, 575.

12. Peter Baker and John F. Harris, "Clinton to Pursue Agenda Through Executive Powers," *WP*, April 11, 1997, A1, A20; and Peter Baker, "Clinton To Seek FEC Ban on 'Soft Money,'" *WP*, June 4, 1997, A1, A9.

13. Thomas J. Weko, *The Politicizing Presidency: The White House Personnel Office, 1948–1994* (Lawrence: University Press of Kansas, 1995), 5, 46, 109–121.

14. Pfiffner, *The Strategic Presidency*, 171–172.

15. On the early stages of the second Clinton transition, see Pfiffner, "Presidential Transitions: Organization, People, and Policy."

16. Al Kamen and Stephen Barr, "Presidential Personnel Chief Promises Kinder, Smoother Transition," *WP*, November 21, 1996, A23.

17. As quoted in the *WP*, December 21, 1996, A16.

18. John F. Harris, "Second Transition to Show if Clinton Learned Lessons," *WP*, November 10, 1996, A1, A20.

19. Peter Baker, "President Taps Bowles, Trouble-shooter and Friend, to Lead Staff," *WP*, November 9, 1996, A1, 14.

20. For more details, see John F. Harris, "Clinton Fills Out Roster for White House Team," *WP*, December 19, 1996, 25. Quotation from Todd S. Purdum,

"The Ungreening of the White House Staff," *NYT*, December 22, 1996, Section 4, 10.

21.   Steven Pearlstein, "Clinton's Cabinet: Dream Team or Trouble?" *WP*, December 22, 1996, H1, H2.

22.   Clay Chandler, "Where Pragmatism and Process Prevail," *WP*, December 14, 1996, A11.

23.   Louis Uchitelle, "An Appointment That Draws No Fire," *NYT*, January 7, 1997, D3.

24.   John F. Harris, "Women's Groups Seek Entry to President's Inner Circle," *WP*, December 3, 1996, A1, A11.

25.   Alison Mitchell, "Clinton Still Studying Choice for National Security Team," *NYT*, December 5, 1996, A1, A16.

26.   See coverage in the *WP* and the *NYT* on December 6, 1996.

27.   "Senate Confirms Richardson as Delegate to UN," *NYT*, February 12, 1997.

28.   Al Kamen, "Many Top Jobs Remain Open in 2nd Term," *WP*, April 14, 1997, A1, A10.

29.   Bill McAllister, "Critical Jobs Still Unfilled by Clinton," *WP*, August 29, 1997, A1, A18.

30.   Margaret Jane Wyszomirski, "Advice for a New Administration: A Review Essay," *Public Administration Review* 49 (July/August 1989): 397–401.

31.   John E. Yang, "Hill Democrats Borrow a Few Themes for Center Looking 'Families First' Agenda," *WP*, June 23, 1996, A19.

32.   Pfiffner, *The Strategic Presidency*.

33.   Ben W. Heineman Jr., "Some Rules of the Game: Prescriptions for Organizing the Domestic Presidency," in *The Presidency in Transition*, ed. James Pfiffner and R. Gordon Hoxie (New York: Center for the Study of the Presidency, 1989), 45–53.

34.   Light, *The President's Agenda*.

35.   See Juliana Gruenwald, "Legislative Success Elusive in Second Term," *CQWR*, January 25, 1997, 234.

36.   For research on the connection between party platform promises and subsequent policy activity, see Gerald M. Pomper, with Susan S. Lederman, *Elections in America* (New York: Longman, 1980), 161. On the platform process, see Stephen J. Wayne, *The Road to the White House 1996* (New York: St. Martin's Press, 1996), 161–164.

37.   Jeff Fishel, *Presidents and Promises* (Washington, DC: CQ Press, 1994), 38–43.

38.   Deborah Kalb, "Democrats, Sensing Victory, Muffle Their Differences," *CQWR*, August 31, 1996, 2467. On the unusually harmonious process of drafting the 1996 Democratic platform, see Deborah Kalb, "Building With Broad Planks," *CQWR*, August 17, 1996, supplement, 33–35.

39.   For a text of Clinton's acceptance speech, see *CQWR*, August 31, 1996, 2485–89.

40.   For a text of the 1996 Democratic National Platform, see *CQWR*, August 17, 1996, supplement, 35–52.

41.   Frank Newport, Lydia K. Saad, and David W. Moore, "The 1996 Election: Americans Stay the Course" in *Where America Stands 1997*, ed. Michael Golay (New York: John Wiley and Sons, 1997), 250.

42.   Scott Keeter, "Public Opinion and the Election," in , *The Election of 1996: Reports and Interpretations,* ed. Gerald M. Pomper (Chatham, NJ: Chatham House, 1997), 108.

43.   William Jefferson Clinton, "Inaugural Address," January 20, 1997. Reprinted in *CQWR*, January 25, 1997, 252–53.

44.   In discussing President Clinton's first-term emphasis on a "new beginning," Crothers argued that Clinton interpreted his 1992 election as a mandate for change. See "Asserting Dominance: Presidential Transition from Out-Party To In-Party, 1932–1992," 809.

45.   William Jefferson Clinton, "State of the Union Address," February 4, 1997, in *CQWR*, February 8, 1997, 380–84.

46.   James Bennet, "Clinton Presents '98 Budget, and a Goal," *NYT*, February 7, 1997, A1.

47.   "FY 1998: Winners and Losers," *WP*, February 7, 1997, A21.

48.   David E. Rosenbaum, "Even With Agreement, A Goal Remains Elusive," *NYT*, February 7, 1997, A10.

49.   Just as Presidents seek to establish a "macro-theme" that underlies and interweaves the selection of discrete issues for their policy agenda, so, too, congressional leaders may set goals and select priority issues that reflect what John Bader calls a "strategic theme." See *Taking the Initiative: Leadership Agendas in Congress and the "Contract With America"* (Washington, DC: Georgetown University Press, 1996), 217–8 and Chapter 6.

50.   See commentary of Peter Baker, "Clinton's Words Show Bipartisanship is Easier Preached than Practiced," *WP*, January 26, 1997, A7.

51.   Peter Baker and Eric Pianin, "Clinton, Hill Leaders Agree on 5 Priorities," *WP*, February 12, 1997, A1, A15.

52.   Adam Clymer, "Clinton and Republican Leaders Agree on Five Goals," *NYT*, February 12, 1997, A1, A12.

53.   Baker and Pianin, "Clinton, Hill Leaders Agree on 5 Priorities," A15.

54.   Jackie Koszczuk, "Gingrich's Friends Turn to Foes as Frustration Builds," *CQWR*, March 22, 1997, 679–81.

55.   Dan Balz and John Yang, "Republicans Set Legislative Priorities," *WP*, March 7, 1997, A10.

56.   George Hager, "Clinton, GOP Congress Strike Historic Budget Agreement," *CQWR*, May 3, 1997, 993, 996–997, quote 993.

57.   Hager, "Clinton, GOP Congress Strike Historic Budget Agreement," quote 997.

58.   Dan Carney, "Differences Not Standing in Way of Juvenile Crime Effort," *CQWR*, April 12, 1997, 845–849, quote 845.

59.   Carney, "As Deal With Clinton Unravels, House OKs Juvenile Bill," *CQWR*, May 10, 1997, 1077–1078.

60.   Jeffrey L. Katz, "GOP Steps Lightly in Response to Clinton's Proposals," *CQWR*, February 15, 1997, 426–429.

61.   Bob Gravely and Eileen Simpson, "Panels Reach Accord to Rework Program for Disabled," *CQWR*, May 10, 1997, 1079–80.

62.   Jeffrey L. Katz, "Fierce Debate Looms as Congress Turns to Social Security Rescue," *CQWR*, January 11, 1997, 127–132.

63.   Steve Langdon, "On Medicare, Negotiators Split Over Policy, Not Just Figures" *CQWR*, February 22, 1997, 488–490.

64.   Alison Mitchell, "Clinton Readies a List of Kennedyesque Challenges," *NYT*, May 18, 1997, A14.

65.   David R. Mayhew, *Divided We Govern* (New Haven: Yale University Press, 1991), 76.

66.   *The White House Bulletin*, April 17, 1997; and Barbara Vobjedak, "Experts Describe New Research on Early Learning," *WP*, April 18, 1997, A3.

67.   James Bennet, "At Volunteerism Rally, Leaders Paint Walls and a Picture of Need," *NYT*, April 28, 1997, A1.

CHAPTER 7

The Irony of the 105th Congress and Its Legacy

ROGER H. DAVIDSON AND COLTON C. CAMPBELL

On January 4, 1995, the 104th Congress burst "out of the blocks at a sprint." For the first time in forty years, Republican majorities controlled both chambers, and the House was intent on acting within the first one hundred days on all ten items of the widely publicized "Contract with America." Lawmakers spent marathon sessions voting on such things as constitutional amendments to balance the federal budget and impose term limits, the line-item veto, unfunded mandates, tort reform, and even internal rules—among other things, applying national workplace laws to Capitol Hill for the first time. Partisans filled the hours with hyperbolic language and debate over the ethics of each other's leaders, principally President Clinton's fund-raising practices and admitted ethical lapses by then–House Speaker Newt Gingrich.

Two years after the Republican revolution, the 105th Congress (1997–1998) promised quietude by comparison, beginning with what one observer called a "legislative lullaby."[1] Republican leaders, plagued by narrow majorities, were unable to legislate effectively. In the House, skirmishes broke out among several factions; a rebel group of two dozen conservative sophomores variously vexed, criticized, and even publicly challenged the Speaker's leadership. Voicing concern that their leaders had become too centrist, too willing to capitulate to President Clinton and the Democrats in budget negotiations, the dissidents even met with Gingrich's four chief deputies in an aborted coup.[2] The solid Republican party organization and disciplined ranks that characterized the early 104th Congress were replaced in the 105th by a disorganized, disconsolate "team."

It was this querulous Republican team that confronted President Bill Clinton, carried to reelection in 1996 by resurgent political fortunes, only to be mired in scandal throughout 1998. The president was able to strengthen his leverage in policy negotiations with Capitol Hill, according to Elizabeth Drew, by successfully "painting the Republicans as extremist because of their proposals for budget cuts" in Medicare and school lunches—programs that help "the middle class as well as the poor—and their efforts to roll back environmental regulations." Additionally, according to Nicol Rae, being on the right side of two government shutdowns helped win back public support, decisively placing Clinton in the driver's seat for reelection while raising doubts regarding the Republican Congress in the minds of voters.[3]

The very qualities that set the 105th Congress apart—its modest policy goals, its narrow majorities and internal strife, and especially in the House its weakened party leaders and ascendant committee leaders—led it to the partisan legacy for which it will always be remembered. This was the House's impeachment of President Clinton in December 1998. It was a bitter partisan climax for a Congress that began with a limited agenda. And it was caused, ironically, by the House's return to "regular order"—which is to say, deference to its committees.

THE 1996 ELECTIONS

Elections provide defining experiences for newly-elected officials, lessons for incumbents who survive, and models for those contemplating future races. In 1994, Republicans were guided by a nationalized platform that many thought hastened their historic takeover of Congress. Not one Republican incumbent was defeated, while thirty-four Democratic representatives and two senators lost their seats. Unhappy with either the congressional process or the policy it produced,[4] voters two years later nearly deprived the GOP of its newfound majority status. The parties fought to a virtual draw; there were no landslides, no mandates to be confidently claimed, and no compelling national messages.

The GOP's near-death experience in 1996 left it with the smallest House majority since 1952. After the 1996 elections, Republicans still outnumbered Democrats by twenty-one (228 to 207), a narrower margin than the twenty-five Republicans had two years earlier (230 to 205).[5] Although Democrats gained seven seats in the Northeast, Republicans continued their march on the South (with a net gain of four seats). In the Senate the Republicans gained two seats for a margin of fifty-five to forty-five. The impact was greater than this gain suggests, according to Drew, "because ideologically the new Republican senators moved the Senate further to the right."[6] But Republicans were still five votes short of the sixty required to shut off Democratic filibusters.

By retaining "control of the House," wrote Drew, "Republicans may have tacked down, but not nailed down, the realignment they were seeking."[7] A simple explanation of the election outcome is elusive given the multitude of possibilities: weak Democratic candidates; voters deliberately splitting their tickets in order to ensure a balance of power—a Republican Congress to check a Democratic White House; or voter backlash against an over-ambitious 104th Congress. It is, however, important to place such results in longer-term perspective. Each successive election is in some sense unique: new voters are added, former voters drop out, and a few even shift their vote from one party to another. The results turn on how many voters fall into each category.

In the 1996 elections the electorate divided itself roughly in thirds: Democrats (37 percent), Republicans (37 percent), and independents (26 percent).[8] Often voters who claim to be independents are in fact "closet partisans" who lean toward one party or the other. Adding these voters to the identifiers of the two parties gave the Democrats a slight edge (47 to 42 percent) in 1996, with about 11 percent true independents. These preferences, as measured by indices of party identification, have remained relatively stable over the past several elections, despite short-term fluctuations.

Party identification remains the most powerful single correlate of voting in congressional elections. In both 1994 and 1996, 77 percent of the electorate were party-line voters, supporting the candidate of the party with which they affiliated. In both of these elections, 17 percent of voters were party defectors, party identifiers choosing a candidate of another party. In both elections, only 6 percent of voters claimed to have no party identification or leaning. This distribution of voters has remained fairly stable since the 1970s.[9]

In 1996, admittedly a very partisan year, better than nine of every ten Democrats and Republicans voted for their parties' candidates; independents' votes split fifty-fifty. Compared with the previous congressional election, the GOP lost support from independents (six percentage points) and from Democrats (three points); their support from those who voted Republican was virtually unchanged.[10]

"All politics islocal," former House Speaker Thomas P. O'Neill Jr. (D-Mass.) used to say. Candidates employ personal styles and issues to appeal to the voters of their districts and states. At the same time local contests are affected by current national events and affairs. In 1996 these included a robust economy and what many considered the excesses of the Republican 104th Congress. The increasing involvement of national party committees and allied interest groups (e.g., labor unions and environmental groups for the Democrats, small business and the religious right for the Republicans) has imposed national coordination upon congressional campaigns, with the result that a mix of local and national forces converge on congressional elections to shape their conduct and their results.[11]

In order to inoculate themselves against the unpopular political idiosyncrasies in Washington, incumbents attempt to separate themselves from the Washington power brokers. In 1996, many Republicans deliberately distanced themselves from the 104th Congress and its record by running their reelection campaigns as independent voices for their districts instead of rubber-stamping then-Speaker Gingrich's policies. Many Republicans of the class of 1994, for instance, "localized" their records by voting intentionally against their party in procedural votes, simply to inflate their overall scores on opposition to the leadership.[12] For example, Representative Phil English (R-Pa.), fighting a tight race for reelection, even boasted about receiving a thank-you note from the White House for helping raise the minimum wage in an ad that read, "Even President Clinton thanked Phil English for his independent action on behalf of working families."[13] Similarly, Republican Senate veteran Mitch McConnell (R-Ky.) took credit for helping to save the school lunch program, and also claimed that he sometimes "goes against what his party is advocating."

Democratic challengers especially railed against the GOP's 104th Congress and its leader, Gingrich. In central Massachusetts' 3rd District, Democrat Jim McGovern coined a winning slogan in his bid to oust sophomore Representative Peter I. Blute (R-Mass.): "If you wouldn't vote for Newt, why would you ever vote for Blute?" And in New Jersey, successful Democratic challenger Bill Pascrell Jr.'s campaign logo showed freshman Representative Bill Martini (R-N.J.) as a puppet on strings held by the Speaker.

Toward the end of the 1996 election campaign, the presidential contest took "an unexpected new turn" that may have profoundly affected control of the House. The disclosure of questionable campaign finance practices in soft-money fundraising by the Democratic National Committee and President Clinton's ceaseless efforts to raise money for his reelection stymied the Democrats' efforts to regain the House. Ironically, noted Drew, voters took out their anger more on Democratic congressional candidates than on President Clinton. In the congressional elections Drew found that "exit polls showed that the eighty-three percent of the voters who decided whom to vote for before the last week of the election favored the Democrats by four percent, while those who decided in the last week favored the Republicans by fourteen percent."[14]

An alternative explanation from political scientists pointed to the Democratic candidates themselves as culprits in the party's failure to retake the House. The candidate recruitment season for 1996 took place in the shadow of the 1994 elections, when Democratic prospects were at a low ebb. Strategically-minded Democratic potential candidates could hardly be blamed for concluding that they should bide their time and sit out their races. As a result, the party fielded fewer "quality challengers" than usual.[15] The Democrats netted an eight-seat gain, whereas eighteen seats were needed for a majority.

In the natural process of membership renewal, voters normally turn relatively few members out of office. Many incumbents leave Capitol Hill voluntarily to retire, to run for another office, or to follow other pursuits. In 1992 and 1994, a combination of voluntary retirements and electoral defeats of incumbent members brought in 196 new representatives and twenty-nine new senators. And the 1996 elections added seventy-four freshman representatives and fifteen new senators.

When the 105th Congress convened, therefore, a majority of House members had been elected in the 1990s. High electoral turnovers in three successive elections made the chamber significantly younger and more junior than it was when the decade began. Less familiar with the institution, the culture, the folkways, and the history of Congress, younger members have often shunned the intraparty or bipartisan comity needed to grease the gears of the legislative process.[16]

The Senate's membership was altered to a lesser degree by recent elections. As in the House, nearly a majority of senators serving in the 105th Congress were elected in the 1990s; though despite respectable turnovers in 1992 and 1994, the average age and seniority remained fairly steady. A high number of retirements in 1996, however, foretold a changing of the guard not unlike that already witnessed in the House.

RETURN TO NORMALCY

The dramatic 104th formed the backdrop for the Congress that followed. Like all Congresses, the 105th flowed from the most recent elections that produced it; indeed, the 1996 elections conveyed fresh messages that influenced incumbents' behavior as well as that of freshly elected members. Campaigns were marked by incumbent protection and, for not a few candidates, a veiled appeal to the status quo. Many Republican lawmakers felt "that if they held the House for the second time in a row," they could retain it for "ten to twenty years."[17] Republicans could use the incumbency advantage "to protect their position and to extend their power—just as the Democrats had for so long."[18] Career-oriented members found that climbing a traditional internal ladder—paying their dues by working through the committee system, earning their stripes by rising through the ranks of the formal party structure, and developing expertise with the support of a caucus of members with shared interests—aids in the pursuit of personal political goals. The 105th emphasized a more traditional model of congressional power, crafting most legislation in committees, with Republican leaders forced to bargain with the Clinton administration. Even freshman Republican members came to Capitol Hill set on working with Democrats to find solutions, a 180-degree reversal from the aggressive reform-minded Class of 1994, who arrived intent on transforming Congress and the nation on their terms.[19]

TAMING THE GOP AGENDA FOR THE LONG HAUL

The Republicans of the 104th Congress arrived with a sense of missionary zeal. "They came to town in January 1995 sweeping all before them, the conquering heroes with justified sense of satisfaction that they could truly change America," said Senator John McCain (R-Ariz.). "Now in 1997," speaking of the House, "they came back, barely keeping their majority and with a wounded leader," McCain said. "I don't know," he continued, "of a greater example of how things can change in this town."[20]

The 105th Congress thus found the Republicans in a chastened mood. With the previous Congress's budget deadlock with President Clinton, internal party disagreements about how to handle pressing agenda items, the collapse of then-Speaker Gingrich's own public support, and the public's discontent with partisan bickering fresh in mind, Republicans gathered to organize the 105th Congress with far less consensus on their agenda, more open divisions among their coalition, tarnished leaders who were somewhat less united than they had been, committee chairs who felt more free to stray from the wishes of the party bosses, and significant differences in the tactics and temperaments of the members. Although, their confidence in the rightness of their cause seemed undiminished.[21]

Many returnees from the Class of 1994 thus tempered their conservatism with a desire to fashion laws through compromise and gain more legislative influence. "I didn't come to Washington to burn all the buildings down," said Representative Roger Wicker (R-Miss.) who had served as class president in 1995.[22] Divided party government, at least for the time being, seemed to foster a rhetoric of cooperation that reflected recognition of the need for bipartisan policy development, especially within committees.[23]

Dubbed the "implementation Congress" by then-Speaker Gingrich, the GOP had a smaller majority presaging an institution seemingly more interested in solutions than partisan agendas. "Making progress on the Republican agenda does not require us to create fireworks," House Majority Leader Richard Armey (R-Tex.) said. "It requires us to simply get down to work."[24] "I think some people are going to have to accept the concept of incremental change, and realize that even if you can't get something this year, you're still closer the next year," noted Representative Ernest J. Istook Jr. (R-Okla.), who two years earlier had initiated a project with leadership support to limit the amount of private money that nonprofit organizations, even such as the Red Cross and the Girl Scouts of America, could spend on "political advocacy."[25]

Two months into the new 105th Congress, House Republicans issued a thirteen-point list of legislative priorities entitled "Creating a Better America for Ourselves and Our Children." The new Republican agenda was far less specific than the 1994 manifesto and embraced no set timetable for implementation. Gingrich was also slow to consult with interest groups on the agenda items.[26] The priorities did not take hold in the Republican conference, mainly because they lacked details and were not vetted by the committee chairs empowered to execute GOP legislation.

Significantly, then-Speaker Gingrich used a special order speech to deliver his agenda message to Republican colleagues. Gingrich would typically deliver such messages "in closed-door meetings of House Republicans, bolstered by written material prepared by the House Republican Conference."[27] Instead, after several months of ceding the agenda-setting role to other GOP leaders during his ethics investigation, Gingrich went to the well from the Speaker's dais to speak before a near-empty chamber. This revived a tactic he had used in the early 1980s to gain prominence in the House, when he used C-SPAN coverage of the House proceedings in his drive to end the GOP's long minority status.

THE TORTOISE BEATS THE HARE: CONGRESS OF "REGULAR ORDER"

The dramatic alteration in majority and minority status was a major ingredient in the legislative pace of the 104th Congress. In shock over losing control, Democrats were slow to adjust to their newfound minority status. At the outset of the 104th Congress, Republicans were determined to pass their strong and aggressive agenda regardless of the degree of opposition.[28]

House Republican leaders put extraordinary pressure on committees to report legislation quickly. To ensure that the committees of jurisdiction moved with speed on the Contract, Gingrich used the leverage of his singular support among the rank-and-file, naming the new chairs of all standing committees, departing in four instances from seniority to lend his support to more activist and committed conservatives. C. Lawrence Evans and Walter J. Oleszek reported that "after one chairman informed Gingrich that his committee was having trouble meeting the contract timetable, the Speaker responded, 'If you can't do it, I will find somebody who will.'"[29] Hearings and markups were often rushed.[30] Party leaders, "and task forces on which inexperienced freshmen predominated, exercised considerable influence on the substance of legislation in committee or through post-committee adjustments."[31] Standing committees were frequently bypassed not only to move legislation more rapidly, but also for other substantive reasons such as circumventing outside committee clienteles.[32]

One hundred days later, House Republicans had passed all but one component of the Contract with America. But this achievement came at a high cost. After the Contract and the first one hundred days were successfully negotiated, some younger lawmakers hinted that they might retire from the House because of the late nights, frenzied pace, and stress that was placed on their families. Others worried about the capacity of members to make intelligent decisions when they were plagued by overwork and little sleep. Deliberation and the quality of legislation suffered. As Barbara Sinclair related, "many Republicans, members and staff alike concede[d] privately that the legislation brought to the floor was sloppy at best; the careful substantive work had not been done."[33] The Speaker and other party leaders expressed sympathy about the hectic schedule, but family-friendly scheduling clearly took a backseat to the need to move an ambitious legislative agenda.

As a routine matter, of course, Congress does not work at such a frenetic pace. Revolutions can be exhausting and difficult to sustain given the institutionalization of certain norms—seniority, apprenticeship, and reciprocity—and with an institution that is sequential, approaching solutions in small, discrete steps, building policy from the bottom up. Elaborate written rules and practices that govern the conduct of both the House and the Senate make it extremely difficult to consider legislation at dizzying speed. By the start of the 105th Congress, Speaker Gingrich agreed to a more regular order of activity: "The Contract with America was a commitment of a legislative minority to a specific set of activities in the first 100 days. This is the commitment of a legislative majority to two years of work. We're going to be pleasant. . . . We're going to have to learn to get things done."[34]

Lawmakers, especially in the House, shrank from a revolutionary agenda and bent to political realities. "Last Congress was a speeding train," asserted a Republican leadership aide. "This Congress is more of a freight train."[35] Another GOP aide added, "We are still struggling to learn how to be a majority, and we have not figured out how the Democrats use the carrot and stick successfully. Until there is change, we are in what is, quote, the status quo."[36]

The 105th was more friendly to members' personal needs. Committees were slow to organize themselves into subcommittees, set their agendas, and even outline broad themes. Both chambers hardly met in January, recessing all but four days. February was not much different; lawmakers were in session just eleven days. Tuesdays were rescheduled for the order of the day, and vote stacking was common. In the first six weeks of 1997, the House was in session just forty-nine hours and the Senate just ninety-six hours, compared to the breakneck 104th Congress, in which 183 recorded votes were held between Opening Day and March 1. From January to March of 1997 there were sixty roll-call votes in the House, eleven of those being on a single subject, term limits, compared to 271 in 1995. The number of bills passed dropped by 25 percent from four years earlier—just sixty-eight bills were passed within the first three months of the 105th Congress, compared to 111 in the 104th Congress—while the days in session declined slightly.[37] Workload comparisons of the first sessions of the two Congresses are presented in table 7.1.

The moderate start produced partisan and factional snipping that the 105th Congress was doing nothing. Democrats had an obvious explanation. "This is not a mechanical problem," declared Representative Barney Frank (D-Mass). "They have nothing to do."[38] Grumbling was heard, especially from some of the hard-core GOP members. "If I had to swear under oath, I would say they don't have a strategy," Representative Jay

Table 7.1: Congressional Workload Comparisons, 1995 and 1997

	104th Congress, 1st session			105th Congress, 1st session		
	House	Senate	Total	House	Senate	Total
Days in session						
	167	211	378	132	153	285
Hours in session						
	1,525	1,839	3,364	1,003	1,093	2,096
Measures introduced						
	3,430	1,801	5,231	3,728	1,840	5,568
Bills						
	2,840	1,514	4,354	3,088	1,568	4,656
Joint resolutions						
	137	45	182	106	39	145
Concurrent resolutions						
	130	36	166	200	70	270
Simple resolutions						
	324	206	530	334	163	497
Measures reported						
	400	249	649	373	248	621
Yea/Nay votes						
	299	613	912	285	298	583
Total measures passed						
	483	346	829	544	385	929
Public bills enacted						
	60	28	88	93	49	142

SOURCE: Data are found in *Congressional Record* (104th Cong., 1st. sess.), Jan. 3, 1996, D1535, and *Congressional Record* (105th Cong., 2nd sess.), Dec. 15, 1997, D1281.

Dickey (R-Ark.) complained of the new agenda. "I would say that the leadership was not being as good in power as it was getting into power."[39] "Even some senior Republicans," according to Richard Cohen, complained that the Speaker did not send clear enough "signals about his plans. 'There is a perception, which I share, that the leaders have not always shot straight with us,' said Representative Joe L. Barton (R-Texas). 'They have had to resort to sleight of hand to bring some bills to the floor.'"[40]

Then-Speaker Gingrich conceded that Republicans had problems. "Managing the process of change is much more difficult than maintaining the status quo," he said. "It is not altogether surprising that we have made mistakes, experienced conflict or doubts, and undergone moments of uncertainty. It is not even surprising that we have, at times, forgotten that we are a team and lost sight of the fact that we all have the same goal."[41]

In fact, the 105th Congress was not necessarily less productive than its predecessor, at least if one compares the first sessions (see table 7.1). To be sure, the pace was more leisurely: the two chambers spent about a third less time in session in 1997 than they had two years earlier. And there were fewer floor votes. But more measures were passed in the two chambers, and more measures enacted into public law, than during the 104th Congress's frenetic first session.

NARROW PARTY MARGINS IN BOTH CHAMBERS

In closely divided chambers, any partisan defections can profoundly affect the outcome of issues. Those outside the parties' mainstream can have great influence. This especially applies to those in the center of the political spectrum: conservative Democrats and moderate to liberal Republicans. Partisan strength in voting is entrenched in what some argue is merely constituency differences; that is, partisans vote together because they represent like political and demographic areas. According to this reasoning, legislators do not follow party lines whenever they feel their party's policies will not benefit their constituents.

Today's Democratic mavericks tend to be from nonminority southern districts, whose voters typically are to the right of the party's mainstream. (Six of them—five representatives and one senator—decamped to the GOP after the 1994 elections.) To hold voter loyalty in these areas, the remaining Democratic officeholders must avoid their party's mainstream course. Fifteen of the thirty-three Democrats who voted with their party less than 70 percent of the time in 1997 were southerners.[42]

Republican mavericks, in contrast, are mostly from New England or the Northeast corridor, where voters generally fall to the left of the party's center. In 1997, all six Republicans who gave 70 percent or less support to their party were northeasterners.

Congress is an institution in which the majority leads. When that majority is sizable, leaders can exercise discretion over what transpires on the House and Senate floors. When the majority is slim, as in the 105th, leaders must work harder to construct winning coalitions. "Majorities are built in Congress, not elected to it," wrote John Manley.[43]

Constructing winning coalitions was not easy for the 105th Congress. Divisions and rifts in the GOP between moderates and conservatives were legislative hurdles—growing pains that normally come with majority status.[44] Often such divisions lead to the emergence of significant and potentially cohesive voting factions based on ideology, region, or particular policy positions. Gingrich and his lieutenants were forced to woo dissident factions in their own flock as well as seek defectors from the opposition in order to negotiate policy matters with the White House.

When political scientists began to do serious roll-call voting analysis in the 1950s, it was obvious that party and ideology were quite distinct ingredients, despite measurable differences between the parties. The major reason was constituency splits within the two parties.[45] In the late 1930s a conservative coalition of Republicans and southern Democrats emerged in a reaction against the New Deal.[46] Historically, this coalition was stronger in the Senate than in the House, but its success rate in both chambers was formidable during the 1938–1964 period—no matter which party controlled the White House or Capitol Hill. The coalition reappeared in 1981 as President Reagan captured votes of conservative Democrats on budget, tax, and social issues, while pulling mainstream Democrats toward more conservative positions on other issues.[47]

The sorting out of the two parties' constituency differences helps to explain a twenty-five year upsurge in lawmakers' party loyalty. Rising numbers of the Democrats' southern flank are African–Americans. The dwindling numbers of Democrats representing conservative districts (including the Blue Dog Democrats) try to put distance between themselves and their leaders. By the same token, the Republican congressional party is more uniformly conservative than it used to be. In the South the most conservative areas now tend to elect Republicans, not Democrats. Elsewhere Democrats have captured many areas once represented by GOP liberals. The decline of archconservative Democrats and liberal Republicans, especially in the House, underlies much of the ideological cohesion within, and the chasm between, contemporary Capitol Hill parties.[48]

Partisan repositioning has shrunk the ideological center in the two chambers. "Democrats are perched on the left, Republicans on the right, in both the House and the Senate as ideological centers of the two parties have moved markedly apart," wrote Sarah A. Binder.[49] In other words, the two parties are more cohesive internally, and farther apart externally, than they were in the recent past; life on Capitol Hill has become commonly acrimonious. The proportion of centrists—conservative Democrats and moderate Republicans—hovered around thirty percent in the 1960s and 1970s, according to Binder.[50] In the mid-1990s, only about one in ten lawmakers fell into this centrist category. The self-named Blue Dogs and the New Democrat Coalition, each claiming twenty-five to thirty-five members, emerged as a powerful voting bloc during the 104th Congress and had the potential to be a powerful voice for compromise in a narrowly divided 105th Congress. So did the moderate Republican groups.

With the 105th Congress's narrow partisan margin, almost any cohesive group was in fact able to wreak havoc in the GOP ranks. Such was the effect of the abortive attempt to overthrow Speaker Gingrich in the summer of 1997. The core dissidents were eleven or so ultra-conservative members, most from the class of 1994, who accused their leaders of abandoning the revolutionary goals typified by the Contract.

The Family Caucus and Conservative Action Team (CAT), successors to the Republican Study Group, were two conservative alliances that experienced a surge in their ranks and in their clout during the 105th Congress. Both groups promote a socially conservative, anti-tax agenda. Although previously excluded from the leadership's weekly strategy sessions, in the 105th they not only had a seat at that table but also sent emissaries to meetings of the moderate Tuesday Group.[51] Comprised of roughly seventy members from all regions of the country, up from fifty in the 104th Congress, CAT took an active role in formulating the Republican agenda, and it enhanced its organizational infrastructure to meet that goal. The group hired a permanent staffer to coordinate its activities and to recruit new members, and even encouraged the creation of a Senate counterpart (SCAT).

Moderate to liberal Republicans, such as those in the Tuesday Group (formerly known as the Tuesday Lunch Bunch), had but forty-five to fifty senior moderate to liberal members, mainly from northeastern, marginal districts, and the newer Main Street Coalition, boasted only thirty members.[52] "The more decidedly conservative bent of the recent Republican majority initially made observers dismiss" the influence of these moderate to liberal Republicans, noted Robin Kolodny.[53]

Their influence enhanced by the narrow GOP majority, these centrist factions were significant to winning coalitions. As Kolodny argued, "liberal Republicans exercised considerable *negative* influence on the congressional agenda championed by the majority of the Republican conference." Tuesday Group members often "removed or blocked controversial proposals" from the common party agenda by pressuring the leadership (by threatening to oppose procedural motions or making speeches on the floor against the party's position), offering motions or amendments on the floor to counteract objectionable measures, or actually defecting from the party's position on several amendment votes.[54]

FEW STRUCTURAL OR PROCEDURAL CHANGES

The House of Representatives adopted for the 104th Congress an extensive set of rules changes which included, among other things, revisions in the House committee system, term limits for House leaders, alterations in floor procedure, and a series of administrative changes designed to cut costs and depoliticize House operations. These changes were the most dramatic alteration in the House procedural environment in two decades. They were intended to make the committee system more accountable to the Republican Conference through the party leaders.[55] On the Senate side of the Capitol, power also was shifting, but with greater emphasis on continuity. Republican senators initially focused on a single unsuccessful reorganization proposal aimed at substantially altering the filibuster rule, but adopted a list of changes from the Mack Task Force later in the session.

THE PEOPLE'S HOUSE: CONTINUED PARTISANSHIP

The extreme centralization of the 104th Congress was a high water mark, but was in no way inconsistent with long-term trends. By the time the 104th Congress adjourned, it was apparent that House leaders, having overreached their powers, needed to placate committee leaders and internal factions, not to mention the Senate and the White House. As the 105th Congress convened, many hard-core conservatives, including the firebrand sophomores from the Class of 1994, had lowered their sights somewhat;

the badly damaged Speaker was striving to salvage some of his lost reputation and power. "As more significant policy divisions emerged among House Republicans in 1996," noted Evans and Oleszek, "committee chairs would retain substantial control over their own agendas."[56] At the end of the 1997 session, Representative David M. McIntosh (R-Ind.) noted of then-Speaker Gingrich, "People will no longer automatically follow him blindly."[57] The Senate leadership, especially new Majority Leader Trent Lott, pursued the classic course of seeking consensus among the Republican Conference members.

Republicans offered only a modest package of rules changes in the 105th Congress. The Republican Conference avoided reforming committees, opting instead for minor procedural streamlining. Committee and subcommittee seats in the 105th Congress are listed in table 7.2. One change was a requirement that committees accept testimony from witnesses only under oath. Dubbed "truth-in-testifying," the new House rule expanded to all committees the practice followed by the House Government Reform and Oversight Committee of swearing in anyone who testified at a hearing. Aimed at nonprofit as well as profit organizations, this requirement directed witnesses to disclose the amount and source of federal grants or contracts they or their organizations had received over the previous three years (House Rule XI, clause 2 (g)).

The rules package contained other changes: a requirement that committee reports include a statement citing the constitutional authority for legislation; that all committee documents be available in electronic form, as far as feasible; stricter rules on limitation amendments to prevent spending cuts contingent on open-ended requests for information; and a repeal of the prohibition on committees sitting while the House is in session without first getting special leave from the House. Members cannot hand out campaign donations on the floor of the House, in the cloakrooms, or in the Speaker's Lobby. The GOP-inspired rule requiring three-fifths majority for House approval to increase income tax rates was amended to two-thirds majority. Finally, members and their staffs were required to submit to random drug tests.

Perhaps more noteworthy were the committee and procedural changes that did not happen. The makeup of the Ethics Committee was much debated, and although the membership of the committee continued to rotate, it was difficult to retain members on it (membership did remain in place in 1996–1997 for the Gingrich ethics case). At issue was whether or not the Committee should delegate the investigatory phase of its work to an outside body such as a temporary, independent commission. For the time being, the committee itself continued to shoulder this burden.

Table 7.2: Committee and Subcommittee Seats: 105th Congress (1997–1998)

SENATE

Committee (year created)	Members	Party Ratio	Sub-Units	Total Seats
Ag., Nutrition & For. (1825)	18	(10-8)	4	50
Appropriations (1867)	28	(15-13)	13	151
Armed Services (1816)	18	(10-8)	6	66
Banking, Housing & Urban Affairs (1913)	18	(10-8)	5	66
Budget (1975)	22	(12-10)	--	22
Commerce, Sci. & Trans. (1816)	20	(11-9)	7	99
Energy & Nat. Resources (1816)	20	(11-9)	4	62
Enviorn. & Public Works (1833)	18	(10-8)	4	54
Finance (1816)	20	(11-9)	5	80
Foreign Relations (1816)	18	(10-8)	7	71
Governmental Affairs (1921)	16	(9-7)	3	47
Indian Affairs (1977)	14	(8-6)	--	14
Judiciary (1816)	18	(10-8)	6	63
Labor & Hum. Resources (1869)	18	(10-8)	4	54

HOUSE OF REPRESENTATIVES

Committee (year created)	Members	Party Ratio	Sub-Units	Total Seats
Agriculture (1829)	50	(27-23)	5	149
Appropriations (1865)	60	(34-26)	13	202
National Security (1822)	55	(30-25)	7	187
Banking/Financial (1865)	53	(29-24)	5	155
Budget (1975)	43	(24-19)	--	43
Commerce (1795)	51	(28-23)	5	174
Science (1958)	46	(25-21)	4	125
Resources (1805)	50	(27-23)	5	139
Transportation (1837)	73	(40-33)	6	212
Ways & Means (1802)	39	(23-16)	5	105
International Relations (1822)	47	(26-21)	5	125
Govt. Reform/Oversight (1927)	43	(24-19)	7	124
Judiciary (1813)	35	(20-15)	5	99
Education & Work Force (1867)	45	(25-20)	5	124

Committee (year created)	Members	Party Ratios	Sub Units	Total Seats
Rules (1880)	13	(9-4)	2	27
House Oversight (1789)	25	(5-3)	--	8
Small Business (1975)	35	(19-16)	4	79
Veterans Affairs (1825)	29	(16-13)	3	59
Standards of Conduct (1967)	10	(5-5)	**	10
Select Intelligence (1977)	19	(9-7)	2	32
TOTALS	801	445-356	92	2178
MEMBERS' AVG.	1.8	56%-44%	3.1	5.0
104th CONGRESS	789		87	2103

Committee (year created)	Members	Party Ratios	Sub Units	Total Seats
Rules & Administration (1947)	16	(9-7)	--	16
Small Business (1980)	18	(10-8)	--	18
Veterans Affairs (1970)	12	(7-5)	--	12
Special Aging (1977)	18	(10-8)	--	18
Select Ethics (1977)	6	(3-3)	--	6
Select Intelligence (1977)	17	(10-9)	--	19
TOTALS	355	196-159	68	988
MEMBERS' AVG.	3.5	52%-48%	6.3	9.9
104th CONGRESS	333		68	1090

JOINT COMMITTEES

Committee (year created)	Members	Party Ratios	Sub Units	Total Seats
Economic (1946)	20	(12-8)	--	20
Library (H/A)	10	(6-4)	--	10
Printing (1846)	10	(6-4)	--	10
Taxation (1926)	10	(6-4)	--	10

*   Independent Member of House counted as Democrat.

** Committee divides into fact-finding and adjudicatory sections in dealing with specific cases of alleged wrongdoing.

Source: Compiled by authors.

Additionally, the GOP Conference rejected conservative proposals that would have limited the latitude of committee chairs. A proposal pushed by Rep. John Doolittle (R-Calif.) and his fellow CAT members would have given the full Conference membership the authority to review the appointment of subcommittee chairs. (These posts are now selected by full committee chairs and are generally based on seniority.) Also dropped was a proposal to strip chairs of the right to hire and fire subcommittee staff.

Finally, the Republican leadership abandoned, probably for good, the more sweeping proposals for overhaul of committees that had been bypassed two years earlier, but were still pushed by some reformers. On November 6, 1996, a GOP reform task force, led by Representative David Dreier (R-Calif.), offered several large-scale jurisdictional and procedural reform plans for the House committee system. Dreier's wide-ranging Task Force Report recommended the elimination of House panels whose membership fell below 50 percent compared to their levels at the end of the 103rd Congress, indicating a drop in desirability. Another proposal was to reorganize the House into eight committees under the headings of budget, economic affairs, defense and international relations, government operations and judiciary, human resources, natural resources, physical resources, and rules. Such a new strategy, the task force conceded, "would significantly disrupt the institutional culture and environment of the House, and it would take several years to assimilate to the resulting changes."[58]

THE SENATE: AN ISLAND OF RELATIVE TRANQUILITY

"Hewing to tradition and its prized status as the more restrained chamber," wrote Michael Wines, the "Senate began its 105th incarnation" with legislative ritual, the exchange "of elaborate courtesies," and "the swearing-in of thirty-four new and reelected members." Referring to the chamber as "an island of tranquillity," Senate Majority Leader Trent Lott (R-Miss.) laid out goals for creating a more genteel Senate, which included requiring senators to show up for votes on time, reducing inconvenience for those who are prompt, and preventing staff members on the floor from talking too much.[59]

Elected Majority Leader in June 1996, Lott was younger, more energetic, and more ideologically conservative than his predecessor, Bob Dole (R-Kans.). Lott instituted a form of leadership similar to his days as Senate Republican whip: congressional party leadership "as a team enterprise."[60] He relied on sharing duties with other elected leaders, attempting to provide more structure but also more openness to leadership endeavors, and striving to include as many senators as possible in party-based activities.

Another noteworthy addition to GOP Conference rules was a six-year term limit for chairs and for ranking members (for a maximum of twelve years). This would have only a delayed impact because current committee chairs are able to keep their posts until 2003. Another new rule stated that

Republicans who chair a committee could not simultaneously chair another committee or subcommittee, with chairpersons of Appropriations subcommittees exempted. This opened up about ten subcommittee slots to junior senators; all eleven Republicans elected in 1994 and five of the eight senators elected in 1996 became chairpersons in the 105th Congress.

A ten-member Reorganization Task Force was headed by Senator Robert F. Bennett (R-Utah). He declared that the filibuster and cloture would be off limits. "We need to separate tradition and continuity from anachronism," said Bennett.[61] The topics explored included biennial budgeting and appropriations cycles, "holds," electronic voting, broadening of committee jurisdictions, the use of task forces, financial management, and scheduling. Some of these items—especially altering senators' ability to delay or halt a bill's progress to the floor by placing a "hold" on it—could potentially affect the chamber in a major way. But the task force eschewed formal hearings or research reports in favor of informal consultations with colleagues.

LEADERSHIP VS. COMMITTEES

Decision-making processes in Congress represent an interaction of committees, parties, and the parent chambers, and the relative importance of each in the policy-making process varies over time.[62] The independent influence of committees varies inversely with the strength and influence of political parties.[63] Committee members must weigh opposing expectations of their parent chamber, their party, and their constituents; generally, the stronger and more disciplined the party caucuses in Congress, the less powerful the role of committees. For example, if the parties' electoral fortunes are tied to issues and decisions, party leaders often assume decision-making responsibilities that otherwise would fall to committees. Conversely, the less cohesive the party caucuses, the more powerful the role of committees. When attitudes on issues are highly fragmented within the party caucus, policy outcomes bear little on party fortunes, and autonomous committees are tolerated and even encouraged.

Practices adopted by the new GOP majority in 1995 continued a long-term weakening of the position of committee chairs. This transformation explicitly reversed the dominant 1950s portrait of autonomous and powerful committees in Congress—encouraged by weak party cohesion—that shaped policies within their jurisdictions in ways that satisfied the parochial interests of committee members.[64] Once in power, House Republicans devised procedural reforms that counterbalanced, and in some cases contradicted, the earlier norm of deference to committees. By giving priority to their party's agenda, committee members are seen to work toward enhancing the party's reputation and to achieving its policy goals.[65]

This party-dominated model is based on the premise that all legislators seek electoral success for their party, which in turn depends partially upon the congressional party's legislative record. The caucuses pressure committee members to behave as agents or instruments of the party. Because they control committee assignments, the congressional parties are able to frame the organization and policy outlook of their committee contingents. Additionally, committees rely on party leaders to schedule their legislation for floor consideration, giving party leaders additional leverage with the committees. These ties create an implicit contract between the parties and their committee members that constrains committee behavior; as a result, the majority party has effective control over committee decisions.[66] And because committee recommendations are constrained by the views of the majority party, committees lack autonomy.[67]

In the 105th Congress, however, committee chairs recaptured important ground in the tug and pull between leadership and committees.[68] To preserve his leadership, then-Speaker Gingrich agreed to changes that expanded committee chairs' power, restoring somewhat the former Democratic majority's model of strong, independent chairpersons and committees coordinated, but not coerced, by party leaders. As a start, he disbanded the Speaker's Advisory Group, an inner cabinet comprised of senior leaders and trusted colleagues, which had became the locus of long-range legislative strategy and agenda planning in the last Congress. At the same time, the larger, more representative GOP leadership group was expanded to include the committee chairs of Budget, Appropriations, Ways and Means, and Rules. As a result of retirements, new full committee chairs were named to the Government Reform and Oversight Committee, the Agriculture Committee, and the Science Committee. These new panel leaders, along with other chairs, were assured of their freedom to develop legislation largely without interference from the leadership of the kind that saw the major pieces of legislation in the 104th (such as Medicare, telecommunication, and appropriations bills) written in the Speaker's "Dinosaur Room" in the Capitol building. Committee chairs, said one congressional aide, "can run free as long as they're on a leash. The difference from the last Congress is that they had a choke collar on."[69]

Acting independently, committee members are freer to respond to the demands of their home constituents or to help important clientele groups achieve their policy aims.[70] More autonomous committees can better control their agendas in the issue areas within their jurisdiction.[71] Their policies are products of the preferences of committee members and their constituencies, rather than something delegated by the floor, the parties, or party leaders.[72]

POLICY CONSEQUENCES

Since the Republican capture of Congress in 1995, warfare between Capitol Hill and the White House has been a constant feature of politics in the nation's capital. Although the 105th Congress offered the hope of decreased conflict, it will forever be remembered for its fiery partisan climax: the impeachment of President Clinton in December 1998.

By the 1996 elections, there was some reason to believe that the Democratic president and the Republican Congress might move toward a working, if not a peaceful, coexistence. For his part, Clinton had moved to the political center, in the process co-opting Republican themes and issues, and neutralizing the GOP's earlier advantages on such issues as crime, welfare reform, minimum wage, and health insurance. Congressional Republicans, for their part, gained some of their objectives but only by making substantial concessions to the White House. Republicans gained political ground by, for example, forcing the president to veto a ban on "partial birth abortions," and to sign welfare reform and the Defense of Marriage Act (DOMA) that prohibited federal recognition of gay unions. Such compromises cooled the unyielding revolutionary spirit that had marked most of the 1995 session. At the same time it enabled Clinton to recover the initiative and, with the aid of Senate Democrats, to frame the legislative agenda. By compromising with Clinton, Nicol Rae has argued, Republicans in Congress were "vindicating the president's claims to represent the center ground in American politics and depriving their presidential nominee [Bob Dole] of valuable ammunition to use against the incumbent."[73]

Republican leadership in the meantime had retreated from the triumphalism of the 1994 takeover. In the Senate, the new majority leader, Trent Lott, was moving cautiously. But in the House the leadership was in open disarray. Speaker Gingrich's ethical problems, and especially his low public approval ratings, reduced his leverage with the rank and file membership. Moreover, the compromises reached with Clinton produced a backlash from those members who formed the core of Gingrich's support: the sizable corps of junior legislators prided themselves as outsiders and made clear their disdain for traditional models of congressional processes. Speaking before fellow Appropriations Committee members, Representative Mark W. Neumann (R-Wisc.) summarized the young turks' position by saying the Committee should "place a higher priority on principle than on passing measures to operate the government."[74]

The outbreak of the scandal involving the president's relationship with Monica S. Lewinsky raised White House–Capitol Hill tensions to an entirely new level of intensity. During the 105th Congress, the focus was almost exclusively on the House. Would it launch a congressional inquiry into the affair? Would articles of impeachment be the result? And would the House act to impeach the president?

When independent counsel Kenneth W. Starr submitted his report on September 9, 1998, the House began a course of action that led eventually to approval of two articles of impeachment. Ironically enough, the very adjustments that marked the 105th Congress's return to "regular order" served to raise the level of partisan warfare and, with it, the likelihood of impeachment.

The most fateful decision, as it turned out, was the adoption of H. Res. 581 which referred the whole matter to the Committee on the Judiciary.[75] As it became more apparent that the House would be asked to take action—but before the Starr report surfaced—Speaker Gingrich floated a proposal for a select panel to conduct the investigation. But his trial balloon was quickly punctured by Judiciary Chair Henry J. Hyde (R-Ill.), backed by his committee members and other committee chairs. In view of the leadership's earlier concessions to committees and their chairs, the Gingrich suggestion had virtually no chance of acceptance. Although select committees had been employed in early impeachment inquiries, Judiciary had processed recent impeachment cases—including the 1974 inquiry of President Richard Nixon and the Watergate affair. Hyde and his colleagues thus had jurisdictional precedent on their side. Moreover, Hyde himself was a figure accorded respect from both sides of the aisle (grudging from Democrats, to be sure). Any deviation in this high-profile case would be interpreted as a slight to a noted leader as well as a threat to committee prerogatives.

Referral of the inflammatory Starr report to the Judiciary Committee, however, was rather like handing matches to a pyromaniac. The committee had long enjoyed a reputation as the most partisan panel on Capitol Hill. The reasons are perfectly clear, and are rooted in the parties' recruitment patterns. Republicans had staffed the committee with staunch conservatives committed to conservative causes within the committee's jurisdiction: tough crime laws, permissive gun regulations, and constitutional amendments on such subjects as abortion, school prayer, flag desecration, and balanced budgets. Liberal Democrats gravitated to the committee in the 1960s to fight for civil rights legislation; more recently, they have been recruited to combat the above-mentioned conservative initiatives.

If the House was partisan, therefore, Judiciary was superpartisan. Committee Democrats in the 105th Congress were on average ten points more loyal to their party than the average for all Democrats (using *CQ Weekly*'s party unity scores). Republicans on the committee were on average more than five points more loyal than their House colleagues as a whole. By the same token, Democrats gave more support to President Clinton and Republicans less support than their party colleagues outside the committee (using *CQ Weekly*'s presidential support scores). As a result, Judiciary was virtually a caricature of Sarah Binder's portrait of the "vanishing middle" of the ideological spectrum. It is no exaggeration to say that there were *no* moderates on the committee, at least as measured by the most commonly used voting indices. There were, for example, none of the party mavericks that so enlivened the Watergate proceedings a quarter century earlier.

The partisan rancor manifested itself in ways both blatant and subtle. Chairman Hyde's choice of David P. Schippers as head counsel for the inquiry, an old friend who claimed to have been a Democrat, was so bitterly anti-Clinton that he helped the minority Democrats circle the wagons in the president's defense. The decision to release Starr's argumentative report immediately—before members had a chance to read, much less consider, the document—encouraged members to stake out their positions before, rather than after, any deliberation or debate had taken place. The raucous demeanor of many members, Republicans and Democrats alike, during the televised hearings merely reinforced the growing conviction of members and the general public that the whole process was tainted by partisanship.

The special House session on impeachment took place, of course, in the wake of the 1998 elections. Republican leadership was in visible disarray. Chastened by the loss of five House seats (after a large gain had been expected), Speaker Gingrich had abruptly abdicated and was exerting no leadership on the impeachment question. His heir-apparent, Appropriations Chair Bill Livingston (R-La.), gave every indication of wanting the issue resolved at the earliest possible moment. Meanwhile, Majority Whip Tom DeLay (R-Tex.), arguably the most effective member of the leadership group, was whipping rank-and-file Republicans to support impeachment. On the other side of the aisle, Minority Leader Richard A. Gephardt (D-Mo.) was carefully building support for the president among Democrats. He was aided not only by the Republicans' ill-concealed zeal, but by the continuing public support for keeping the president in office.

In the end, the votes on the four articles of impeachment—the last actions taken by the 105th Congress—were mainly along partisan lines. Of the 1,740 votes cast by House members on the four articles of impeachment—two of which were adopted—a total of 92 percent followed partisan lines; Republicans supporting the president's impeachment, Democrats resisting it.[76] It was a partisan conclusion to a Congress than had initially promised a more moderate demeanor.

CONCLUSION

Unlike the partisan intensity that characterized the 104th, party cohesion in the 105th was less pronounced and the inter-party warfare less visible, visceral, and confrontational. Such a fluid environment offered greater opportunities for members to be creative and entrepreneurial, but also posed greater risk that members' gambits would fail for their misjudgments. The long-term trends—mainly strengthened party leaders with the capacity to influence or bypass committees—seem likely to survive. As Barbara Sinclair has pointed out, the trend toward leadership management of legislation predated the Republican takeover and is likely to survive temporary leadership setbacks.[77]

Much of the "unorthodox" behavior of the Republican majority in 1995 was reversed or modified in 1996, as the full impact of the American governmental system and the two-year House election cycle became apparent. These constraints on congressional change, according to Rae, are a perfect late-twentieth-century illustration of the precepts set out by James Madison's celebrated *Federalist* essays Nos. 10 and 51.[78] A new popular majority was elected to control the branch of government closest to the people, the House of Representatives, reflecting widespread popular demands for change and reform. To a large extent the new majority was able to fulfill its mandate by confirming the shift in the direction of American public policy toward economic and social conservatism, and by implementing significant institutional reforms of Congress. As the Republican program of the 104th Congress began to encounter significant popular resistance the constitutional checks provided by the Senate and the presidency arrested the Republicans' "revolution."[79] Further, as Republicans began to approach reelection in 1996, they found themselves compelled to fall back on the same incumbency protection tactics that characterized congressional elections in the last two decades of Democratic rule—accommodation, compromise, and attention to local concerns, rather than intense agenda change and implementation.

The impeachment debates and votes in late 1998 tended to obscure this readjustment. They highlighted the most partisan aspects of the contemporary Congress, and diverted attention from the moderating influences. Partisanship remains potent in Washington policy-making, even when both Republicans and Democrats strive to move toward the ideological mean.

NOTES

1.   Quotations from Guy Gugliotta, "In the Cradle of Republican Revolution, a Legislative Lullaby," *WP*, March 1, 1997, A4.

2.   Juliet Eilperin and Jim Vande Hei, "Some Wounds Never Heal: Today's GOP Leadership Has Roots in 'Guerilla' Warriors of the 1980s," *RC*, October 2, 1997, 1.

3.   Elizabeth Drew, *Whatever It Takes: The Real Struggle for Political Power in America* (New York: Viking Penguin, 1997), 44; and Nicol C. Rae, *Conservative Reformers: The Freshmen Republicans and the Lessons of the 104th Congress* (Armonk, NY: M.E. Sharpe, 1998), 169.

4.   John R. Hibbing and Elizabeth Theiss-Morse, *Congress as Public Enemy: Public Attitudes Toward American Political Institutions* (New York: Cambridge University Press, 1995).

5.   The figures include Rep. Bernard Sanders (I-Vt.), who commonly votes with the Democrats.

6.   Drew, *Whatever It Takes,* 237.

7.   Drew, *Whatever It Takes,* 238; also see 240, 47.

8.   Regina Dougherty, Everett C. Ladd, David Wilber, and Lynn Zayachkinsky, eds., *America at the Polls 1996* (Storrs, Conn.: Roper Center for Public Opinion Research, 1997).

9.   Norman J. Ornstein, Thomas E. Mann, and Michael J. Malbin, *Vital Statistics on Congress, 1997–1998* (Washington, DC: CQ Press, 1998), 74–75.

10.   Dougherty et al., *America at the Polls.*

11.   Thomas Edsall, "Issue Coalitions Take on Political Party Functions," *WP*, August 8, 1996, A1; and Ruth Marcus, "Outside Groups Pushing Election Laws Into Irrelevance," *WP*, August 8, 1996, A9.

12.   Rae, *Conservative Reformers*, 207.

13.   Howard Kurtz, "On the Defensive, Republicans Go Their Own Way in Ads," *WP*, October 3, 1996, A10.

14.   Drew, *Whatever It Takes*, 196, 241.

15.   Gary C. Jacobson, "The 105th Congress: Unprecedented and Unsurprising," in *The Election of 1996*, ed. Michael Nelson (Washington, DC: CQ Press, 1997), 143–166, at 154.

16.   Craig Winneker, "Forty Years of Conflict," *RC*, May 15, 1995.

17.   Quotations, Drew, *Whatever It Takes*, 4–5.

18.   David R. Mayhew, *Congress: The Electoral Connection* (New Haven: Yale University Press, 1974); and Morris P. Fiorina, *Congress: Keystone of the Washington Establishment* (New Haven: Yale University Press, 1977).

19.   Carroll J. Doherty and Jeffrey L. Katz, "Firebrand GOP Class of '94 Warms to Life on the Inside," *CQWR*, January 24, 1998, 155–163.

20.   Dan Balz, "Subdued GOP Resumes Lead with Eye to Past; Party Retained Hold on Power, Lost Consensus on Agenda," *WP*, January 8, 1997, A9.

21.   Rae, *Conservative Reformers.*

22.   Quoted in Doherty and Katz, 159.

23.   Christopher J. Deering and Steven S. Smith, *Committees in Congress*, 3rd ed. (Washington, DC: CQ Press, 1997).

24.   Quotations from Laurie Kellman, "Armey Takes a Larger Role," *Washington Times*, February 28, 1997, A1, A13.

25.   The term, according to the measure, included "carrying on propaganda, or otherwise attempting to influence legislation or agency action, including, but not limited to, monetary or in-kind contributions, preparation and planning activities, research and other background work, endorsements, publicity, coordination with such activities of others, and similar activities." *Congressional Record*, August 3, 1995, H8385.

26.   Laurie Kellman, "Gingrich's New Agenda Excites Few Republicans," *Washington Times*, May 18, 1997, A1.

27.   John E. Yang, "Gingrich Revisits Backbench Strategy: Speaker Makes Use of C-SPAN, Empty Chamber to Deliver Message," *WP*, March 18, 1997, A10.

28.   James G. Gimpel, *Fulfilling the Contract: The First 100 Days* (Boston: Allyn and Bacon, 1996).

29.   Quoted in C. Lawrence Evans and Walter J. Oleszek, *Congress Under Fire: Reform Politics and the Republican Majority* (Boston: Houghton Mifflin Company, 1997), 120.

30.   Barbara Sinclair, *Unorthodox Lawmaking: New Legislative Processes in the U.S. Congress* (Washington, DC. CQ Press, 1997), 226.

31.   Sinclair, 226.

32.   Roger H. Davidson, "Building the Republican Regime: Leaders and Committees," in *New Majority or Old Minority? The Impact of Republicans on Congress*, ed. Nicol C. Rae and Colton C. Campbell (Lanham, MD: Rowman & Littlefield, 1999), esp. 79–80.

33.   Sinclair, *Unorthodox Lawmaking*, 226.

34.   Quoted in Dan Balz and John Yang, "Republicans Set Legislative Priorities," *WP*, March 7, 1997, A10.

35.   Jennifer Bradley, "Democrats Hit GOP Work Pace," *RC*, March 6, 1997, 1.

36.   Jennifer Bradley, "Democrats Ready a Welcome Back Attack," *RC*, April 7, 1997, 1.

37.   Bradley, "Democrats Ready a Welcome Back Attack."

38.   Quoted in Bradley, "Democrats Hit GOP Work Pace."

39.   Quoted in Kellman, "Gingrich's New Agenda Excites Few Republicans."

40.   Quoted in Richard E. Cohen, "Beginning of the End," *NJ*, July 26, 1997, 1516–1517.

41.   Quoted in Cohen, "Beginning of the End."

42.   Calculated from *CQWR*, January 3, 1998, 36–37.

43.   John F. Manley, "The Conservative Coalition in Congress," *American Behavioral Scientist* 17 (December 1973): 223–247, at 224.

44.   Charles E. Cook, "The Onus to Beat 'Do-Nothing' Rap Falls to Chairmen," *RC*, May 12, 1997, 6.

45.   Julius Turner, *Party and Constituency*: Pressures on Congress (Baltimore: Johns Hopkins University Press, 1951).

46.   Manley, "Conservative Coalition"; Barbara Sinclair, *Congressional Realignment: 1925–1978* (Austin: University of Texas Press, 1982); and Mack C. Shelley, *The Permanent Majority: The Conservative Coalition in the United States Congress* (Tuscaloosa: University of Alabama Press, 1983).

47.   Robert J. Donovan, "For America, a New Coalition?" *Los Angeles Times*, July 6, 1981, A4.

48.   David W. Rohde, "Electoral Forces, Political Agenda, and Partisanship in the House and Senate," in *The Postreform Congress*, ed. Roger H. Davidson (New York: St. Martin's Press, 1992).

49.   Sarah A. Binder, "The Disappearing Political Center," *The Brookings Review*, Fall 1996, 36–39.

50.   Sarah Binder's definition of centrists in "The Disappearing Political Center" is those members who are closer to the ideological midpoint between the two parties than to the ideological center of their own party.

51.   Juliet Eilperin and Rachel Van Dongen, "The Insider's Guide to House Factions," *RC*, January 20, 1997, 1.

52.   Other caucuses represent the hard-core partisans on both sides of the aisle: e.g., the Mainstream Conservative Alliance, the Congressional Black Caucus, the Progressive Caucus, and the Hispanic Caucus.

53.   Robin Kolodny, "Moderate Success: Majority Status and the Changing Nature of Factionalism in the House Republican Party," in *New Majority or Old Minority?*, 153.

54.   Kolodny, "Moderate Success," quote 154, also 158–159.

55.   Evans and Oleszek, *Congress Under Fire*, 129.

56.   C. Lawrence Evans and Walter J. Oleszek, "Procedural Features of House Republican Rule," in *New Majority or Old Minority?*, 124.

57.   Alison Mitchell, "Gingrich Emerging From Self-Exile, Humbler, Wary and Thinner," *NYT*, October 27, 1997, A18.

58.   Juliet Eilperin, "Committee Reform Fervor Fades as New Drier Report Highlights Obstacles to Eliminating More House Panels," *RC*, November 14, 1996, 10.

59.   Michael Wines, "The 105th Congress: The Senate; Manners Will Matter, Leaders Caution," *NYT*, January 8, 1997, B8.

60.   Barbara Sinclair, "Partisan Imperatives and Institutional Constraints: Republican Party Leadership in the House and Senate," in *New Majority or Old Minority?*, 36.

61.   Helen Dewar, "Will Brass Spittoons Survive Move to Modernize Senate?," *WP*, January 15, 1997, A17.

62.   Deering and Smith, *Committees in Congress*.

63.   Colton C. Campbell and Roger H. Davidson, "Coalition Building in Congress: The Consequences of Partisan Change," in *The Interest Group Connection: Electioneering, Lobbying, and Policymaking in Washington*, ed. Paul

Herrnson, Ronald Shaiko, and Clyde Wilcox (Chatham, NJ: Chatham House, 1998), 119–123.

64.   Kenneth A. Shepsle, "The Changing Textbook Congress," in *Can Government Govern?*, ed. John Chubb and Paul Peterson (Washington, DC: Brookings, 1989).

65.   D. Roderick Kiewiet and Mathew D. McCubbins, *The Logic of Delegation: Congressional Parties and the Appropriations Process* (Chicago: University of Chicago Press, 1991); Gary W. Cox and Mathew D. McCubbins, *Legislative Leviathan: Party Government in the House* (Berkeley: University of California Press, 1993); Barbara Sinclair, *Legislators, Leaders, and Lawmaking* (Baltimore: Johns Hopkins University Press, 1995); Sarah A. Binder, "The Partisan Bias of Procedural Choice: Allocating Parliamentary Rights in the House, 1789–1900," *APSR* 90 (March 1996): 8–20.

66.   Deering and Smith, *Committees in Congress*.

67.   Kiewiet and McCubbins, *The Logic of Delegation*; Cox and McCubbins, *Legislative Leviathan*.

68.   Deering and Smith, *Committees in Congress*.

69.   Damon Chappie, "105th Congress Gets Ready for Business: GOP Changes Style, But Not Its Leadership," *RC*, November 21, 1996, 1.

70.   Richard F. Fenno Jr., *Home Style: House Members in Their Districts* (Boston: Little, Brown, 1978); Fiorina, *Congress: Keystone of the Washington Establishment*; Barry R. Weingast and William Marshall, "The Industrial Organization of Congress," *Journal of Political Economy* 91 (1988): 775–800.

71.   Kenneth A. Shepsle, "Institutional Equilibrium and Equilibrium Institutions," in *Political Science: The Science of Politics*, ed. Herbert Weisberg (New York: Agathon Press, 1986); Weingast and Marshall, "Industrial Organization."

72.   Deering and Smith, *Committees in Congress*.

73.   Rae, *Conservative Reformers*, 190.

74.   Cohen, "Beginning of the End," 1517.

75.   Jeffrey L. Katz, "Politically Charged Vote Sets Tone for Impeachment Inquiry," *CQWR*, October 10, 1998, 2712–2715.

76.   Calculated from CQWR, December 22, 1998, 3372.

77.   Sinclair, *Unorthodox Lawmaking*.

78.   Rae, *Conservative Reformers*.

79.   Rae, *Conservative Reformers*.

Epilogue

Harvey L. Schantz

The most notable political development during the second Clinton administration was the House impeachment of the president. On December 19, 1998, the 105th U.S. House voted two articles of impeachment against Bill Clinton for grand jury perjury in testimony concerning his relations with Monica Lewinsky and Paula Jones, and for obstruction of justice in the Jones sexual harassment lawsuit. The 106th U.S. Senate, however, on February 12, 1999, acquitted Clinton on both articles.

In both chambers of Congress, the pattern of the vote demonstrated the importance of congressional political parties and the hazards of divided government for presidents. In the House, the grand jury perjury and obstruction of justice articles of impeachment drew only five Democratic supporters, but was voted for by 223 and 216 Republicans, respectively. In the Senate, neither article of impeachment attracted a single Democratic vote, but they drew 45 and 50 Republicans, respectively. Clearly a Democratic Congress would not have brought Clinton to the brink of removal from office.

A second significant political development was the loss of seats by House Republicans in the 1998 midterm election. In November 1998, the Republicans retained control of the U.S. House, but the five-seat Democratic gain was the first pickup of seats for the president's party at midterm since 1934, and only the second such gain since 1862. Many congressional Republicans blamed Speaker Newt Gingrich for the loss of seats, and three days after election day, Gingrich declined to run for the Speakership in the newly elected Congress. Dennis Hastert (R-Ill.) became the new Speaker on January 6, 1999, at the outset of the 106th Congress.

A number of politicians emerged from the 1998 election with heightened prospects for election 2000. In New York State, First Lady Hillary Rodham Clinton effectively campaigned for successful Democratic senate candidate Charles Schumer, and thus positioned herself for a senate candidacy of her own. Meanwhile, Texas Governor George W. Bush Jr., was reelected by a large margin and quickly became the front-runner for the Republican presidential

181

nomination. Jeb Bush, a younger brother, was elected governor of Florida, further demonstrating the appeal of the Bush name in the growing sunbelt states.

For the most part, impeachment and electoral politics have overshadowed policy during the second Clinton administration. Nevertheless, the advent of a balanced federal budget has greatly altered the domestic policy environment. In the summer of 1997, the president and Congress reached a historical agreement for a balanced federal budget by fiscal year 2002, but that goal has already been achieved due to the growing economy. Currently the policy debate is over how to use the federal surplus. Most Republicans would like to offer tax cuts. President Clinton and most congressional Democrats would like to keep tax cuts to a minimum and use the surplus money to stabilize Social Security, Medicare, and fund other federal programs, including farm aid. A possible solution to the policy impasse would be to use the surplus to lower the national debt.

The political stakes in the budget surplus debate are great. In 1990, President George Bush permanently lost important credibility with the electorate by agreeing to raise taxes in a budget deal with the Democratic Congress. Both parties are wary of conceding any political ground, and both advocate solutions most supportive of their traditional constituencies. Policymaking in the remaining time of the Clinton administration will be tied to position-taking for the 2000 elections.

List of Contributors

Emmett H. Buell Jr. (Ph.D., Vanderbilt University, 1972) is a professor of political science and director of the Richard G. Lugar Program in Politics and Public Service at Denison University. He has written numerous articles and book chapters on presidential nominating politics and is the co-editor of *Nominating the President* (1991).

Colton C. Campbell (Ph.D., University of California, Santa Barbara, 1996) is an assistant professor of political science at Florida International University. He has served as a Congressional Fellow of the American Political Science Association and has received a Dirksen Congressional Research Grant. Campbell is coeditor of *New Majority or Old Minority? The Impact of the Republicans on Congress* (1999).

Milton C. Cummings Jr. (Ph.D., Harvard University, 1960) is a professor of political science at Johns Hopkins University. Cummings has been a Rhodes Scholar, Guggenheim Fellow, and for six years was on the staff of the Brookings Institution. His many books include *Congressmen and the Electorate: Elections for the U.S. House and the President, 1920–1964* (1966); *The National Election of 1964* (1966); *The Patron State: Government and the Arts in Europe, North America, and Japan* (1987); and *Democracy Under Pressure: An Introduction to the American Political System*, 8th ed. (1997).

Roger H. Davidson (Ph.D., Columbia University, 1963) is a professor emeritus of government and politics at the University of Maryland, College Park, and visiting professor of political science, University of California, Santa Barbara. From 1980 to 1988 he held the post of Senior Specialist in American National Government and Public Administration with the Congressional Research Service, U.S. Library of Congress. He is co-author of *Congress and Its Members*, 7th ed. (2000); and coeditor of *The Encyclopedia of the United States Congress* (1995).

Douglas B. Harris (Ph.D., Johns Hopkins University, 1998) is an assistant professor of government, politics, and political economy at the University of Texas at Dallas. He is author of "The Rise of the Public Speakership," *Political Science Quarterly* (1998); and "Dwight Eisenhower and the New Deal: The Politics of Preemption," *Presidential Studies Quarterly* (1997). He was a 1995 recipient of a Dirksen Congressional Research Grant, and has been a visiting assistant professor of political science at Colgate University and Johns Hopkins University.

Garrison Nelson (Ph.D., University of Iowa, 1973) is a professor of political science at the University of Vermont and senior Fellow at the McCormack Institute, University if Massachusetts, Boston. He is the editor of the two-volume set *Committees in the U.S. Congress, 1947–1992* (1993). He regularly provides ideological rankings of all Members of Congress to National Journal Inc. for use in their biennial editions of *The Almanac of American Politics*.

Harvey L. Schantz (Ph.D., Johns Hopkins University, 1978) is a professor of political science at the State University of New York, Plattsburgh. He has served as a Congressional Fellow of the American Political Science Association and as a Visiting Fellow at Yale University. He is the editor of *American Presidential Elections: Process, Policy, and Political Change* (1996).

Margaret Jane Wyszomirski (Ph.D., Cornell University, 1979) is Director of the Arts Policy and Administration Program at Ohio State University and a professor on the faculty of both the School of Public Policy and Management and of the Art Education Department. Her most recent book is the co-edited volume *The Public Life of the Arts in America* (2000). She is also the co-editor of *Executive Leadership in Anglo-American Systems* (1991), and co-editor of *America's Commitment to Culture: Government and the Arts* (1995). Wyszomirski has been a past or current member of the editorial boards of *Governance, Journal of Policy Studies, Presidential Studies Quarterly*, and *The Journal of Arts Management, Law, and Society*.

Index